"Special Trust and Confidence"

"Special trust and confidence in your loyalty, integrity and ability"
are terms of commendation used in the letters of appointment for
Ambassadors and High Commissioners, and signed by the Governor General.

"SPECIAL TRUST AND CONFIDENCE"
ENVOY ESSAYS IN CANADIAN DIPLOMACY

Edited by
DAVID REECE

Carleton University Press

Copyright © Carleton University Press, 1996

Printed and bound in Canada

Canadian Cataloguing in Publication Data

Main entry under title:
    Special trust and confidence : envoy essays in
Canadian diplomacy

Includes bibliographical references and index.
Includes some text in French.
ISBN 0-88629-292-1

    1. Diplomatic and consular service, Canadian.
2. Canada—Foreign relations—1945- . 3. Diplomats—
Canada. I. Reece, David, date-

FC242.S62 1996   327.71'009'045   C96-900694-2
F1029.S62 1996

Cover Design: Your Aunt Nellie
Typeset: Mayhew & Associates Graphic Communications, Richmond, Ont.
Front cover photo: The laying of the cornerstone for the new Canadian High Commission in Islamabad, Pakistan, February 1971.

Carleton University Press gratefully acknowledges the support extended to its publishing program by the Canada Council and the financial assistance of the Ontario Arts Council. The Press would also like to thank the Department of Canadian Heritage, Government of Canada, and the Government of Ontario through the Ministry of Culture, Tourism and Recreation, for their assistance.

CONTENTS

ACKNOWLEDGEMENTS — *viii*

INTRODUCTION
David Reece — *ix*

1. BREAKING GROUND IN BUDAPEST, 1978-1982
   Dorothy Armstrong — *1*

2. MAKING THINGS HAPPEN AT THE UNITED NATIONS
   William H. Barton — *17*

3. INDOCHINA: FROM DESK OFFICER TO ACTING COMMISSIONER
   Arthur E. Blanchette — *33*

4. CLOSING A MISSION: CYPRUS, 1970
   Gordon Brown — *49*

5. PLAYING FOR TIME: SOUTH AFRICA, 1969-1972
   Harry H. Carter — *69*

6. OTTAWA, ROME, BRUXELLES, 1972-1984 : QUELS DÉFIS?
   D'Iberville Fortier — *85*

7. LES OTAGES DE STANLEYVILLE
   Interview de M. Michel Gauvin par M. D'Iberville Fortier — *103*

8. EN AMBASSADE AU MOYEN-ORIENT DE 1970 À 1974
   Jacques Gignac — *115*

9. ASSIGNMENT IN CHINA: 1984-1987
   Richard V. Gorham — *133*

10 A FOREIGN SERVICE OFFICER AND CANADA'S NUCLEAR POLICIES
    J.G. Hadwen   *155*

11 CRISIS MANAGEMENT IN NATO: THE POLISH CRISIS, 1980-1981
    John G.H. Halstead   *177*

12 MOSCOW, 1980-1983: THE SECOND COLD WAR
    Geoffrey A.H. Pearson   *189*

13 AFRICA AND THE CARIBBEAN: INITIATIVE AND INFLUENCE
    David Reece   *199*

14 FROM PAKISTAN TO BANGLADESH, 1969-1972:
    PERSPECTIVE OF A CANADIAN ENVOY
    John Small   *209*

15 NATIONALIZATION IN GUYANA
    J.A. Stiles   *239*

16 A NEW BASE FOR PROMOTING CANADA'S INTERESTS IN JAPAN
    J.H. Taylor   *255*

17 CULTIVATING RELATIONS WITH SADDAM: 1986-1988
    Erik B. Wang   *269*

ILLUSTRATIONS

1	Ambassador Armstrong with Janos Kadar, Hungary, 1982	*13*
2	P.M. Trudeau, Ambassador Barton and Robert Kaplan, New York, 1978	*26*
3	High Commissioner Brown at Kyrenia, December 1968	*50*
4	Outside Soweto, 1971	*74*
5	Le roi des Belges et le nouvel ambassadeur, septembre 1980	*93*
6	L'empereur Hailé Sélassié, accompagné par l'ambassadeur Gauvin, 1966	*109*
7	Ambassador Gorham and Li Xiannien, 1985	*146*
8	Karachi: Fall 1952	*159*
9	Geoffrey Pearson with Wayne Gretsky and Vladislav Tretyak, 1981	*193*
10	President Kaunda and High Commissioner David Reece: Lusaka, Zambia, 1988	*203*
11	High Commissioner Small with Sultan M. Khan, Pakistan, 1971	*216*
12	High Commissioner Stiles and P.M. Forbes Burnham: Georgetown, Guyana, July 1971	*250*
13	The Canadian Embassy residence in Tokyo	*257*
14	Chancery of the Canadian Embassy in Tokyo	*261*

ACKNOWLEDGEMENTS

TO PROFESSOR Michael Brecher and the late John Holmes, who provided ideas and inspiration for this work.

To Dr. John Flood, President and CEO, Carleton University Press, his Senior Production Editor, Jennifer Strickland, and his Administrative Assistant, Suzanne Williams. They were excellent coordinators and producers of a book comprising a multitude of skilled authors, diverse topics, and chapters in either English or French. They received valuable assistance from the Reader who assessed the manuscript for the Press, and from the copy-editor, Noel Gates.

I am especially grateful to one author, John Stiles, who provided me with wise help and counsel during a complicated operation.

David Reece
Odessa, Ontario
October 1996

INTRODUCTION

DAVID REECE

THESE SEVENTEEN ESSAYS reflect the geography of Canada's pursuit of our national interests through the exercise of diplomacy. These interests are as wide as the world. They include the settlement of international disputes, peacekeeping and peace-making, and economic aims. The essays illustrate the role of the ambassador and staff in the diverse programs of embassy work: political, trade, aid, immigration, consular, information, cultural, security—especially important in some countries—and last but nevertheless essential, administration, which can be a potential nightmare in a difficult foreign environment.

The essays show how Canadian representation abroad has grown steadily and fruitfully since the end of World War II, at which time we had only a few thin bands of diplomacy stretching to Asia, Europe, the U.S. and Latin America. Since then we have spread a web of Canadian diplomacy into many countries of diverse political complexion including sundry ex-colonies in Africa, Asia and the Caribbean. Our embassies in Commonwealth, Francophone and other developing countries are an important feature of Canadian interests and diplomacy. The multiplication of new countries since World War II sometimes requires Canadian envoys and embassies to look after our interests in two or more countries through dual accreditations.

In addition to accounts of bilateral diplomatic missions, essays are included on the work of Canadian delegations to multilateral fora: the UN in New York, NATO in Brussels, the International Commission in Cambodia and arms control negotiations in Vienna.

The essays cover a long time span and a wide variety of activities. They are all written by diplomats who have served as ambassadors or high commissioners (the term used in Commonwealth countries for envoys from other Commonwealth countries). One point they make is that an envoy is not a dog on a chain. He receives instructions from Ottawa but he often has a need to embellish and adapt these orders from HQ in order to take account of an evolving local situation. Recommendations from the ambassador and staff can be an important ingredient in Ottawa's subsequent instructions to them; and the swift development of an important situation may sometimes require the ambassador to take action without reference to Ottawa for lack of time. There are, moreover, a myriad of minor, ongoing cases in which reference to home base is unnecessary. The embassy's consular role naturally takes on vital importance in times of major unrest, riot and rebellion in the country concerned.

Sometimes—but not frequently—an envoy has to disobey orders from home base, in whole or in part, if he decides that imperative and urgent local exigencies compel him to do so. But no ambassador wants to do this very often—for his own sake! On the whole, Ottawa and the posts abroad mesh their efforts harmoniously, sometimes after a dialogue characterized by constructive tension between views formed from differing vantage points. The head of mission is not always aware of all the policy factors that have to be reconciled at HQ, but overall harmony is furthered by the rotational nature of the foreign service. Except for a few political appointees, Canadian envoys usually spend as much time in Ottawa as in the field. They know the inherent problems faced at home.

Preparation of an embassy's economic and political reports is a major task. In addition to the embassy's judgement and assessment they often contain the gist of information that helped shape those views, namely: confidential discussions with local ministers, officials, businessmen, other diplomats and international functionaries. This is one reason why diplomatic reports are decidedly not, as some have asserted, mere repetitions of what is in the newspapers. Making arrangements for Canadian visitors and then guiding them is another important responsibility of the envoy and his staff. These visits are often of particular value in the trade and aid fields, where practical decisions can stem from on the spot assessments and parley.

It has been suggested that this book may fill a lacuna because most books about foreign policy and its history are written from the viewpoint of the capital as the centre of policy making. I and my fellow authors believe the essays do indeed provide new and useful material about the role of the envoy and his staff in the creation and in the implementation of Canadian and international interests. The ambassador is not a dog on a chain, but a harmonious partner, the external wing of Canadian policy.

I

BREAKING GROUND IN BUDAPEST
1978-1982

DOROTHY ARMSTRONG

THE HUNGARY OF 1978, the year of my arrival, seemed to me the best possible version of what I particularly wanted to observe at close quarters, an East Bloc country still anchored in Marxist theology and state-controlled economics, but somehow more accessible and more humane than the rest. This impression was relative, of course. The Communist infrastructure was still in place, all institutions being dominated by the Party. There was a pervasive secret police, a controlled press and a Parliament which, in spite of its splendid gothic spires, was little more than a rubber stamp. Phones were tapped, producing a tell-tale echo, and diplomats without special "safe rooms" in their offices resorted to paper and pen for their confidential discussions, the evidence being later shredded for safe disposal. Not surprisingly, special permission had to be sought well in advance before Hungarians could accept invitations to dine at a Western embassy. At the heart of this web and ensuring its continuance were the 80,000 Soviet occupation troops distributed with their missiles throughout the countryside, about whom no one spoke.

Yet Hungary was undeniably the most liberal country in USSR-dominated Eastern Europe at that time, the result of a brilliant balancing act engineered by Janos Kadar, Party Secretary and undoubted ruler of Hungary. Over the years he had won the right to open up and experiment domestically in return for Hungary's faithful allegiance to Soviet foreign policy goals. It was a bargain not easily won, and the Hungarians had constantly to work at it by sending delegations to Moscow year after year to argue the case for each step forward. Promising no more revolutions would have been Kadar's ultimate bargaining chip.

His motivation had probably much to do with wishing to make it up to his fellow Hungarians for what looked like an act of treachery in 1956—and some fairly rough years of repression until the amnesty of

1963—by offering them a decent life once he had consolidated his authority. Reconciliation became his motto ("Those who are not against us are with us") and by the late 1970s an astonishing transformation had taken place. Kadar, once universally loathed, was able to mingle unafraid in a crowd and was now believed to be able to win a free election, an unheard-of situation anywhere else in Eastern Europe.

Among his early reforms was the New Economic Mechanism of 1968 (NEM), a cautious step toward a market economy which allowed a certain amount of decentralization, some private enterprises and individual ownership of plots on state farms, moves which helped Hungary become the only net exporter of agricultural products in the COMECON, eliminating food line-ups in the process. Since as a precautionary measure these new concepts continued to be cloaked in Marxist terminology, they also produced a certain amount of confusion and scepticism, and became the butt of NEM jokes like the one about two joggers who decide to take a swim in a nearby pool. As one prepared to dive from the high board the other shouts, "Wait, there's no water in the pool." "So what?," his friend yells back, "I can't swim anyway." Though radical in the context, it was only a halfway house meant to deal with the obvious inefficiencies of the communist system; it had a rocky ride and fell into disrepute through conservative pressure, only to be revived at the end of the 1970s.

There was no real political freedom, but the intellectual atmosphere had become considerably more relaxed. The arts scene was a vibrant one, with over twenty theatres in Budapest producing everything from Shakespeare to modern drama, abundant avant-garde sculpture, painting and dance (not a trace of socialist realism here) and as one might expect, a wide choice of musical offerings. Directors like Miklos Jancso and Istvan Szabo ("Mephisto") were producing films as metaphors, set in another historical time and place, which were really sharp political and social criticisms of the current regime. Often close to or right in the danger zone, they were saved by international acclaim. Writers and the media were even more delicately placed, and though officials insisted that there was no censorship, in reality a very powerful self-censorship prevailed. Intellectuals knew which were the untouchable topics and those who stepped beyond the pale were simply unprinted or unemployed. There was therefore little harassment or imprisonment of the kind regularly endured by their confreres in other parts of the communist world, although the small group of dissidents,[1] throwing discretion to the winds with their street corner *samizdat*, could look forward to periodic raids.

Despite warnings about leaving politics to the Party, there was the "Microscope" political cabaret, balancing on a high wire as satirists nightly took chances with their careers by lampooning the establishment in surprisingly deep cuts. There was a whiff of danger and excitement about the place, and with a bit of Hungarian I was drawn there irresistibly to find out what was really going on. Western political scientists who were amazed at the extent of the cabaret's risk-taking finally concluded that the regime had decided that if people spend the evening laughing at them they are unlikely to go out and make another revolution.

Such was Hungary in 1978, a country intriguingly poised between East and West, moving slowly, imperceptibly forward to a future only dimly imagined, and in contrast to the exhilarating turbulence of *Solidarity* about to erupt next door, along another path, more akin to convergence. A concept much debated in the 1960s it envisaged East and West moving closer together through trade, investment and human contacts. Considered utopian in view of the general agreement that fundamental change had to await real movement in the USSR—a most unlikely prospect in the era of Brezhnev—the idea fell into disfavour, but in fact the Helsinki Final Act of 1975 laid the groundwork for just such a process and the Hungarians were quite prepared, pending some miracle in Moscow, to take full advantage of the opportunities being offered by détente. For example, travel for Hungarians was being made easier, and in particular trips to Austria (always their private dream model) became commonplace. Stalled family reunification questions began to be settled quickly and smoothly. For my part, I too was anxious to take advantage of the new possibilities opening up.

BEGINNINGS

The advent of a woman ambassador in Budapest had some of the trappings of celebrity, producing what turned out to be a false sense of euphoria. While an early presentation of credentials is regarded by some as flattering to the new arrival's country, I had decidedly mixed feelings about being summoned to the President only days after disembarking from the aircraft and while still jetlagged. This was due to energetic staff work on the part of one of my officers, for which I was grateful in principle, but the fact was that faced with a looming credentials ceremony, I had nothing to wear. The small air shipment containing the requisite clothing had not arrived and when it did there was every prospect of it languishing in customs, I was told, for some days.

With considerable anxiety I explained this situation to Protocol, who regretted that the ceremony's date was irrevocably fixed. Could I not borrow something? Given the time I had spent that summer agonizing over the appropriate costume, the answer was *no*. Male ambassadors had their regulation morning coat and striped trousers, or the elaborate gold-braided uniform favoured by the British and French. But what did women wear? No one really knew. The black wool suit and fur hat (a reference to one of our export industries) finally decided upon were just a guess, but at this point I was not to be deterred. Considerable pressure was applied, the trunk surfaced the afternoon before the event, and I was able to sally forth, perspiring in the late October heat wave, but reasonably confident that I could cope with the small, informal ceremony promised.

Instead, I walked into a Presidential reception room ablaze with klieg lights and alive with technicians from both local television channels. The day held other surprises, including the inspection of a military guard and the placing of a gigantic wreath (over a metre across) on the cenotaph at Heroes' Square. After a brief moment of panic during which I decided I might have to drag it, two white-gloved soldiers stepped forward to carry it on my behalf, the beginning of my active career of wreath-laying in Hungary.

Thus, although my first days went by in a heady atmosphere that gave me the impression I might be able to accomplish great things, my curiosity value soon faded. While I remained the only woman Head of Mission throughout my four years there, the reality was that though I was always received with the greatest courtesy, no special privileges or attention were thereafter accorded me. On the contrary, not many weeks had passed before the Hungarian Foreign Ministry released a list of its "priority countries," an unusual move that at least made the situation quite clear, namely that Canada placed last with Australia, far below the socialist brethren, neutrals, developing countries, and the EEC. (The United States enjoyed a special position because of its superpower status, but more importantly because the American Ambassador of the day had been the one to return the Crown of Hungary[2] after its long exile in Fort Knox. With such a hero and his exceptional access it was impossible for the rest of us to compete, though he was always generous in sharing information with his Canadian colleague.) Coincidentally, it happened that the Hungarians' view of our position was approximately mirrored by Ottawa's own disinterest. Part of the problem was that we were such latecomers: our Embassy had not opened until 1972 with a Chargé d'affaires, the last of the Western group, and there had been only one previous ambassador. We had little profile, and I knew that I was going to have to make a major effort for anything I might win on Canada's behalf.

BILATERAL DIPLOMACY

As one of their primary tasks ambassadors are expected to make contacts at the highest echelons, particularly among the eco-political establishment— the better to incline them to your own government's policies and views. Those of us with a NATO connection, however, were routinely denied access to the Politburo,[3] which was the real seat of power in Hungary. We were enjoined to leave them to the important business of running the Party (i.e., the country) and encouraged instead to call on the next level down, which meant Ministers and senior officials. This did not include the Ministers of Defence or the Interior, where sat the Soviet KGB "uncles."

The Foreign Ministry was, of course, open to us—along with Trade, Agriculture and Culture—but even then, with all the good humour with which we were received, we usually had the impression that we were not getting the complete picture (to make up for this, NATO ambassadors met regularly to exchange information). In those days our views were fundamentally opposed on most foreign policy issues in any case, and there would come a point early in our discussions when I would come up against the brick wall of Soviet-style orthodoxy to which the Hungarians were deeply committed. However, the promotion of détente through the Conference on Security and Cooperation in Europe (CSCE) was an exception for them: the more this succeeded the freer they were to liberalize at home, and here we found a meeting ground. Indeed the Hungarians played an active and progressive role among the East Bloc group in their willingness to move forward, particularly on human exchanges under Basket III provisions.

Regular bilateral political discussions are a key element of diplomacy, providing momentum and life-blood. As newcomers we had a good deal of basic ground to make up and this was the forum of choice, kept alive in our early years by a senior official on each side who was personally interested. When such individuals move on, as is often the case, it is up to the ambassador to provide the continuity and to keep those regular talks on the agenda.

Meanwhile, other avenues were being explored. Our commercial relations were at an early stage, but trade and investment promotion was, and is, a priority for all Canadian missions. Agriculture was already our most active sector (a number of enterprising Canadians having gone ahead without waiting for an embassy to materialize) and Canadian cattle stock was being used extensively to upgrade the local varieties on Hungary's state farms. Almost coinciding with my own arrival was the last air shipment of a herd of Holsteins. Thereafter, in a leap of technology, an individual with a black case rushing from aircraft to refrigerated facilities was the preferred method of transport.

I travelled to several of these state farms, which, as the engine of much of the country's economic success—thanks to the NEM reforms—had privileged access to Western machinery and an unusual degree of self-management. All were equipped with laboratories and white-coated technicians to operate the artificial insemination programs. On one memorable afternoon a bowl filled with small vials was handed to me with the remark, "Ambassador, you are now holding a future herd of cattle in your arms," an experience that I recall as being almost mystical.

Our most remarked Canadian visitor in that particular field was associated with a more direct technique. A breeder of bulls on a farm near Toronto, she had sold one to a state farm and wished to check on his performance. She also happened to be the daughter of the British film actor Leslie Howard who had been, contrary to all appearances, Hungarian in origin, and who remained a cult figure in Hungary through regular TV festivals of his old movies. Chic in black velvet, she created a sensation in state farm circles that afforded Canada welcome attention for some time to come.

PIONEERING

If we had essentially "arrived" in agriculture with thriving sales of poultry and livestock, it was in the more lucrative industrial sector that we particularly wanted to make a breakthrough. Hungary was of course locked into COMECON's economic arrangements for well over 60 percent of its trade. Of the rest, West Germany predominated and the competition was keen among a wide spectrum of other countries for the limited hard currency at Hungary's disposal. Canadian businessmen found the bureaucratic red tape of the state trading system and the unfamiliar language fairly daunting, so there were relatively few of them. It was our job to persuade them that new opportunities were opening up in this market and to give all support to those who accepted the challenge to show at Budapest's trade fairs and to profit from them by facing the competition. Among the provinces it seemed to us that Alberta showed the greatest initiative.

During these years we tried for the big league through the first major bids by Canadian firms in the industrial sector, worth millions of dollars. Stelco of Hamilton was promoting its latest innovation, the so-called coil box (which involved a new steel rolling process) for Hungary's major steel plant at Dunaujvaros. Ambassadors, by their presence and because of what they represent, can sometimes influence a sale. To this end I paid several "corporate liaison" visits to the factory and its senior management, becoming a familiar figure among the blast furnaces. It is of historical interest that we did win the contract, though the sale was delayed over a year by foreign exchange shortages; however, the "box" was ultimately so successful at increasing production and lowering costs at the plant that Stelco was encouraged to fan out elsewhere in Eastern Europe.

Quicker results were achieved with the Velan sale of valves for Hungary's first nuclear power plant. Things did not go well toward the end of this negotiation and I was asked to intercede personally. I did so, in the full knowledge that important commercial decisions were in the end decided on political grounds in Hungary and that, once we were in the club of recognized suppliers, the rest would come more easily. In my call on the Trade Minister I argued that we had never yet been awarded a major contract and that surely, if they were serious about our bilateral relations, it was Canada's turn. We had the skills and the know-how. When he finally said "Why not?" I knew that it had been enough to swing the decision in our favour, and the Velan tender became our first major contract in Hungary.

It was clear that we needed the kind of support and backing that a Chamber of Commerce could provide, but no single COMECON country had enough trade with Canada at the time to attract such an organization on a national level. As an alternative we launched the idea of a Canada-East Europe Trade Council covering the entire region, and this became the subject of a letter-writing campaign to all the likely movers and shakers in Canada that I thought might be able to help. It was to have a happy ending: the Council was formed about two years later, and led eventually to the active Canadian-Hungarian Chamber of today. Although this phase developed after my departure, the *ex post facto* type of satisfaction one derives from such advances is an integral part of our diplomatic experience.

Because this was Hungary there was another leading angle and that was culture, which in this small central European nation was deeply, even passionately, bound up with national identity. In fact, it was not too much to say that an embassy's cultural performance had a direct bearing on how its country was regarded by the Hungarians generally and could even have an impact on something so seemingly unrelated as an economic contract. This symbiosis was not easily explained at home and there was reluctance to accede to Hungary's request for a cultural agreement. Believing firmly in the power of cultural diplomacy we therefore resolved to take what initiatives we could even without formal arrangements. This meant that we would have to depend on borrowing attractions destined for larger nearby posts.

By keeping an eye on the schedules of what was going where, we managed to negotiate and reroute a Tom Forrestal exhibition for the Fine Arts Museum (the first major Canadian art show held in Hungary) as well as the West Coast "People of the Cedar." Carleton University had already begun a scholarship exchange with the University of Budapest, but when I discovered that Marshall McLuhan was much revered by the students as an American I felt that immediate action was needed. About this time a young Hungarian scholar came forward who had, to my amazement, just completed her doctoral thesis on the works of Hugh MacLennan, though Canadian literature was still very little known in Hungary. We were subsequently able to persuade her and the authorities to launch the first CanLit seminar at the University. In these instances, book gifts always help to get things moving and Ottawa's policy in this regard has always been very sound.

In those days there were close links between the Kodaly Institute and enthusiasts for the Kodaly method in Canada, but except for a small "new music" group that included the well-known flautist Robert Aitken, we were not successful in luring orchestral or chamber groups to Hungary. This was a disappointing state of affairs in a country that positively reverberates with music, but we did try to make up for it by inviting Canadian soloists living elsewhere in Europe to come and give house concerts at our Residence. Television reflected Hungarian life itself, the news and political programs being predictable and somewhat tedious, while the music and artistic content were invariably of high calibre. Musical programs began to be exchanged after a memo of understanding was signed between

Magyar Radio and the CBC in 1980, and our Embassy supported efforts that led to national evenings on television in both countries.

The occasion of an agreement to be formally signed between Hungary's Academy of Sciences and our Social Science and Humanities Research Council provided an opportunity to demonstrate the variety of a diplomat's tasks. Arriving ten minutes before the ceremony, I noted that the flag marking the Ottawa delegation's position was the old Ensign, defunct since 1965. With no great optimism the attendant and I rooted quickly through shelves of flags in a storage room. Finding nothing and with three minutes to go, I ran down a steep flight of steps to where the official car was sitting in a light rain, snatched the standard from its holder, raced back and placed a damp maple leaf flag in position on the desk just ten seconds before both delegations filed in.

THREATS

Receiving threatening letters and facing the possibility of being kidnapped or held hostage is one of the less palatable aspects of diplomatic existence. Diplomats do not brood about this (it would make life unbearable) but do take all possible precautions and then put the matter from their minds, going about their daily routines as before. In January 1980, we were unexpectedly put on alert after the so-called "Teheran Caper" in which several Americans were hidden and then helped to escape by Canadian diplomats while the U.S. Embassy in Iran was under siege. When this was discovered the Iranian Foreign Minister, Ghotbzadeh, went public in a speech inciting Iranians everywhere to "get" a Canadian ambassador in revenge for the humiliation. All of us in the field were immediately instructed by headquarters to approach our host's protocol department and ask for special protection.

Somewhat sheepishly under the circumstances, I did so, being in the ironic situation of asking to be shadowed by the communist police instead of complaining about them, although in fact the regime by this time was relying mainly on electronic surveillance. Because of the number of Iranian students in Budapest, Protocol was happy to oblige with a police guard which circled the Embassy during the daylight hours and followed my car for some months thereafter until the whole affair died down. The hostages were released in Iran and in a twist of fate Ghotbzadeh himself was executed. My escorts disappeared, and I almost missed them.

A CONSULAR CASE

Consular work is full of human unpredictability—how can Canadians think up so many ways to get into trouble?—and yet it presents problems that are usually so solvable that most of us remember our consular apprenticeships with something like pleasurable nostalgia. An unusual case, toward the end of my posting, illustrated a significant feature of the Hungary of that day. A young Canadian was arrested for espionage after being caught photographing a Soviet military base. His story was unconvincing and he languished in jail awaiting trial while we secured him legal counsel, extra food and paperbacks. A fifteen-year sentence was standard for this serious charge, and his prospects did not look good until I received a phone call from a senior Foreign Ministry official with whom I dealt regularly. "After all the work you and I have done over the years to build up our bilateral relationship," he offered, "we shouldn't let this sordid little incident spoil it, should we? Have him out of the country by midnight and we'll forget it." We did, and asked no questions about the rule of law.

THE DSB AND THE NEW CHANCERY

Our daily lives in Budapest were ruled by an organization known as the Diplomatic Service Board (DSB), essentially a branch of the Interior Ministry, which decided on your staff (who were obliged to report regularly to them) and when and if you received maintenance at your quarters or embassy. They worked on a political priority basis, of course, and being some distance from the top necessitated on our part many a *démarche* to get us moved up the waiting list for hot water or virtually anything else.

Coming on the scene so late in the day we had to struggle mightily to get a decent roof over our heads, since most of the good buildings had long since been snapped up by earlier arrivals. Housed in a somewhat down-market residential apartment featuring small, dark rooms on several floors it was not easy to operate efficiently or to keep up morale in such disconnectedness. However, I had an excellent small corps of officers (two of whom have since become Heads of Mission in their own right) and although the first person pronoun is often used in this narrative they were very much a part of all our endeavours. While an ambassador must be the guiding force who integrates all the embassy's work, it is clearly the team that counts. Being in somewhat difficult circumstances on several fronts made our satisfaction all the greater when we enjoyed our modest successes.

We had high hopes when told that we were being assigned a 19th-century villa for our future Chancery, but the decaying and abandoned structure, surrounded by a forest of weeds, with which we were presented was enough to discourage the most confirmed optimist. It was to be a joint renovation: the Hungarians would be responsible for the exterior façade and we for the interior, a seemingly simple equation that in fact involved years of negotiations, special Heritage Board demands, and worst of all, a complete stoppage of work for a year while the construction firm dropped us in midstream to renovate the Opera House.

Getting the reluctant workers started, visiting the site daily to keep them going and trying to save the lawn and statuary for future generations all took energy, buoyed by the hope that I would one day sit in a beautiful new office. It was not to be. The splendid Chancery opened, after long travail, only in 1984.

In this, as with all our efforts in Hungary, we attempted to win goodwill through official functions at the Residence, a time-honoured practice for diplomats everywhere because it works so well. These occasions were always much appreciated by the Hungarians, who never forgot how to enjoy themselves whatever the political climate. Among my most successful ventures were what I was told later were the first embassy dinner dances since World War II. It hardly mattered that some had never learned to dance, this not being a pastime ever encouraged by the Party.

ON VISITS AND ACCESS

The National Defence College
Visits open doors and the National Defence College (NDC) was always particularly welcome at any Canadian embassy. The one planned for June 1979 was a first for Hungary, however, and far from being a sure thing. There was no question of my calling on the Defence Minister—a phantom as far as we were concerned—and the Foreign Ministry was initially cool to the idea of a 55-strong NATO invasion. That would surely raise eyebrows in "certain quarters." I pointed out what an excellent opportunity this would be for the Hungarians to demonstrate their professed attachment to détente, and in any case the NDC tour group always

included several non-military members. This appeared to ease matters and the visit was approved, that is until it was revealed that it was not strictly bilateral, and that other nationalities (British, Australian and American) were on the course. This sent the visit off the rails, and it took more lengthy negotiations to come up with an ingenious, if rather silly formula: the ambassadors of those three countries could each write a letter of invitation to their respective compatriots. They agreed, and the tour was on, finally.

Receiving the NDC as visitors is surely one of the pleasantest experiences a Head of Mission can have, as is indeed that of having a military attaché on staff. Their training and discipline ensure that things go forward like clockwork, once the local ambassador becomes used to the military maxim that unless one is five minutes early, one is late. The group was warmly welcomed and appeared to appreciate their program, even if the defence component was not as substantial as they found it elsewhere, since military installations were closed to Westerners.

We had hoped to make their last evening one to remember, and had arranged a buffet reception on board a Danube pleasure boat. In keeping with the spirit of the post-Helsinki years, we had included the military attachés of all the NATO member countries as well as those of the Warsaw Pact who were assigned to Budapest. It was a convivial occasion, floating serenely down river in the sunset, past the monuments of the lovely old city, and the camaraderie among the two opposing camps, enjoying their essential humanity, had a special poignancy in the light of hindsight. Only a few months later the Soviet invasion of Afghanistan, which shattered détente, meant that all such scenes were to be only a memory for years to come.

THE MINISTER

A visit from one's Foreign Minister is the jewel in the crown of an embassy's work and we all strive, even agitate for one. This is the ultimate signal that your government cares about the host country and new and important opportunities for access present themselves as a result, both during the visit and afterward. First, however, it was my task to secure agreement from a preoccupied Ottawa, realizing that many other colleagues were trying for the same thing. This had to be done over many months by pointing out that Hungary had never, in its history, had such a visit from Canada and, further, that we were the only western nation at

Ambassador Armstrong with Hungarian Party Secretary Janos Kadar at an official reception in 1982. Discussion centred around his economic reforms.

that point which had never acknowledged Hungary's attempts to liberalize through a Foreign Minister's visit. Never liking to be too conspicuously absent Ottawa agreed, and in the event the operation lived up to all expectations, with Mark MacGuigan, then Secretary of State for External Affairs, playing his part with professionalism and enthusiasm.

The ultimate accolade accorded a visitor to Hungary in those years was to be received by Janos Kadar, though this was normally restricted to heads of state and government. I attempted to argue that our visit, being an historical precedent, was a special case deserving of such attention. Nevertheless, it was not until the last moment that word came through and we all filed into Kadar's office at Party Headquarters at 10:00 a.m. to be offered a whiskey and a fascinating dissertation on Kadar's version of 1956 and world events. For example, he claimed that he went over to the Soviet side during the revolution to stop the fighting and save Budapest from further destruction. "It is my hope," he said, "that some day Hungarians everywhere will understand." (On this, only time will tell.)

He also informed us that he was actively seeking better relations with the West, but "we don't have to shout it from the rooftops, do we?"

The visit, among other things, called forth from the Ambassador what might be called the holistic approach to diplomacy, i.e., the single Head of Mission, while accompanying the Minister everywhere, participating in discussions, press conferences, and so on, had somehow at the same time to see to the official dinner at the Official Residence that evening, and ensure that the table seating plans, food, wines, and flowers were worthy of the occasion. Of more enduring importance was the return visit by the Hungarian Foreign Minister to Canada the next year, which was proof that the exercise had given our relationship a momentum that it had lacked before, and that a new phase had indeed begun.

TOWARD PLURALISM

While Hungary at this time was not a severely repressed society, neither was it a democratic one. MPs of the only Party met ritually twice a year in their impressive Parliament to approve decisions made by the Politburo without any pretense of real debate. But something was happening behind the scenes which was developing like a kind of embryo of the democratic process. Throughout the year standing committees of Parliament met and held hearings, very discreetly, until in 1981-82 the machinery came alive over an environmental issue.

Pressed by the need for cheaper energy, the government had announced plans for the first nuclear power plant at Paks, using outdated "Eastinghouse" technology. This did not reassure the population, and the first civic action protests began, not in demonstrations, which were still banned, but through hearings held by the parliamentary environmental committee. These were in fact so effective that the legislation governing the installation had to be amended to markedly strengthen the safeguard provisions, to the best of my knowledge the first time popular pressure had brought about governmental change in communist Hungary. [4]

Significantly, it was another environmental issue in 1987-88, the projected hydroelectric dam across the Danube between Gabcikovo in Czechoslovakia and Nagymaros in Hungary (which threatened much beautiful and touristically important countryside) that mobilized Hungarian society in a way that would never have been allowed for more openly political reasons. The public's opposition to this scheme, including the hundreds of thousands of signatures collected, was an historic milestone along the road to democracy and led ultimately to the project's cancellation on the Hungarian side of the undertaking. Though this decision later resulted in a legal struggle with the newly constituted Slovakia, which sent the issue to the International Court of Justice, the political significance of that mass popular protest remains.

As early as 1982 the idea had been introduced of allowing several candidates to stand in certain electoral constituencies, all of course for the Communist party. But the signs were clearly there and it only needed the openings offered by *perestroika* to propel the Hungarians (more smoothly than some others, perhaps) along an evolutionary path, with a sudden rush at the end as the Soviet system began to collapse. In 1989, with Kadar gone from the scene, Budapest legalized free assembly and a multiparty system, the only instance of a communist regime voluntarily giving up its monopoly role.

Today much has changed and Hungary is indeed a democracy, still in a state of transition that is not without pain, but on the right track. Much too has changed in our bilateral relations. Canadian ambassadors, representing a country that is among its most important investors, now find themselves in the happy position of pressing on open doors everywhere.

NOTES

1. Most of us would have liked to get closer to them but since this would have complicated their lives even further, we Western diplomats were cautious, even covert, in our few contacts.
2. The centuries-old Crown and regalia had been taken by runner to the U.S. armed forces while the Soviets were at the gates of Budapest in 1945.
3. I was eventually granted an interview with the lone woman member, and in my fourth year, with Gyorgy Aczel, cultural czar and French speaker.
4. I except the 1956 revolution, which I believe was the real trigger that began the steady process of liberalization. It was far from being a failure.

Dorothy J. Armstrong joined the Department of External Affairs in 1957. She served abroad in New Delhi, OECD Paris and Bonn and was Canadian Ambasssador to Hungary from 1978-82. In Ottawa Ms. Armstrong worked for the Policy Analysis Group and from 1974, directed the North-West Europe Division. In 1983 she was "Foreign Service Visitor" at the University of new Brunswick, then returned to Ottawa to serve as Director of Commonwealth Affairs. In 1986 she was appointed Ambassador to Denmark and Greenland, where she opened a Canadian Consulate in 1987. Ms. Armstrong returned to Canada in 1991 and was a senior policy advisor until 1993.

2

MAKING THINGS HAPPEN AT THE UNITED NATIONS

WILLIAM H. BARTON

ARTICLE I OF THE UNITED NATIONS CHARTER sums up the purpose of the Organization—to make the world a better place to live in—in three short paragraphs, and concludes with a fourth: "To be a centre for harmonizing the actions of nations in the attainment of these common ends."

Put that way it sounds simple, but, as anyone who has tried to make things happen at the UN well knows, the reality is vastly different. The eminent UN scholar, Inis Claude, once compared the Organization to a carpenter's plane with each member government having a hand on it, and each pushing to attain its own goals. To the extent that enough hands push in the same direction there is progress, but all too often the result is stalemate, or even regressive movement.

Operating in the UN milieu is not for everyone. Nothing happens without long and tedious negotiation. Decisions are normally expressed in the form of resolutions, adopted by whatever body is concerned with an issue. Most UN bodies have large memberships straddling all regions of the globe and a wide range of views on what is desirable. Even if only half the membership elects to speak to a single item it means a three-day debate.

To get a resolution adopted you must build a supportive constituency of sufficient size to have it carry the day, either by vote or by consensus. You do this by recruiting as representative a group of delegations as you can to join as co-sponsors, and use them as emissaries to influence other delegations in the regional groups they belong to. The capacity of all parties to this process to haggle, not just over points of substance, but over every word and punctuation mark, has to be experienced to be believed. Often the final product of the negotiation looks only remotely like what you started with.

In addition there is the problem of quids for quos. The delegations you are seeking to enlist have their own projects, which they will expect you to support. All too often you are faced with a difficult choice. What price are you prepared to pay for success?

In a sense, the working life in any UN institution is like a poker game. It is important to play by the rules, but a good player has to use guile and bluff while still maintaining a reputation for fairness and keeping one's word.

The UN Institute for Training and Research once published a collection of essays, written by ambassadors who had served as presidents of the Security Council. It was entitled *Paths to Peace: The UN Security Council and its Presidency*[1] and was edited by Davidson Nicol, the Executive Director of the Institute, himself a former ambassador (of Sierra Leone). Each ambassador wrote about great decisions which had been reached during their incumbencies. Needless to say, in each case it emerged that the result was due to the author's efforts and diplomatic skill. With reference to what follows let it be understood that during the time that I had the privilege of heading the Canadian missions to the UN in Geneva and New York they had (and I am sure they still have) highly competent and dedicated staffs which worked with great effectiveness. Credit for what we accomplished must deservedly be shared by the whole team.

At any given moment, Canadian missions to the UN, whether in New York, Geneva, Vienna, or elsewhere, are pursuing a number of goals. The package varies, depending on the state of the world and the concerns of the Canadian government. It also varies with the times of the year, depending on which UN bodies are in session, but it will always include the following elements:

- Canadian involvement in major political issues (including economic issues), e.g., Bosnia or Somalia, or the Uruguay Round in the GATT. In such cases the missions concerned will be dealing with the Security Council, the UN Secretariat, the missions of other governments, and other UN agencies, such as the High Commissioner for Refugees, the GATT, the International Atomic Energy Agency, or any of the Specialized Agencies. This could involve also our Missions in cities where UN agencies are based, for example, Geneva and Vienna. When we are serving a term on the Security Council, which happens about once in a decade, this membership becomes an overriding responsibility.
- Canadian concerns about the management of the organization, including our aspirations to be elected to UN bodies, the way the business of the General Assembly or its subordinate bodies are being conducted, the effectiveness and efficiency of the Secretariat, etc. These issues are not glamorous, but often they are important and can have a material effect on the way the UN functions, and the way it is perceived by the public.

- Support of Canadian candidates for positions on UN bodies or secretariats. This is a difficult and troublesome area, but one which often has political ramifications, both at home and in our dealings with other delegations and with the Secretary-General.

In the following sections of this essay I will describe some typical Canadian involvements in each of the three areas mentioned above, that occurred during the time I was our representative to the UN in Geneva and New York.

CANADA AND THE REVIEW OF THE NON-PROLIFERATION TREATY, 1975

In 1968, over one hundred governments became parties to the Nuclear Non-Proliferation Treaty. It was the product of a lengthy negotiating process which had been going on for many years, and in essence was a bargain between the governments possessing nuclear weapons and those which did not. In exchange for forswearing nuclear weapons the non-nuclear states were to receive technical assistance in the peaceful uses of atomic energy (including peaceful nuclear explosions, which were still deemed to have potential value at that time). In addition, the nuclear weapons states undertook to pursue negotiations in good faith on disarmament and the ending of the nuclear arms race.

But there were unresolved problems. Only three of the nuclear powers (United Kingdom, United States and USSR) were parties to the Treaty. France took the position that the only solution to the nuclear menace lay in the cessation of the production, and the destruction of stockpiles, of nuclear weapons. The mainland Chinese government was at that time not represented at the United Nations. A number of other governments which had the potential to become nuclear powers also refused to become parties to the agreement.

The Treaty provided that review conferences should be held in Geneva every five years after it had come into force, "with a view to assuring that its purposes and provisions [were] being realized." Since the Treaty came into force in 1970, the first review conference was held in the spring of 1975. The Canadian government then, as now, regarded the Treaty as a major accomplishment in progress toward nuclear disarmament, and was anxious that the review conference should adopt a strong declaration of support. But many delegations felt that there were major shortcomings in the way the Treaty was being implemented and were determined to take advantage of the conference to press their case.

The president of the conference was the distinguished and redoubtable Swedish Minister for Disarmament, Inge Thorsson. She was experienced in chairing such meetings and knew all the major players, but she found almost immediately that, although none of the parties wanted to destroy the Treaty, there were strong convictions about what should be happening to carry out its purposes and provisions.

The developing countries felt strongly that they were being short-changed on the technical assistance front, especially in the area of peaceful nuclear explosions. They also were indignant that the nuclear powers were not showing due diligence in their negotiations to end the nuclear arms race, and that the security guarantees for non-nuclear states were inadequate. Their sense of resentment was fuelled by their conviction that the importance attached by the developed countries, and the nuclear powers in particular, to getting conference agreement to end the proceedings with a positive declaration gave them a powerful weapon for wringing concessions from them.

The nuclear powers did want an endorsement of the Treaty but these major powers were not prepared to make concessions to the developing nations. As usual, the position of Canada and most of the developed nations that were not nuclear powers was in the middle. Canada and some of the others had increased their contributions to the technical assistance program of the International Atomic Energy Agency, in an effort to demonstrate that we took seriously the treaty obligation to respond to the needs of the developing countries, but we were not willing to join them in what we felt was an unproductive effort to improve security guarantees.

The work of the conference was carried out in three drafting committees, and stalemate became evident almost from the start. After weeks of argument we were running out of time, and the prospect of ending up in disarray began to loom large. The prospects for the kind of declaration we wanted began to look dim indeed.

At this point, after talking things over in our delegation, I went to see Mrs. Thorsson and suggested that a small group from delegations of Sweden, Australia and Canada work in secrecy to produce a declaration which would attempt to find middle ground on the main issues. Then, the day before the conference was to end, she should call a plenary meeting, express concern at the absence of agreement, and put the declaration on the table as a "President's Text." She recognized the inherent risk in the proposal but without hesitation agreed that we should go ahead.

Our little drafting group started to work at once in the Canadian mission, well away from the Palais des Nations where the conference was being held, and when the opportune moment arrived Mrs. Thorsson confronted the conference with her text. The effect was dramatic. No one wanted to disown the president, but the major protagonists were furious. In the end the conference adopted the declaration but then put on the record the reservations of delegations. The list was long and the interventions were vituperative, but as we had anticipated the declaration was what went to the General Assembly, and the reservations disappeared in the filing cabinets of the Secretariat.

For many years we kept a discreet silence on how the very positive Declaration of the 1975 Review Conference was achieved. Apparently similar tactics were unnecessary at the twenty-five year review conference in 1995.

CANADA AND THE NAMIBIAN INDEPENDENCE NEGOTIATIONS 1977-78

At the 1976 session of the General Assembly Canada and Germany, as members of the "Western Europe and Others Group," were elected to two-year terms on the Security Council for the period 1977-78. At almost the same moment, the United States elected a new government, and early in the New Year Andrew Young, the former mayor of Atlanta and a close colleague of Martin Luther King, was appointed ambassador.

Shortly after he arrived, a meeting of the Western members of the Council (Canada, France, Germany, U.K. and U.S.) was convened at our mission, to discuss what issues were likely to confront us, and what positions we might take. The Canadian mission was a popular place for meetings because we had a good conference room and we were close to the UN. It gave us a useful edge in negotiating because as hosts, by default, we often chaired the meetings.

I had expected that our most immediate preoccupation would be the Middle East, but Andy, as he quickly became known to everyone at the UN, had other concerns. It was common knowledge that the African delegations would be leading another charge, demanding action by the Council, including sanctions under Chapter VII of the Charter, on the complexity of Southern African issues, including Rhodesia, Apartheid in South Africa, and Namibia. Andy argued that a simple reiteration of opposition by the Western members would be detrimental to the reputation of the Council. It was obvious that he was not comfortable with the thought that he would have to oppose his African brothers.

Inspired by Andy we came up with a dual approach: on the one hand we would try to persuade the African delegations that, instead of having a contentious debate over Southern African issues, ending with a Western veto, we should attempt to shape a declaration for adoption by the Council, built on areas of agreement and having a strong and positive thrust. Such a declaration, as a considered expression of the convictions of the Council, would have an important impact on world opinion.

If the African delegations would accept this approach we, for our part, would undertake to use all avenues at our disposal—as major trading nations dealing with South Africa—to find a solution to the problem of Namibia. It will be recalled that Namibia (South-West Africa) had been mandated to South Africa at the end of World War I. After the UN had been established the mandate should have been replaced by a UN trusteeship agreement, but South Africa had refused to comply. Eventually the Security Council declared that the mandate was terminated and that the UN was responsible for the administration of the territory, but short of using force, which it was not prepared to do, it was unable to give effect to its decision.

Our proposal would involve South African acceptance of a plan, consistent with the guidelines laid down by the Security Council, to hold free elections at an early date, leading to the establishment of Namibia as an independent state recognized as such by the UN. It carried with it an implicit undertaking to use economic pressure to encourage South African acceptance, and when we referred our negotiating proposals to our governments I was not at all sure that the British and German authorities would go along. However, my doubts proved groundless.

As soon as we got clearance from our capitals we held a series of consultations with the African members of the Council, and with the so-called Front-Line States (the African countries abutting South Africa). Our plan raised serious problems for them. It foreclosed early action in the Council on an issue of cardinal importance to all African States. Moreover it envisioned negotiations over Namibia with a government which in their view had no legal basis for being a party to the dispute. In the end, however, the possibility of real progress over Namibia encouraged them to accept.

Just as we were getting ready to try our proposal on the South African government it announced a program to give Namibia independence—South African style. We urged the South Africans to call a halt to their plans in favour of one which would result in an independent government universally recognized, rather than another Transkei. At the same time we told the South African ambassador that if his country persisted in going ahead, Western governments could not be expected to keep on resisting retaliatory action in the Security Council. To our relief the South African government agreed to engage in the negotiations.

The Western group had now become known in the corridors of the UN as "the gang of five." (The Chinese foreign minister suggested to me that it would be more appropriate to be called the gang of four plus one.) We prepared a draft of the kind we had in mind for an affirmative South African declaration, but it was rapidly shown to be a non-starter. Discussions with the Africans continued throughout the spring, but the text fell far short of the minimum the Africans could accept. Things stayed quiet during the summer doldrums, but by autumn a succession of events, including the death of Steve Biko, a series of detentions and prison deaths, and the suppression of the anti-apartheid South African press, made action by the Africans in the Council inevitable. They produced a package of four resolutions, three of them involving the imposition of sanctions, and one of a more declaratory nature which could be lived with.

The Western members of the Council shared the general repugnance to developments in South Africa, but there was no way that the U.K., with its economic involvement in South Africa, could have acquiesced in punitive sanctions under Chapter VII of the Charter, even if the U.S. and France, the other members of our group with a veto, had been prepared to go along. We looked hard for something we could do that would show our outrage but would, at the same time be tolerable to the British, and finally came up with the idea of a compulsory arms embargo under Chapter VII of the Charter. The practical effect of such an embargo would be minimal, but as a political gesture it would be significant.

This led to a time-consuming round of consultations with our governments, and unfortunately meant that we had to pursue stalling tactics in the Council, where the debate was becoming more and more highly charged every day. When the issue finally came to a head the Western nations voted against the sanctions resolutions (which meant that these proposals were vetoed by the U.K., U.S. and France) and supported the declaratory resolution.

By this time we had received approval to submit our resolution imposing an arms embargo, but the Africans were so angry with us that they spurned it. However, after a day or so of cooling off and a rewrite by the Indian ambassador which made it more acceptable, the resolution was adopted on November 4, 1977. It was the first time that action under Chapter VII had been taken against a member-government of the UN.

While all this was going on we were also working out our ideas for a Namibian agreement. As it turned out this initiative proved to be the major preoccupation of our delegations, and indeed of the Council, during 1977-78. During the next sixteen months, as we wrestled with the problems of developing a plan and selling it to the parties, we found our efforts threatened with collapse on an average of about once every three weeks.

The basic components of the plan had to ensure that the guerilla warfare along the frontier between Namibia and Angola would come to a halt; that the blacks who had fled the country would feel it was safe to return; that the 20,000 to 30,000 South African troops stationed in Namibia would be reduced to a minimum, so that the possibilities for intimidation during the voting process would be eliminated; that the possibility of intimidation by the police and civil administration would also be neutralized; and that the electoral and constitutional measures required to establish an independent government could be carried out in a manner that was perceived by the international community to be fair. In working out the plan we drew extensively on the practical experience of our military, police and civil administration experts.

We decided at the outset to entrust the detailed negotiations to a so-called "contact group" consisting of the deputies of our five missions. The Canadian member was Paul Lapointe. We reached agreement on the main elements of our plan without much difficulty. But then came months of fine-tuning the language, modifying details, and vigorous salesmanship to convince the parties concerned that their vital interests were taken care of. This was where personal friendships, good relationships between delegations, and continued evidence of good faith paid off.

The contact group made five trips to Africa; Sam Nujoma, the head of the South-West Africa People's Organization [SWAPO] (and now President of Namibia), came to New York for consultations on three occasions, and the South African foreign minister came twice. The five western foreign ministers (in our case Don Jamieson) had lengthy joint consultations with both sides and with the Front-Line States (Angola, Zambia, Botswana, Tanzania and Mozambique).

In April 1978 South Africa announced acceptance of our plan, but we had not yet obtained the agreement of SWAPO. Sam Nujoma had come to New York, and we were doing our best to convince him that he too should sign on when the South Africans launched a fierce raid on SWAPO headquarters in Angola. Nujoma immediately broke off talks with us and returned to Angola.

It took a month for the situation to cool off to the point where consultations could be resumed. With the aid of the Front-Line States SWAPO was finally persuaded to accept the Western plan on July 12, and at the end of July, 1978 we brought two resolutions before the Security Council. The first resolution authorized the Secretary-General to develop a proposal for holding elections and launching a constitutional process for the independence of Namibia. The Secretary-General's proposal would, in effect, be the plan which we had developed and which had been approved by the two sides. The second resolution affirmed the view of the Council that Walvis Bay was an integral part of Namibia and undertook to lend its full support to the initiation of steps necessary to ensure the early reintegration of Walvis Bay into Namibia.

The adoption of the principal resolution would mark a turning point in the Namibia negotiations, so the Council meeting acquired some ceremonial significance, and seven foreign ministers planned to participate. July was Canada's turn to preside over the Security Council, and Don Jamieson was looking forward to being in the chair. Unfortunately for him the Queen chose that moment to visit Newfoundland so he had to go home to host a dinner for her, and I had the privilege of presiding. The resolution was adopted by thirteen votes to none, with the USSR and Czechoslovakia abstaining. The Walvis Bay resolution was adopted unanimously.

In accordance with the decision of the Council, the Secretary-General submitted his plan for ensuring the early independence of Namibia through free and fair elections under the supervision and control of the United Nations, and it was approved by a resolution adopted the following September.

When our term on the Security Council came to an end (December 31, 1978) the prospects for early implementation of the UN plan looked good. Sad to say, at that point things started to go wrong, and as it turned out more than ten years passed by before the political obstacles could be overcome. However, at long last the plan, essentially unchanged, was put into effect and carried out successfully.

The success of the Namibia negotiations was due to the cooperative efforts of the five Western delegations. Each of our allies had special interests in the region, and sometimes needed to be encouraged not to allow those interests to block the path to our goal. On one occasion, when the South Africans were being particularly difficult and we began considering limited sanctions the British almost broke ranks with us, but in the end group solidarity won out and the South Africans backed off from their position. The Front-Line States played a pivotal role in persuading Sam Nujoma that he should accept the plan. As Canadians I think we can take satisfaction from having made an important contribution. In particular, the Front-Line States regarded us as a friendly voice in the councils of the Western group.

IMPROVING THE OPERATION OF THE GENERAL ASSEMBLY

The General Assembly operates under rules of procedure that have been honed and refined over the years to take account of both political and administrative considerations, and are probably as good as an organization of the character of the UN can expect. Moreover, proposals for

Prime Minister Trudeau in New York, accompanied by Ambassador Barton and the Hon. Robert Kaplan (left), en route to consultations with the Secretary-General over stalled disarmament negotiations, 1978.

changing the rules are always contentious and can be relied upon to produce lengthy and heated debate.

Within the rules there is a great deal of room for ensuring that the business of the Assembly is conducted efficiently and efficaciously, but they can just as easily be abused or exploited, so that proceedings bog down in a morass of time-wasting frustration. In this process the role of the president of the General Assembly is critically important. If pressure is not maintained by the president himself, and by chairmen of committees, to start meetings promptly, proceedings can be delayed unconscionably. The penchant of some delegates for abusing points of order has to be kept in check and constant attention has to be paid to maintaining an effective pace of debate.

Unfortunately, the president of the 1978 Assembly did not provide the leadership which is essential for the expeditious conduct of business and, as the session drew to a close, delegations were so exasperated that they all came together to hold an indignation meeting. Of course we could not attack the president himself—instead, the focus of complaint was on the rules of procedure. The Secretary-General (Kurt Waldheim) attempted to respond, and undertook to bring proposals for revision to the 1979 session of the Assembly for consideration by the membership.

In January 1979 we (the Canadian mission) held a post-mortem on the events of the Assembly just concluded. It seemed to us that if we were to avoid a repetition of the 1978 fiasco something more was called for than reliance on the Secretary-General's undertaking. At best his proposals would not surface before June, and no one would look at them until the opening of the Assembly in September. They would then be referred to the General (steering) Committee for study and, by the time it had dealt with them, the Assembly would be at least half over.

On the basis of analysis I took a hard look at my representation allowance and invited the heads of eighteen delegations which I felt were influential in the various regional groups to a luncheon at a restaurant near the UN. I also invited the Undersecretary-General responsible for General Assembly Affairs, together with his deputy.

I outlined to them our appraisal of what would happen to the Waldheim review, and suggested an alternative. I proposed that we set up an informal working group right away, with a mandate to review the rules of procedure (and the precedents for the way they were applied) and come up with practical reforms where appropriate. I also suggested that it should be decided at the outset that we would not waste time arguing about reforms that were contentious, and that we would confine our efforts to areas of basic agreement. We should keep the members of the regional groups to which we belonged informed about what we were doing, and in due course clear the results of our efforts with them. We could then pass on the final product to the Secretary-General with the expectation that, when it finally reached the General Committee, it could be approved and put into effect at the beginning of the session.

Our proposal was greeted with enthusiasm by all present. The working group was set up immediately, and the Undersecretary-General named his deputy as secretary. By then it was pretty well established who the next President of the Assembly would be, so we briefed him fully on our plan. The working group finished its efforts by April, and they were cleared informally by the regional groups. The Secretary-General embodied our recommendations in his proposals to the Assembly, and they were adopted without controversy by that body during the first week of its 1979 session.

The adoption of the changes was dealt with as a matter of administrative routine, and the way they had come about was known only to those who had been involved. I am not even sure whether our own Minister of External Affairs was aware of the role of the Canadian mission, but it was a classic example of what can be done when the will for action is present, and I still look back on that project with personal satisfaction.

GETTING OUR SHARE OF THE ACTION—UN APPOINTMENTS FOR CANADIANS

When it comes to placing Canadians in UN bodies there are two arenas of activity. The first relates to elective posts, such as the heads of Specialized Agencies and appointments to the International Court of Justice and the International Law Commission. If they are to have any prospect of success, campaigns for these positions need to be launched years in advance, and the candidate needs to become known in the milieu in which he or she expects to operate. On more than one occasion (fortunately I was only peripherally involved), the Canadian government has launched campaigns which violate these rules, and has ended up a bad loser. The trouble is that officials who advise that it is an unwise strategy are accused of lacking loyalty. Then, when they do their best in support of a losing cause, they are blamed for not having tried hard enough.

At times, however, we do it right. There was never any doubt that Maurice Strong would be the first Executive Director of the UN

Environment Program, and I am sure that this was also true of the recent appointment of Elizabeth Dowdswell to the same position. The situation with respect to appointments to the UN Secretariat is another story. The UN Charter specifies that "the paramount consideration in the employment of staff and in the determination of the conditions of service shall be the necessity of securing the highest standards of efficiency, competence, and integrity. Due regard shall be paid to the importance of recruiting the staff on as wide a geographical basis as possible." Inevitably the geographic requirement has acquired great weight and forced compromises in the search for quality.

I do not know exactly how the current senior hierarchy is structured, but in my time it was a given that certain Undersecretary-General appointments went to nationals of the major powers. There is intense competition for all posts at the level of director and above, and the Secretary-General cannot ignore the demands of member governments whose nationals are under-represented in the Secretariat. Ambassadors have learned that they have to be aggressive in their approaches on behalf of their candidates, and I have no doubt that making these appointments is one of the least attractive features of the Secretary-General's job.

During my term at the UN we were fortunate in having a distinguished Canadian, Dr. George Davidson, as Undersecretary-General in charge of management. He had been recruited on the personal initiative of Kurt Waldheim when the latter became Secretary-General. In addition there were a number of Canadians in relatively senior positions who had been with the Secretariat since its early days. We were also called upon from time to time to provide people with technical skills required by the Secretariat.

In 1978 there were two positions about to become vacant for which we had strong candidates. The first was the head of the World Food Program. We were major contributors to the program and we were convinced that we had a first-class nominee. The problem was that the appointment was in the joint purview of the Secretary-General and the Director-General of the Food and Agriculture Organization, and the latter individual was not on good terms with the Canadians on his governing body.

The second appointment would be to the directorship of the Human Rights Division. Our nominee was a distinguished legal scholar with an established reputation in the human rights field. We lobbied vigorously in favour of both candidates, both in the Secretariat and with other delegations which might be tempted to run alternative nominees. But as the time for decision arose, I knew that I would have to press our case with the Secretary-General himself.

I was aware that he had recently had an encounter with one of my ambassadorial colleagues, who had threatened to suspend payment of his country's budgetary contribution unless he got satisfaction. I was not prepared to go that far, but I knew that I would have to show determination to the point of being contentious.

When the time came, our discussion was as unpleasant as I had anticipated. I stressed the qualifications of both candidates and the prominent role played by Canada, both in human rights and in food aid. Our most effective bargaining lever was our very substantial contribution to the World Food Program and I pressed the point as hard as I could, short of making an outright threat. The Secretary-General, for his part, pointed out that we were well-represented in the Secretariat, and told me a tale of woe about his problems in dealing with the Director-General of the FAO. The meeting ended with his undertaking to let me know shortly about his decision.

A week later he called me in and told me that our nominee for the World Food Program would be appointed, but that we would have to give up on the Human Rights assignment. I have often wondered what deal he made with the Director-General of the FAO to get him to go along. I wonder also whether we would have been successful if we had been seeking only one appointment.

The problems we encounter in attempts to place Canadians in the UN Secretariat are repeated in each of the UN Specialized Agencies, except that the opportunities are even more limited, and the Directors-General, in many cases, are more entrenched. The Canadian government has a vigorous program for identifying good candidates and pressing for a fair share of jobs, but it is a frustrating task.

•

In this essay I have attempted to illustrate by example the kind of work that Canadian representatives at the United Nations do to achieve the objectives set out by the government. The work is quite different from that involved in relations with individual nations, which is carried out through our embassies. It requires alertness and aggressiveness in inserting oneself into the unceasing informal negotiations between groups of delegations on every issue before the Organization. Wheeling and dealing is the name of the game, and having a wide circle of acquaintances in the fifty or sixty influential delegations is essential.

Major breakthroughs come only rarely and by and large you have to be satisfied that small victories will ultimately contribute to the attainment of the better world that all nations seek. Some people find this to be disheartening and disillusioning. As a response let me quote the words of a great Canadian diplomat, Hume Wrong. This is what he said: "disillusionment, in its literal sense of the absence of illusions, is a good thing. It should mean that we see more clearly, not that we have lost hope." This is the essence of diplomacy at the UN and the spirit that must motivate all who work there.

NOTE

1. Nicol, Davidson (ed.), *Paths to Peace: The UN Security Council and its Presidency* (New York: Pergamon, 1981).

William H. Barton served in the Canadian army in World War II, retiring with the rank of major. He joined the Defence Research Board in 1946 and was seconded to External Affairs in 1952, where he served in the Defence Liaison I Division. He was permanently transferred to External Affairs in 1954. Mr. Barton was Counsellor of the Canadian Embassy in Vienna from 1956-60. Returning to Canada, he was appointed head of Defence Liaison I Division but was reassigned in 1961 as Counsellor, and later as Minister, of the Canadian Mission to the UN in New York. In 1964 he was appointed head of United Nations Division and in 1970 became Assistant Undersecretary to the Department. He was appointed Ambassador to the UN office in Geneva in 1972, and from 1976-80 was Ambassador to the UN in New York. Mr. Barton served twice as President of the UN Security Council and was awarded the Order of Canada in 1994.

3

INDOCHINA: FROM DESK OFFICER TO ACTING COMMISSIONER

ARTHUR E. BLANCHETTE

ON MY RETURN in April 1953 from my first posting, Mexico City, where I had spent nearly five years, with some expectation of continuing to work in the Latin American sector, I came up against one of the Department's first personnel requirements: adaptability and flexibility.

On reporting for my next assignment to Evan Gill, the chief of personnel, a kindly man under whom I was to serve later in South Africa, he rather apologetically said that an unexpected vacancy had occurred in the Far Eastern Division. They needed somebody fast for the Indochina-Southeast Asia desk and that was where I was to report the following Monday morning. This was Friday, so I had all of a weekend to try to prepare for my next assignment. We were still in the hotel at the time, house-hunting, awaiting our furniture from Mexico, and so on. Fortunately, the hotel was near the main branch of the Ottawa Public Library, where I borrowed such few books as they had on the subject.

On Monday morning, I duly reported to the Head of Division: Chester Ronning. I did not know it at the time, but I was extraordinarily lucky. He was one of the most outstanding men under whom I would have the good fortune of serving: knowledgeable, kindly, approachable, friendly, helpful. I remember to this day how, not long after my arrival in the Division, he handled my first memorandum to the Minister. He must have noticed that I was nervous when I brought it in to him for consideration. He leaned back in his chair, rested his feet on his desk, and said: "Arthur, read it to me." I proceeded to do so with some trepidation. He listened intently and said: "Arthur, that's fine. Give it to me." And he signed it then and there. He had won a friend for life.

The work of a desk officer can be quite fascinating, especially when a war is beginning to reach a climax, as was the case in Indochina at the time. In addition, the Division was an agreeable place to work in. It was a genuine pleasure to work for Chester Ronning. He seemed to have a particular talent for bringing out the best in people. At least he did so with me and my service with him remains embedded in my mind as one of the happiest periods of my professional life.

Fighting had broken out in Indochina towards the end of 1945, as France sought to re-establish its presence in its former colony and its forces came up against those of the Vietnam Independence League (Vietminh). Its leader, Ho Chi Minh, had proclaimed the Independence of Vietnam in Hanoi on September 2, 1945, following the surrender of Japan and its withdrawal from the peninsula. Until 1949 France was able to maintain its position fairly easily but, with the victory of Mao Zedong's armies in China that year, fighting became more intense and its hold began to weaken.[1]

Historically, Southeast Asia had not been an area of direct interest to Canada. Commercially, the relationship was relatively slender, although the Trade Commissioner Service had for many years maintained an office in Batavia, capital of the former Dutch East Indies (now Indonesia). Politically, connections were virtually non-existent.

During the early post-war period, the government's outlook on Indochina reflected this situation, and on the whole it was rather aloof. Nevertheless, France's efforts to regain control of its former possessions in Indochina could be viewed somewhat testily in Ottawa at times; they were considered primarily in the NATO context, as weakening France's participation in the Alliance during its vital growing stages.[2]

As a result of this general outlook Indochina was not a priority issue in the Department during the late 1940s and the subject was dealt with on a part-time basis, mainly by one of the Far Eastern Division's five officers. Even as late as 1953, when I arrived in the Division, Indochina was still a part-time assignment; my mandate also included much of the rest of Southeast Asia. I worked closely with a desk officer in the European Division who, among other things, handled the NATO aspects of France's war in Indochina. Both of us dealt with the French Embassy in Ottawa when necessary.

By the end of 1953 this position of relative detachment was rapidly changing. The French defeat at Dienbienphu, in May 1954, which rendered France's continued presence in the peninsula virtually untenable, made Indochina an emergency subject. In the aftermath of Dienbienphu, the newly elected government of Pierre Mendès-France sought urgently to disengage from the conflict, and it was agreed that the question would be dealt with during the Geneva Conference on Korea, which had been decided upon some time before.

Thus, concurrently with the meetings on Korea, in which Canada took full part on the basis of its contributions to the UN cause, negotiations were also held on Indochina from May 8 to July 21, 1954. Canada did not participate officially in these negotiations, although Canadian delegates to the Korea Conference were on occasion involved informally in some of the discussions. At the official level, Canada's main representatives in Geneva were Chester Ronning and John Holmes.

What had been a position of relative calm was abruptly and unexpectedly shattered on July 19, 1954. I remember it vividly. Without any warning, we learned from media sources that the co-Chairmen of the Conference, Anthony Eden and V.M. Molotov, had opted for Canada as one of the members—along with India and Poland—of the three International Commissions for Supervision and Control, established at Geneva to oversee the settlements agreed upon with respect to the three countries in Indochina.

Far Eastern Division was caught by surprise as much as anybody else. I recall that divisional officers had two reactions when we heard the news. The first was to get as much information as possible about what might be involved, and an urgent telegram was immediately sent up from the Division for dispatch to Canada House in London forthwith. The reply, received the same day, confirmed the fact that an official invitation could be expected and gave as much information as could be provided on the basis of enquiries in London, which was relatively little. The second reaction was that, if Canada had in fact been so invited, the request would be almost impossible to refuse, given the government's internationalist outlook. [3]

We learned later that it was Premier Chou En-lai of China who had nominated Canada for the task. Belgium had been considered for a while, but was not accepted. Why Chou En-lai proposed Canada is uncertain. Many think that Chester Ronning, who spoke fluent Chinese and was friendly with Chou En-lai, may have had something to do with it. [4]

Ronning makes no mention of this in his memoirs and seems never to have spoken to anybody in the Department about it. In any event, if he was involved, he has much to answer for! Staffing the Indochina Commissions became the single biggest administrative and personnel problem that the Department had to face during the next 20 years.

The official invitation from Eden and Molotov reached the Department on July 21. A policy matter of such importance soon gyrated to departmental levels far higher than those of a desk officer. The initial telegram to Canada House and the circulation of its reply were about my last real involvement on the policy side of the question, which quickly absorbed the attention of the department's most senior officers and the cabinet.

It soon transpired that our forecast of the government's acceptance of the invitation was right, although the decision was not an easy one. Many years later I learned from Paul Martin, who had been Minister of National Health and Welfare during the 1950s and who later became External Affairs Minister, that most cabinet members were far from enthusiastic about the prospect. He told me that most were "very much of two minds" about accepting the burden, including Prime Minister St. Laurent, who was "very much opposed." Trade Minister Howe was "quite sceptical," he added, and so too was Agriculture Minister Gardiner. He, Martin, was in favour and so too was Lester Pearson, then in charge of External Affairs, although neither, Martin explained, was really enthused about accepting such a responsibility in an area that Canada knew very little about. It was Pearson who "carried the ball," Martin added. St. Laurent, who had "great respect for Pearson," allowed himself to be persuaded and the other members of the cabinet followed suit. Martin remarked that, in his recollection, during that week Eden had been after Pearson "persistently" to accept. In Martin's view, the invitation was accepted more out of a sense of duty, in the interests of peace in Southeast Asia, than anything else. [5]

Acceptance of the invitation was made public on July 28 and the pace in the Division and elsewhere in the Department became quite frenetic. The Cease-Fire Agreements for North, Central, and South Vietnam were scheduled for July 27, August 1, and August 11 respectively. August 11 therefore became the target date for the beginning of Commission operations, which left very little time for preparations and planning, staffing and other administrative and logistical arrangements, not only in External but also, particularly, at National Defence. [6]

India, as chair, urgently convened a preparatory meeting of the participants, to take place in New Delhi from August 1 to August 6. In the Department, many administrative, financial and personnel decisions were required fast. There were many meetings with National Defence regarding its manpower contribution and role. It was agreed early on that, because of the terms of the Cease-Fire Agreements, specifying a considerable number of fixed and mobile inspection teams throughout Indochina, the National Defence component would be much larger than that from External Affairs but that, owing to the political implications, External would be the lead department in the operation.

I recall one meeting in particular with National Defence. It was held in the Undersecretary's office in the East Block. Very senior staff officers from National Defence were there. The main topic of discussion was the size of its eventual component in the field. At one point, a senior general asked Dr. R.A. MacKay from External Affairs, who was chairing the meeting: "How many bodies will be needed on the ground out there?" "Bodies?" queried a rather startled Dr. MacKay, "Bodies on the ground?" "Yes. Bodies," was the reply. It was Brigadier (later Major-General) Rothschild, if I remember rightly, who explained. He had been dealing with External Affairs quite a bit and knew our language and ways. "Mr. Chairman. How many people, how many service personnel, may be required in Indochina?" "Oh. I see," replied Dr. MacKay.

The consensus which emerged from the meeting was that a personnel component of several hundreds from National Defence would be required. We were not far wrong. The meetings in New Delhi eventually determined that the Canadian and Polish contingents of each Commission would have to be approximately 165 to 170 each, of whom about 135 or 140 would be military and the remainder civilian. The Indian component would have to be a good deal larger; India would be supplying not only military personnel, but also the general administrative and communications secretariat, along with the related support staff required for the common services of each Commission. Because of the urgency, Canada's first servicemen were sent to Indochina from Korea.[7]

It was at this point, mid-August 1954, that I left the Indochina Desk. Personnel had determined that, pending the arrival of our ambassador to Egypt, I should be posted to Cairo as chargé d'affaires to open one of the three new embassies in the Middle East that the government had decided upon, the two others being in Beirut and Tel Aviv. Cairo was scheduled to be operational by early October.

Pre-posting briefings were set up for me; inoculations were required; and in those days one travelled by ship. My family and I reached Alexandria from New York, after nearly four weeks on the high seas, in time to meet the deadline. The rest of the Cairo team from External consisted of Bill Graham, an excellent administrative officer, and Angie Waterman, an extremely competent and versatile secretary. We were all on board an American Export Line freighter, the *Excambion*. Elizabeth MacCallum, Canada's first woman head of post, was also on board. She was on her way to Beirut to open the new post there. The Commercial Secretary, Mac Dale, had preceded us by a few days and met us at the docks.

To open an embassy, by the way, is not as easy as it may sound. In Cairo, it meant finding suitable offices for the post and housing for the incoming ambassador and our own families, hiring competent local staff, making banking, communications, and other arrangements, and so on: all in new surroundings. We were very busy. Fortunately, French and English were in common use and interpreters were available, but some Arabic would have done no harm. We were also very lucky. We found just the sort of property that the Department preferred as a chancery. The government eventually bought it and, after all these years, our Embassy is still located in the building we found.

This was a lively time to be in Cairo. Colonel Nasser had just achieved power. Nationalization of the Suez Canal was in the offing. The great High Dam at Aswan was the subject of intense bargaining among the great powers, with the Soviets winning out. Thus, not only were we busy setting up a new post, but also frantically trying to keep Ottawa abreast of what was going on.

Four years went by until my next exposure to Indochina. During the interval, after about a year and a half in Egypt, I served 15 very happy months with Evan Gill in South Africa, which came to an end in early July 1957, when he was posted to Accra as Canada's first High Commissioner to Ghana. I then became acting High Commissioner until the arrival of the new High Commissioner in March 1958, at which time I was almost at the end of my posting.

I fully expected to be recalled to Ottawa, but towards the end of April, 1958 I received a telegram from Personnel asking whether I would be willing to go to Phnom Penh for a while, on my way home, as Acting Canadian Commissioner and head of our delegation to the International Control Commission for Cambodia.

I accepted, and in due course, in early July, 1958 reached Phnom Penh by train, via Singapore and Bangkok. Shortly after my arrival, I received a letter from the Cambodian Minister of Transport asking me to come to his office in order to give him my reactions to my ride on his trains. When I called, I learned that I was the first diplomat to reach Phnom Penh by train in a very long time.

The trip was made from the Thai border on an *Autorail Michelin*, a small, noisy, smelly, diesel-propelled two-car unit, and I had been seated with all the locals and their chickens and other animals. I badly needed a wash and change of clothing on arrival! Yet the train had come in on time. I had reached Phnom Penh safe and sound; and had in the process managed to see a lot of the countryside. An interesting introduction to life in Cambodia. What more could one ask for? So I said generally nice things to the Minister about his trains. He was very pleased.

At the office, the morning following my arrival, I found a very small post indeed. Since the establishment of Prince Sihanouk's government in 1957 things had calmed down a good deal in Cambodia. A cease-fire had been in place for some time. Troop withdrawals had taken place. Population movements had been completed, as had exchanges of civilian refugees and internees. Elections had been held and a fairly stable government had come into being. There had been no really serious incidents for quite a while. In other words, the objectives of the Geneva Agreement respecting Cambodia had been achieved.

In the circumstances, Ottawa argued that the Commission had successfully completed its mandate and should accordingly be disbanded. Prince Sihanouk thought otherwise and insisted that it remain in place, as a measure of protection for his country. India and Poland agreed and, finally, so too did Ottawa, albeit reluctantly. In so doing, however, it decided to considerably reduce the size of the Canadian delegation. [8]

I was the only External Affairs officer there, with a secretary, Gertrude Moreau, and a clerk/accountant, André Doucet, also from the Department. The National Defence component was larger. It was headed by a lieutenant-colonel and included a chief warrant officer, Mr. Fenton, as he was called, and on occasion a sergeant and a varying number of corporals. During most of my posting, our military advisor was Roy Oglesby. A local staff of interpreters, messengers and drivers, provided by the Cambodian government, was also on hand. The need for interpreters was compelling; Khmer is an isolated tongue spoken by relatively few people in the world. The need for messengers and drivers reflected the poor telephone system in Phnom Penh. A letter or note by messenger or driver was by far the most expeditious way to communicate effectively.

On the subject of communicating, one of the corporals taught me a very good lesson shortly after my arrival, and I am in his debt to this day. At one point, mid-morning, I felt the need for a cup of coffee. It was one of the prerogatives of the corporals to brew it and I asked for a cup somewhat along the following lines or in some similar convoluted way: "Corporal! Wouldn't it be nice to have a cup of coffee." Five minutes went by, ten minutes, and no coffee. Finally I went into the corporal's quarters and asked: "Corporal! Where's my coffee?" "Sir," he asked. "Did you want coffee?" I said: "Yes!" "Sir!," he replied. "Why didn't you say so?"

So, then and there, I gave him a set of good, plain, direct instructions: coffee every morning at 10 o'clock, with sugar, and I got it served faithfully every day with a flourish! I have warm recollections of that corporal.

On the basis of the Geneva Agreements, the Indochina Commissions were empowered only to inspect incidents and observe conditions. They had no executive mandate and no powers of enforcement. They could only report infractions and difficulties to the Geneva Conference co-Chairmen and members for consideration and possible action. For such Commission action as was possible unanimity was required, although minority reports could be submitted to the co-Chairmen. When a vote was scheduled, which during my time in Phnom Penh was rare, I would follow the general guidance I had received from Ottawa on the occasion of the posting. If a question was unexpected, unusual or sensitive, which happened very infrequently when I was in Phnom Penh, I would consult External.

Commission work was on the wane in Cambodia, as the Sihanouk government was getting into its stride. The Commission met rather spasmodically during my posting. Nevertheless, it was during these meetings and my frequent contacts with the Indians and Poles that I got an insight into their outlooks and mindsets.

Canadians serving on the Indochina Commissions generally expected the Poles to be intransigent and rigid in their support of North Vietnam and the Communist cause. For instance, while I was in Phnom Penh, not once did they take a neutral or anti-North Vietnam stand. Yet, despite ideological differences, I found that the Poles—although unwavering in outlook—tended to approach questions, to justify their positions on problems, in terms of logic and thinking processes that were essentially Western in conceptualization and background. Also, their daily lives, their general deportment, their dress, reflected Western patterns and practices. I, for one, found the Poles to be rather more like us than I had expected.

Administratively, they ran their component of the Commission much like ours, albeit more stiffly. Actually, except for the Commissioner and military advisors, most of the subordinate Polish staff in Phnom Penh during my posting were devout Catholics. Most went to mass and communion regularly, more so than some Canadians I know! Also, many knew several languages and were quite well versed in Western literature. They tended to use French with me. A few spoke English and served as interpreters for the Polish Commissioner, who spoke French but no English and required interpretation during Commission meetings or when dealing with our chairman.

While the Poles on the Commission may have been unwavering in their support of Communism and North Vietnam, they were not necessarily so with respect to the Russians, at least on a personal basis. I vividly remember a fist fight between a Polish military advisor and a Russian military attaché during a reception at the Soviet Embassy! Both had had a bit too much to drink and, before they could be separated, each had done quite a bit of damage to the other. I later learned that it was the Pole who started the fight and that it was not about a woman, as one might have thought, but reflected the deep hatred that many Poles felt for the Russians. I rather expected that the Polish major might have been recalled or transferred after the incident. But no; he remained *en poste*. Boys will be boys, even in Poland!

In the case of the Indians, I found their thought processes, and their way of approaching things, to be quite different. They tended to deal with Commission problems more convolutedly, more indirectly. This doubtless reflected both the complexity of their long historical relationship with the countries of Indochina and the importance of the peninsula as a facet of their country's regional interests, but probably it also derived from the way in which they had been brought up to approach questions and to think about and solve problems generally.

In addition, caught at times as they were, as the country chairing the Commission, between the Canadians and the Poles, they had of course to tread warily. Sometimes the chairman would agree with us, and sometimes he would agree with them: almost as if it were a balancing act. However, because things were much quieter in Cambodia than in Vietnam and there was much less Commission work to do, we in Phnom Penh did not experience to the same degree the sharp and persistent tensions among the Canadians, Indians, and Poles, that were characteristic of the Control Commission in Vietnam. [9]

In their personal lives, the Indians reflected of course the values, the interests, the dress, the deportment, the social stratification of the East. A small incident illustrating this comes to mind. One morning, during a Commission meeting, the Indian chairman (a major-general) needed a file. "Subahdar!", he shouted towards the next office, "Get me file number such-and-such." The subahdar came in, saluted smartly, got down on his knees, opened the bottom drawer of the desk behind which the general was sitting, drew the file, stood up, saluted smartly again, placed the file on the desk, and said: "Sar! [*sic*] File number such-and-such." He didn't even get a thank-you. Almost simultaneously, the Polish Commissioner looked at me and I looked at him, while this was going on. We both raised our eyebrows—almost together—stared at the ceiling and struggled not to burst out laughing. The Indian Commissioner looked at the two of us with no little puzzlement, as we proceeded to study file number such-and-such.

Thus, I for one found on balance, that despite sharing common parliamentary institutions and democratic government, as well as the English language, the Indians turned out to be much less like us than I had expected.

Fortunately, as the Commission's work dwindled, Colombo Plan activities got into swing. By the time I left Phnom Penh early in August 1959, the post's military component had been considerably reduced and, in essence, the Canadian delegation had become a small aid mission, with some political and economic reporting on conditions in Cambodia, and very occasional Commission meetings that dealt largely with administrative and other internal Commission matters.

CIDA experts in fisheries and in water and forest management were arriving. Shipments of medical equipment and supplies were being prepared. Scholarships for Cambodians in Canadian universities and other institutions were being provided and suitable candidates had to be found. Preliminary consideration of the great project to develop the vast Mekong River Basin was getting under way. Regrettably, it did not materialize but I hope that some day it will; its benefits for the entire region would be immense. [10]

Aid was big business in Cambodia, and Prince Sihanouk nursed it zealously. He encouraged rivalries in this respect between the Americans and the Soviets in particular, and he also played other countries off against each other as well. The Soviet Union and the United States tended to go in for rather showy large-scale projects. The Chinese too did so on occasion, but more typically they would often send their experts into the fields to show how irrigation and rice production might be improved. Australia's aid programs resembled ours: basically technical assistance. The French, Czechs, and Japanese were also active.

In February 1959, *The Economist* ran the following gem about aid to Cambodia from one of its correspondents who had recently visited the country.

Theoretically, it will soon be possible for a lucky Cambodian pedestrian, who has been knocked down by a Polish steam locomotive, travelling to a port constructed by the French, on a railway built by the Chinese, to be rushed in an East German ambulance, driven by a Japanese-trained chauffeur and fuelled by American petrol, along a highway built by the Americans, to a modern hospital erected by the Russians and staffed by nurses using Czech medical equipment, who have been educated under the Colombo Plan. [11]

There was thus plenty of scope for Sihanouk's machinations and many observers at the time thought him to be quite mad in his convolutions. There is no doubt that he could be mercurial and unpredictable. Nevertheless, as I reported to Ottawa at the time, he was nobody's fool and there seemed to be a good deal of method in his madness. [12]

He was managing quite successfully to wangle development assistance for his country from a wide variety of sources and in an extremely broad range of activity. The country was generally peaceful. Its economy was progressing. Development was taking place. In short, while Prince Sihanouk was at the helm, Cambodia survived not too badly. Tragedy struck his country later on, after he was ousted. [13]

Canadian relations with other Western aid donors were close. I personally felt most at home with the Australians, whose general approach and outlook tended to resemble ours. U.S. and British embassy officers would sometimes come around to Candel, as our delegation was called, to enquire about what the Commission was doing and so too would the French. However, as Commission work had dwindled quite sharply, there was not really much to tell.

Prince Sihanouk's government kept a generally firm hand on the countryside and it was possible to visit most of it by car, except for the far north and northwest where the *Khmers rouges* had camps, as they still do to this day. The roads were not all that they might have been, but I managed to get around quite a bit in order to show the flag. I was thus able to visit not only several provincial cities but also, of course, the great ruins at Angkor Wat, and many lesser known sites, more isolated and less striking, but perhaps more appealing and in certain ways more romantic because they were less frequented and less well restored.

In his own inimitable and lively way Prince Sihanouk made life for the diplomatic corps, Commission officials and senior public servants somewhat more bearable. A hospitable and accomplished host and a musician of talent, he would fairly often invite us to dinner at the Palace, where he not only wined us and dined us, but also sang to us, and the orchestra—often under his baton—played some of his own compositions. On occasion, he would organize superb performances of the Royal Khmer Ballet in the Palace compound.

It was at one of those dinners that I acquired a spurious reputation for cool-headedness. At one point I had received instructions from Ottawa to oppose Commission involvement in a matter of personal interest to Prince Sihanouk himself. Ottawa reasoned, on the basis of the facts, that what he really wanted was an endorsement by the Commission of his position on what was essentially a matter of internal Cambodian politics. I followed my instructions. India and Poland supported Prince Sihanouk and he soon learned that Canada had not. There was, therefore, no formal Commission involvement. I said to myself: "You've not heard the last of this."

One week went by. Two weeks and still no response from the Palace. Perhaps I was out of the woods, I thought. But I had overlooked Prince Sihanouk's long memory. A few weeks later, at one of his dinners, at about midnight, he called for silence and started to talk. At one point he singled me out and launched on what could only be called a diatribe. I do not know what he said, because at almost the very moment that he began to point in my direction one of the batteries of my hearing aid gave out! I was fairly close to him and could not change the batteries inconspicuously. So I stood still. I could see that he was agitated but I could not hear a word! He eventually calmed down, turned his attention elsewhere, and I quickly changed batteries. It was at that point that the Australian minister came up to me and said: "My! You External Affairs types are really cold fish!" The French ambassador remarked: "Mais, cher collègue, quel sang froid!" Apparently Sihanouk had been quite personal and biting in some of his comments. Not wanting to disillusion my friends, I basked in their praise.

Incidentally, several weeks later, as my posting was coming to an end, I sent a note to the Palace by messenger seeking an appointment for the customary farewell call. I received no reply. As I said above, Prince Sihanouk had a long memory. I was sorry about his refusal to see me because, despite his quirks, I rather admired him.

As an aside on the subject of diplomacy and hearing, I may mention that the great French foreign minister, Talleyrand, once made a very perceptive comment during the Congress of Vienna in 1815. At an early procedural meeting of heads of delegation, to which he had been invited alone without advisors, Talleyrand noticed that Prussian business was being handled not so much by the head of Prussia's delegation, State Chancellor Hardenberg, who normally dealt with much of his country's foreign policy, but by Humboldt, his deputy. It was explained that Hardenberg, who suffered from deafness, had decided that Humboldt's presence was required because of this hearing impediment, to which Talleyrand replied somewhat along the following lines: "Oh! Yes! Where ailments are concerned, we all have our infirmities and should take the greatest possible advantage of them. Prince Hardenberg knows very well how to use his infirmities." Very well, he was told, he could bring advisors with him the next time. Talleyrand had won his first point.

An early childhood fall had left Talleyrand with a club foot and at times he used his limp to advantage. I suspect that Hardenberg may have tended to hear only what he wanted to hear: Il faut se servir de ses infirmités! [14]

Daily life in Phnom Penh was certainly easier than in Hanoi or Vientiane. In North Vietnam, life was beset by all the problems typical of a communist country, coupled with those normally accompanying a pervasive and all powerful military regime, which in addition had just won a considerable victory. Life in Hanoi was particularly oppressive psychologically, whereas in Laos the problems were more physical. Vientiane was a small, distant, rather neglected outpost with few amenities, while in much of the Laotian countryside, where the inspection teams had to operate, the practical conditions they faced were those of the jungle. Saigon, like Phnom Penh, was much better and tended to be used by Commission colleagues, whether Canadian, Indian, or Polish, as a rest and recuperation haven.

Nevertheless, all this was rather relative. Health and sanitary conditions throughout Indochina left much to be desired, as was indicated by the long list of required pre-posting inoculations and injections. Safe drinking water was a constant problem. Much care had to be taken about food, which was easier said than done, since most Commission personnel had to live in hotels, such as they were, and depend on restaurants, when available. These difficulties were aggravated by pervasive year-round mosquitoes and constant high heat and humidity that could test the patience of a saint and in addition rot shoes and clothing, unless special steps were taken to air them regularly. Air-conditioning was rare during this period, but there were some alternatives. The French had left behind them their *Cercles Sportifs* with tennis courts, swimming pools, and so on, to which Commission personnel had access.

The same trying conditions also affected Commission work. In addition to the mosquitoes, high heat and humidity, we had to endure office space that in Phnom Penh and Vientiane at least was quite rudimentary, with technical equipment on the primitive side, and in close contact with counterparts around the table whose positions could at times be intransigent and unwavering. Compromises were virtually impossible, which could be quite frustrating.

There was no parallel for this experience at that time, either in the United Nations context or at NATO, or elsewhere, where Canadian delegates were accustomed to negotiations conducted with the most contemporary equipment available, in comfortable surroundings, and with at least some allies around the table.

As a general conclusion to these recollections of a fairly distant past, membership in the Indochina Commissions was undeniably a daunting challenge administratively and politically. But at the same time it was a professional plus for External Affairs. The Department acquired a reservoir of officers and staff who had had to acquire skills in management techniques and the art of negotiating under the most trying conditions, and also to develop procedures for dealing quickly with complex questions in difficult circumstances. It is interesting to note here the number of contributors to this volume who served in Indochina as young officers.

There is no doubt that the Department's experience on the Commissions was to stand it in good stead later on as the Cold War progressed and we had to deal with such serious issues as disarmament and nuclear proliferation, East-West relations, the Law of the Sea, the international aspects of federal-provincial affairs, and problems with France, among others.

NOTES

Files referred to in this chapter are located in the National Archives of Canada.

1. See James Eayrs and Douglas A. Ross for background in, respectively, *In Defence of Canada, Indochina: Roots of Complicity* (Toronto: University of Toronto Press, 1983) and *In the Interests of Peace* (Toronto: University of Toronto Press, 1984).
2. For background, see "Canada's Policy on Indochina," a memorandum prepared in the Far Eastern Division, November 16, 1953, on Department of Foreign Affairs (previously External Affairs) File No. 50052-40. (File 50052-40 is the basic file on Indochina for this period and is in many volumes.) The memorandum is printed as Document 1079 in Donald Barry, ed., *Documents on Canadian External Relations*, Volume 19, 1953 (Ottawa: Canada Communications Group) at pages 1580-82. See also, in File 50052-40, referred to above, under April 1953, "Indochina as a NATO Problem" and "Possible Developments at the Current NATO Council Meeting."

3. File 50052-40, under July 19-21, 1954 carries this correspondence in detail.
4. *In Defence of Canada*, p. 50, gives an account of how this may have come about. See also John Holmes, *Shaping the Peace, 1943-1957*, Volume 2 (Toronto: University of Toronto Press, 1982) p. 205, for background.
5. Personal conversation with the Hon. Paul Martin, Sr., August 5, 1988.
6. Both Eayrs and Ross analyze the announcement at pages 56-57 and 87-90, respectively, of their books. See also file 50052-40 for the full text of Canada's acceptance of the invitation and related documents.
7. File 50052-40 provides a detailed account.
8. See John Hilliker and Donald Barry, *Coming of Age 1946-1968*, Volume 2 of *Canada's Department of External Affairs* (Montreal and Kingston: McGill-Queen's University Press, 1995), 115-21.
9. Reporting comments by Pamela McDougall, a former Ambassador to Poland and Deputy Minister of National Health and Welfare, who served in Vietnam during the late 1950s, *bout de papier* (Ottawa: Professional Association of Foreign Service Officers) Winter-Spring issue, p. 26, gives a good account of these tensions, as well as of the living conditions prevalent in Vietnam at the time.
10. Department of Foreign Affairs File 11038-AG-40 deals with Canadian-Colombo Plan activities in Cambodia.
11. *The Economist*, February 14, 1959.
12. See File 50052-C-2-40. Phnom Penh letter No. 202, September 8, 1958.
13. For a general account of the political situation and economic conditions prevailing in Cambodia during the 1950s, see David J. Steinberg et al., *Cambodia* (New Haven: HRAF Press, 1957). The HRAF Press published a sequel by Steinberg in 1959. The Library of Congress in Washington, D.C. has also issued country studies on Cambodia from time to time.
14. See Duff Cooper, *Talleyrand* (London: Jonathan Cape, 1932), Chapter 10 and Harold Nicolson, *The Congress of Vienna* (London: Constable, 1946), Chapter 9. Both authors relate this incident.

Arthur E. Blanchette joined External Affairs in 1947. He was Indochina desk officer during the mid- to late-1950s, then served as the head of the Canadian delegation to the International Control Commission in Cambodia. Subsequently appointed Ambassador and Permanent Observer to the OAS in Washington, Mr. Blanchette also served as Ambassador in Tunisia and Libya. For many years he has represented Canada at the Pan-American Institute of Geography and History, a specialized agency of the OAS. Three of his books on Canadian foreign policy between the years 1955 and 1993 have been published by Carleton University Press.

CLOSING A MISSION: CYPRUS, 1970

GORDON BROWN

JUST OVER A YEAR after arriving in Cyprus, I closed the doors of the Canadian High Commission on instructions from Ottawa. Until 1969, few heads of Canadian diplomatic posts had had this unpleasant experience: for most who had to close shop, the necessity had arisen at the outbreak of war, in enemy territory, with the rules of the game well defined by international custom. To pull up stakes in a friendly country is far more difficult because no rules exist. Diplomatic relations that have been entered into with solemn professions of mutual respect are terminated because the financial wizards of a country tell their government that it must economize and it is decided that the foreign ministry must join in the economy drive.

And, so, a mission or two or three are chosen for the axe. The country's diplomats then have to adduce reasons for closing those missions, reasons which often are transparent because a government cannot admit to being broke and cannot tell another country that it is of no consequence. So the rationale usually stretches the truth. And this makes the task even less agreeable. It was like that in Nicosia, Cyprus, in 1969.

Closing Nicosia had always been a possibility, because the Canadian High Commission had never been "established" in a formal sense as a post; all of its job positions had been borrowed from elsewhere in the Department of External Affairs when the post had been created in March 1964, a few days in advance of the arrival of the first Canadian troops. It was the understanding then that the post would remain as long as the troops were there: when I came to Nicosia, I knew that it was intended to close the post if the Canadian contingent in the United Nations Force in Cyprus (UNFICYP) were to be withdrawn.

When this would happen was a moot point. Some thought that it might be in two or three years, near the end of my tour of duty in Cyprus. Others believed that it would be earlier. At the meeting of heads of European posts in London, in January 1969, I joked that my aim was to

A visit in December 1968 to the reconnaissance platoon of the Canadian contingent at Sami House, near Kyrenia. High Commissioner Brown is talking with Lieutenant-Colonel Jean Riffou and other members of the Royal 22nd Regiment.

achieve the first post closing since that of the mission in St John's, which became redundant when Newfoundland entered Confederation. I was quite prepared to work towards the termination of Canada's presence in Cyprus but, to ensure that I would look at that possibility objectively, I asked only that, if the post were closed, I be given another assignment abroad. This was readily agreed to by the departmental powers-that-were in November 1968, although the promise was to be lost in the confusion that surrounded the decision to close the mission and the way in which it was executed.

Pierre Elliott Trudeau was to have more impact on the Department of External Affairs than any of us suspected when he became Prime Minister in April 1968. We thought that he would bring fresh ideas to Canadian foreign policy and to the style in which we should conduct it. What we did not realize was that he had some antipathy toward senior members of the foreign service.

In ordering the review of foreign policy in 1968, Mr. Trudeau explained that there was no commitment to change but only to re-examine the premises on which policy was based. But it was soon apparent that membership in NATO was in jeopardy and that relations with Europe were regarded as unimportant when compared with those with China and the Soviet Union. While this alarmed senior officers of the Department, they failed to assess what the Prime Minister really wanted and to adjust to the new bench-marks that he set. There was also a failure to ensure that he understood the role of the Department. The first months of contact did nothing to establish the credibility of the foreign service in the eyes of the Prime Minister. As Bruce Thordarson was to write:

If Mr. Trudeau was generally sceptical of civil servants, he was particularly critical of the Department of External Affairs. Other departments he viewed as excessively conservative: External he seemed to regard as largely irrelevant. He seemed to believe that the main function of Canada's diplomatic service was to collect and despatch information.[1]

The early stages of the review of policy towards Europe, an exercise known as "Stafeur," occupied the Department throughout the second half of 1968. The initial draft of the report was the central item on the agenda of the London meeting of heads of posts which coincided with the 1969 conference of Commonwealth Heads of Government; it was the first time that they—and we—were exposed to the new Canadian Prime Minister. As Secretary of State for External Affairs, Mitchell Sharp was the chairman of the heads of post gathering; but during his frequent absences at the Commonwealth meeting his Parliamentary Secretary, Jean-Pierre Goyer, led the discussions.

Stafeur's draft report examined the bases of the Canadian relationship with Europe in great detail. It argued that the institutional framework of the relationship had served us well for almost two decades and should be continued, more or less unchanged. This was not what Trudeau and Goyer wanted to hear. They regarded the report as a rigid, conservative defence of the status quo, devoid of imaginative thinking. They found that the report gave no hint of any departmental feeling for a new approach to problems or awareness of the new ideas which Mr. Trudeau and the inner group of his cabinet and staff prided themselves on. These were serious flaws, but the Department's error was compounded by its failure, in the writing of the report, to observe the newly promulgated procedures for the presentation of material to the Prime Minister. Mr. Trudeau thus became convinced that the foreign service was opposed to change of any kind. It must be admitted that the Department almost invited this criticism, even if it did not merit the punishment that the Prime Minister was to inflict.

I saw Mr. Trudeau in action for the first time at the London meeting when he spoke to the heads of post. There were about two dozen of us present, one woman and 23 men, whose responsibilities ranged from those exercised at the important capitals of London, Bonn and Paris to the comfortable posts of Berne, The Hague and Lisbon and down to my small hornets' nest at the eastern end of the Mediterranean. The Prime Minister's opening words were condescending: foreign service officers were always considered an intelligent group of civil servants, he said, and it was a new experience for him to meet so many distinguished members of the service at one time. He remarked that he knew more first and second secretaries than ambassadors and he was concerned that the junior officers were excluded from policy-making. He wondered—"I am talking off the top of my head but I do know these people and what they are thinking"—whether ambassadors encouraged them to think about policy, the way he wanted his ministers to do. It was his impression that the brainpower of the juniors was not being employed, that the windows were closed. This ploy by the 49-year-old Prime Minister, associating himself with the younger group of the foreign service, did not sit well with an audience, whose average age was 53, even though it included some of the oldest heads of post in the service.

Mr. Trudeau continued by giving notice that the very basis of our policies had to be examined and that we had to determine what was best for Canada and why. Foreign policy had to reflect the geography of Canada, its size and economic strength and the existence of the two founding groups; policy remained to be defined in new conditions and with reference to new areas of technology. Meanwhile, he asked himself, were our diplomats doing the right things? Were they emphasizing only the traditional diplomatic role or did they know the young Canadian artists in their countries? Were they aware of the importance of multinational corporations in limiting or influencing the foreign policies of countries? Were they following developments in cybernetics and electronics?[2]

It was a most impressive performance. But it was disturbing. Only later did I learn that Jean-Pierre Goyer had helped to sharpen Trudeau's doubts about us. At the first meeting I had formed the impression that Goyer regarded the officers of the Department present as members of a professional establishment resentful of change. He had reported to the Prime Minister that the cream of Canadian diplomats had not come up with a single new idea during the meeting. In terms of the review of foreign policy that meeting had been a failure; for the Department the consequences were to be even more serious.

While relations with NATO were a principal target of the policy review, the very future of the armed forces was also at stake. If the forces were to be reduced, then the continued participation of Canada in the peacekeeping force in Cyprus was also in question. In addition to the Department, the Committee on External Affairs and National Defence of the House of Commons had been put to work on the review of foreign policy. On February 11 I learned that the Committee would visit Cyprus a month later as part of a swing through Europe to look into peacekeeping and NATO and to examine the options of disarmament (in Geneva) and neutrality (in Stockholm).

The visit took place on March 10-11 or, more precisely, for 25 hours from 4:30 p.m. on the 10th until 5:30 p.m. on the 11th. Ian Wahn, the chairman of the Committee, was the leader of the thirty members making up the group, which included many distinguished parliamentarians. They were briefed at the United Nations headquarters by General Martola, the Finnish commander of UNFICYP, and Dr. Bibiano Osorio-Tafall, the Special Representative of the United Nations Secretary-General. Then, at Camp Maple Leaf, leaders of the Greek- and Turkish-Cypriot sides made strong endorsements of the need for a Canadian military presence and Brigadier-General E.M.D. ("Ted") Leslie—the Canadian deputy to General Martola—and I also made presentations.

My pitch was solidly in favour of continued Canadian participation in UNFICYP. After setting the scenario for peacekeeping in the long and involved history of the island, I spoke about the current intercommunal talks between Greeks and Turks and the part that had been played by the United Nations in bringing them together. I made the point that the possibility of renewed fighting must not be discounted; in these circumstances, the role of UNFICYP was perhaps even more important than it had been before the talks began.

The job of peace*keeping*, I argued, had to continue so that the more delicate enterprise of peace*making* might be undertaken. I went on to say:

This enterprise involves the search for a reasonable and workable arrangement under which the Greek-Cypriot majority and the Turkish-Cypriot minority may live and work in peace. Such an arrangement must obviously provide the Turkish-Cypriots with every assurance that their cultural, linguistic and religious individuality will be protected and enabled to flourish. It must also provide the one community with assurances that the other community will not obstruct the governing of the state or the development of the economy. These are difficult objectives but their attainment is made even harder by the need to satisfy Greece and Turkey that their national interests in Cyprus will be safeguarded. And going beyond that, the ultimate solution of the Cyprus problem must be viable enough—at the very least—to withstand scrutiny in the world at large and particularly at the United Nations. All of these factors make it seem unlikely that peacemaking will be a rapid process."[3]

Continuing, I said that I did not claim that the High Commission played a direct role in the task of peacemaking although the possibility that it might should not be ruled out. However, the High Commission did provide diplomatic support to the Canadian contingent and to the peacekeeping efforts of UNFICYP whose political heads consulted us frequently.

I felt that I had been speaking to the converted for many of the parliamentarians assured me before they left the next day that they were convinced of the need for continued Canadian participation in the peacekeeping force. They seemed, too, to take for granted the continued presence of a Canadian diplomatic mission as long as Canadian troops were on the island.

As spring progressed and I planned for a week of consultations in Ottawa in late May, I became more and more persuaded that a case existed for placing the High Commission in Nicosia on a permanent basis. I believed that a settlement of the island's problems would not be achieved in the immediate future and might take several years. Meanwhile, our office was doing much more than providing diplomatic support to the peacekeepers. Canadian trade with Cyprus was assuming some importance, having reached an annual level of nearly a million dollars. Immigration had grown to about five hundred a year and consular work was increasing, as more Canadians visited Cyprus and more Cypriots arrived in Canada. The post was a link between Canadian missions in Arab countries and the embassy in Israel. In time of war in the Middle East Cyprus would be a safe haven. Other considerations mattered: Cyprus was in the Commonwealth and its strategic position made it important to the Western alliance. For all these reasons, I was certain that we should establish the small High Commission on a permanent footing, giving that action a high priority and, if necessary, precedence over the setting up of new missions elsewhere.

My enthusiasm for this thesis was crushed within hours of my arrival in Ottawa on May 21. Those in the Department of External Affairs who dealt with Cyprus and Europe preferred that the question of Nicosia's permanence or impermanence should not be raised in days of defence cuts—days too, I learned, of the possible abolition of some of our own posts. Although the parliamentary committee had expressed support for peacekeeping, it seemed that there were elements within the cabinet who did not want us to stay in UNFICYP. The possibility of posts being closed came to mind the next day when I was told by a senior officer that we were not being given the money to run the foreign service at its current level, let alone paying for new posts and rising salaries and allowances. If we were not allowed the funds, he said, something would have to give. My informant remarked that budgetary problems were not the only ones for the Department in the Trudeau age: because of the new style of government, the Department had not made a policy recommendation for months. A friend at National Defence, which was about to be decimated, spoke bitterly about the centralization of power in the Prime Minister's office and, within the cabinet, in a few ministers. My friend opined that there was a direct parallel between the predicaments of National Defence and External Affairs. Military bases would be closing. Why not diplomatic posts too?

Throughout June and into July there was little word from Ottawa to suggest that the High Commission would not remain open. On July 17, with the Department's agreement, I renewed the lease on the official residence for another year and wrote in my diary: "I presume we will still be here: the Cyprus problem is certainly no closer to solution."

I was on leave on August 13 when I heard Prime Minister Trudeau's announcement that he would reduce the civil service by 25,000 over the following two years and freeze the budgets of government departments. It was all in the interest of fighting inflation, he said. My only reaction at the time was that the Ottawa merchants would be worried: the curbs on spending did not seem to have any direct relevance for me. When I returned to Nicosia, however, the austere wind from Ottawa was felt in a letter notifying us of a general cut of ten percent in our allowances for representational activities.

About that time I also received a report from a Canadian newspaper on the austerity program. In it Mitchell Sharp was quoted as describing as speculative a rumour that the External Affairs budget would be cut by two million dollars annually. The news article also quoted an "inside source" as claiming that the Department planned to cut or close eight embassies or consulates, including three in Latin America. A few days later, a military visitor from Ottawa told us that Nicosia had been listed in a newspaper story on posts which might be closed in the next year. The courier bringing our diplomatic bag from Ottawa that week also conveyed the rumour that we were on the short list for closing. I decided that the time had come to seek confirmation and, on 15 September, wrote to the head of the office dealing with political-military affairs in the Department to ask what was up. Planning was necessary, I said, if we were to close: we had to try to minimize the harm to bilateral relations with Cyprus, overcome difficulties which the Canadian contingent would encounter without diplomatic support, and avoid undue hardship to personnel.

A few days later, the first official indication that something was amiss came in a telegram cancelling my secretary's impending posting and the move of her replacement. On the strength of this, I sent an "immediate" priority telegram to Ottawa, using the gist of the arguments in my previous letter to the Department and asking to be brought into the picture. Other posts must also have heard of the list of posts to be chopped and made the same request for, on September 22, there came an unclassified telegram signed by Mitchell Sharp acknowledging the rumours. He deplored the speculation, saying that "it cannot but cause largely unnecessary and certainly premature concern." He went on to tell us that the conclusions of the departmental study of savings would "shortly" be brought before the Cabinet. The message concluded: "The interest and concern of departmental personnel are very much in our minds and will be taken fully into account, and I can assure you further that decisions when taken will be communicated to you as soon as possible."

September ended before we heard anything more definite than this. Meanwhile, Ted Leslie had communicated his views to the Chief of the Defence Staff in Ottawa on the need to maintain a High Commission as long as there was a Canadian contingent in UNFICYP. One of his arguments was that the diplomatic presence constituted a deterrent against the Cypriots making trouble for the Canadians, which prompted me to say to Ted that, as the deterrent was exercised by my occupying my chair, it might be called backside diplomacy.

Early in October, the reports that Nicosia would close became more solid. It was also learned that between forty and sixty foreign service officers were being rusticated, about twenty of these by means of an early retirement scheme of doubtful legality. The gloom in the Department, we heard, was deep. There was a matching gloom in my small office. The circumstances hardly encouraged us to maintain routine reporting on the Cyprus situation or to cultivate contacts. Why, I asked myself, keep up our "presence" if we were going to pull out? The Department replied to my mid-September letter to confirm that Nicosia was on the list and that, while it would be premature to consider the post axed, we should think about "precautionary measures." I commented in my diary: "So much for consultation between the department and posts."

A day later—Sunday, October 12—the orders of execution at last arrived. I was informed in a telegram that, on the 14th, it would be announced that the post in Nicosia would be closed along with six others: Berlin, Santo Domingo, Montevideo, Quito, Vientiane and Phnom Penh. This action was "essential" to achieving the government's intention "to combat inflation by containing federal government expenditures." I was instructed to pass immediately a message from Mitchell Sharp to the Cyprus government.

The Minister's message began with the words: "As a result of a decision to effect significant economies in the Government's operations," it was necessary that the resident mission in Nicosia be withdrawn. Yet, the message went on, Canada attached the greatest importance to the continued development of relations with Cyprus in all fields and, above all, to the maintenance of ties as members of the Commonwealth. To prove that we would continue to care about the problems of the island republic, arrangements were proposed for Canadian representation by one of our diplomatic posts nearby.

The cold, peremptory communication contained not one suggestion, let alone expression, of regret. It was left for me to add that. I sent a reply to Ottawa to say that I would deliver the message the next day and followed this telegram up with a reminder that others besides the Cypriots, especially the United Nations Secretary-General, should know of our intentions.

I saw Nicos Dimitriou, the Acting Minister of Foreign Affairs, at noon on Monday, October 13 to deliver the message. As instructed, I explained how the closing was solely for "important reasons of economy" and that we placed great value on our continued relations with Cyprus. The instructions also required me to state that the action should not be interpreted as reflecting any abatement of our deep concern to see an early solution of the Cyprus problem or any lessening of our willingness to search for that solution. Nor, the script continued, did the action imply any decision with respect to the nature of Canada's participation in UNFICYP.

Mr. Dimitriou said that he was sorry to hear the news. He observed that, in its five years in Nicosia, the Canadian High Commission had done much for the development of relations between Canada and Cyprus. But he regretted more that, like the Canadian decision to pull troops out of Europe, this decision seemed to reflect a turn by Canada towards isolationism and a withdrawal from the role in world affairs that we had played so well for the past 25 years. He also made the cogent observation that foreign expenditures, such as those for an embassy, had little to do with domestic measures to fight inflation.

The instructions from Ottawa had said that a message from Prime Minister Trudeau to President Makarios would follow. I asked the Foreign Minister to arrange for me to call on the Archbishop and was given an appointment for the 15th. Overnight, however, messages arrived advising us that the public announcement of the closing of missions was postponed because Ottawa wished to be able to consider any representations that might be made by the governments concerned. The Department was anxious that our intentions be kept secret; in the event of a leakage, we were to say that no details would be announced until the governments concerned had made their views known. As it would have been untrue to assert that we had invited comments from the Cypriots, I phoned Chris Veniamin, the Director-General of the Foreign Ministry, to tell him that it seemed that Ottawa might be susceptible to pressure. He saw President Makarios and called me afterwards to express "His Beatitude's surprise and concern." The President, he said, believed that there should be a resident Canadian diplomatic mission because of the Canadian contingent, with which the High Commission worked so closely, thus making an effective contribution to peacekeeping, to the Commonwealth link and to Canada's place in the Western world with which Cyprus needed close ties.

While all this was going on, the Department asked us to submit a plan for the closing of the High Commission. I proposed that we should remain operational until December 15 when the Security Council would have extended the UNFICYP mandate for another three to six months. Then, I suggested, we could run down our activity over a two-week period and spend January disposing of leases, furniture and files. We had been asked not to bother the Department with administrative questions, a request which I found ironic when the objective of the entire exercise was to save taxpayers' money.

A bizarre contribution to the mood of the day came on October 15 with the announcement by the Prime Minister of the establishment of a Canadian diplomatic mission to the Vatican and the appointment of Dr. John E. Robbins as its first head. The timing of the announcement disturbed me. Why was the Canadian government adding salt to the wounds of the Cypriots and others by broadcasting the opening of the Vatican post at this time? And how could the government be so callous as to appoint a 66-year-old from outside the service when there was talk of firing much younger career officers as part of the economy drive?

The Turkish-Cypriot leadership gave me their reaction to the notification of the post closing on October 17 in the form of a letter from the Vice-President, Dr. Fazil Kuchuk, to Prime Minister Trudeau. The Canadian High Commission and the Canadian contingent, he said, had been instrumental in bringing peace to the island and their influence would be equally important in assisting with a final solution. The High Commission had been valuable to the people of Cyprus and particularly to the Turkish community. It was not a persuasive plea.

The next day—a Saturday—we received the long-awaited message from Mr. Trudeau to President Makarios. It was clear that it could no longer be delivered because its case had been overtaken by developments and so, in an immediate reply, I proposed some changes. Much later I was to learn that my telegram was not received by the departmental desk officer for a week; it was a communications failure which, in retrospect, seems a normal event in a situation that was becoming messier by the day. Although we were under orders from headquarters to observe secrecy about the closing, we were being bombarded with *un*coded telegrams on housekeeping matters—messages in clear language directing us to wind up our leases on the chancery at 15A Heroes Street and the residence at 8 Epaminondas Street, to count our china and pots and pans, to report the condition of vehicles and furniture, and so forth—messages that gave the game away.

Although pressure had been put on the Canadian government in Washington, London, Athens and Ankara to keep the post in Nicosia open, Ottawa remained unmoved. In his press conference of October 15 on the opening of the mission to the Holy See, the Prime Minister had been downright cavalier. He said:

We will have to close other embassies abroad. I suppose Mr. Sharp will be announcing them as part of his guideline application. I would not like to give the examples now. I believe certain countries have been contacted but until Mr. Sharp announces it and until they have agreed or resigned themselves to it,

I don't want to give examples. But if you look at the lists of our diplomatic posts abroad there are some and perhaps several which are of very, very little importance to Canada. We think that the Vatican will give us much more grass roots information about the countries of the world than these particular posts which we will have to close. And that's the whole objective of the guidelines. It is not just to save money, it is in order that we use the money ... more efficiently.... We are closing some posts which are not giving us the results we need in the diplomatic area and we are opening others.... We do not have posts to sort of flatter the other guy. We should have them in order to help Canadians, either travellers or the Government, to follow its policies and its international developments.⁴

"So much," I wrote in my diary, "for (1) the Cypriots (2) the Canadian contingent to UNFICYP and (3) peacekeeping. Let alone some of our friends." I added that I would like to think that a review of the usefulness of the Vatican post would be made within a year or two, but knew that it would not be.

The formal reply of Acting Foreign Minister Dimitriou to my note to him of October 13 was delivered on October 18. It contained no new arguments. "Surprise and deep concern" were once again expressed. Mr. Dimitriou wondered whether our decision might not be misconstrued at a stage when the Cyprus problem was turning to a new and critical phase. Our association in the Commonwealth was referred to as was Canada's exemplary record in UN peacekeeping. I felt that the note lacked bite.

Mitchell Sharp scheduled a press conference for October 21 at which it was intended that he would announce the names of the missions to be closed. In the event he confined himself to the remark that the posts were not in countries where Canadians visited. We found that statement—an echo of Mr. Trudeau's reference to helping Canadian travellers—amusing because the Cypriots called the UNFICYP troops "permanent tourists" and we had 584 of them. Multiplied by 365 days of the year, that amounted to a lot of Canadian tourism.

On October 23, we received a message stating that, although careful consideration had been given to the representations of the Cypriots, there would be no change in the decision. I was given discretion to tell the Archbishop and so I acknowledged the instructions and proposed the text of a note that I would deliver to him. This, I suggested, might be done early in the following week. The air had been cleared, I thought: we were indeed closing and had cut through the fog created by Ottawa. I was wrong. That evening a highest priority ("flash") telegram asked that the Cypriots not be spoken to because it would be inconsistent with a remark made by Mitchell Sharp to the press to the effect that a public announcement of the closing of missions would need to be deferred to give an opportunity for the government of Canada to consider representations from various quarters. So we were again back behind the smokescreen.

The "flash" message had advised me that it was not thought that there would be any change in the plan to close Nicosia, but I would be told as soon as possible. It would have to be soon because, earlier in the day, we had learned that *The Times* of London had carried a story naming Nicosia as one of the posts to be closed. It was a clever article because it linked the Canadian withdrawal from the International Control Commission in Cambodia and Laos with that from peacemaking in Cyprus. It had the earmarks of a Foreign Office plant and I speculated to myself that it would force Ottawa's hand.

On October 24, I called on Foreign Minister Spyros Kyprianou, who had just returned from a visit to Washington and the United Nations General Assembly in New York. He said that he had learned with sorrow of the Canadian decision and could not believe that it was for economy reasons. He deplored the possibility that we would go because we and the British were the only Commonwealth countries with resident diplomatic missions in Nicosia and, moreover, the only UNFICYP contributors represented by envoys on the spot. Our withdrawal would leave Cyprus with only the British High Commission to turn to and the Cyprus Government did not relish that situation. But what concerned Mr. Kyprianou most was that when our decision became public, it would give rise to serious misunderstandings and misinterpretations. He said that the Archbishop had made this point to him that morning and expressed dismay at the probable public reaction to the move. Nobody would believe that Canada could not afford a resident diplomatic mission. Invidious comparisons, he continued, would be drawn between our closing in Nicosia and opening in the Vatican and several other places. Viewed against the background of the Cyprus problem, he said, our decision to pull out would be taken as proof that we regarded the problem as insoluble. It would also be conjectured that we would follow up by withdrawing from UNFICYP.

The Foreign Minister had marshalled his arguments better than anyone else I had heard from. He asked me to report his views and expressed the hope that the decision would be reversed.

On October 28, yet another telegram came from External Affairs to confirm the finality of the decision to close the High Commission. I was instructed to convey this to the President, while emphasizing our continued interest in the Cyprus problem and our willingness to contribute by any means at our disposal to the search for a satisfactory settlement. The message warned me that no public announcement had yet been made by the Secretary of State for External Affairs and it was hoped that the Cypriots would not comment publicly; it was especially hoped that there would be nothing along the lines that Foreign Minister Kyprianou had followed in his meeting with me. Clearly his home-truths had discombobulated the myth-makers at headquarters.

On October 31, I called on President Makarios to deliver a note on the "final" decision. Makarios was gentle, saying that he did not want to make comments that could be taken as interference in Canada's internal affairs. But he expressed concern about the Commonwealth aspect. He asked how much money we would save by closing the mission and, when I replied that it might be a quarter of a million dollars a year, he responded archly: "Not very much, is it?"—and asked about our economic problems. When I turned the conversation by relating that Mr. Trudeau had established priorities such as national unity, the President referred to the visit earlier in the week of the French Undersecretary of State for Foreign Affairs, Count de Lipkowski, and came out with this: "Mr Lipkowski told me that the position of French-Canadians is that of second-class citizens and that the recent Ottawa legislation doesn't change this." Was Mr. Trudeau really French, the Archbishop asked. I tried to straighten him out on the Prime Minister's lineage and the important role of French-speaking Canada in our society and the federal government, especially within the Cabinet.

The President did me the honour that day of accompanying me from his office to my car. His last words to me were that he would "pound Mr. Trudeau very hard" about the post closing when they next met. That was not to be for some years, by which time—to paraphrase Mr. Trudeau—the Archbishop had resigned himself to the loss of the Canadian High Commission.

The English-language daily *Cyprus Mail* carried an account of the closing of the mission on November 4. It was triggered, we learned later, by the announcement of the post closings which had been made in the House of Commons by Mitchell Sharp the previous day. The Minister said of my post:

We propose to close our resident High Commission in Nicosia. Our relations with Cyprus and any diplomatic assistance required by our forces there can be provided for effectively through dual accreditation of the Canadian representatives to a neighbouring country. There is no connection between this decision and the question of our continuing participation in UN peacekeeping forces on the island. Canada remains deeply concerned in the search for a solution of the Cyprus dispute and is willing to make whatever contribution it can to the settlement of the problem.

And there was—at last—a hint of regret: "These actions have been taken with the utmost regret and after long and careful study. They are dictated by the need for economy and do not reflect any lessening of Canada's interest in the areas concerned or suggest that our relations with them have diminished in importance. The governments concerned have been notified."

Finality, it seemed. But it was not. A few days before we had learned through a request for an aircraft clearance that Mitchell Sharp would spend an hour at Nicosia airport on Friday, November 14, en route from Tel Aviv to Cairo during a tour of the Middle East.[5] After checking with the Foreign Ministry, I sent a telegram pointing out that the Cypriots would want to extend courtesies and suggesting that Mr. Sharp might wish to use the opportunity to reassure them on the closing of the mission. The Department replied that if courtesies were customary, they would have to be accepted—but no fanfare was wanted. I arranged to keep the stopover event small. The Cypriots, however, had every intention of using the occasion for one last attempt to have us maintain our office.

Those early November days were poignant for the small Canadian diplomatic community. I noted in my diary after a reception at the Ledra Palace Hotel:

Many people spoke to me about the closing of our office. Nothing nasty whatever: they express sorrow, shock and surprise and ask with obvious bewilderment why we are doing this to them. I try to hide behind the simple answer that it is a domestic political decision and that we personally are also very sorry that it has been taken. Nobody believes that economy has anything to do with it.

Eleftheria, the principal Greek-language newspaper, carried an editorial on November 9 speaking of its sorrow at the action. The editorial employed an argument that had not previously been used elsewhere, although hinted at by the Archbishop to me: "Canada's diplomatic representation could also help the island in another way. Canada can understand our external problems perhaps better than any other country because the separatist tendencies of one of its provinces are causing trouble there too." Concluding, *Eleftheria* once more regretted the decision and hoped that it would be rescinded "for the sake of mutual interests."

The brief visit of the Secretary of State for External Affairs to Cyprus took place during the lunch hour of November 14. Aboard the Cosmopolitan aircraft of the Canadian Armed Forces with the Minister were Marcel Cadieux, Undersecretary of State for External Affairs, some other officials and a number of Canadian journalists. The meeting with Foreign Minister Kyprianou took place in the VIP lounge of the airport terminal building. Besides Mr. Kyprianou, Chris Veniamin, Director-General of the Foreign Ministry, and George Pelaghias, Chief of Protocol, were present on the Cypriot side. Marcel Cadieux and I were with Mr. Sharp.

Mitchell Sharp began the exchange by telling Mr. Kyprianou that the decision to close Nicosia was dictated solely by economic considerations and had nothing to do with political factors. Mr. Kyprianou responded with the Cyprus government's case why we should not close, using arguments that were familiar to me. He asked Mr. Sharp to reconsider the decision. Before replying to that point, my Minister observed that, although the External Affairs budget had been cut, that of the Canadian International Development Agency had not been touched and there was money available for aid. Mr. Kyprianou retorted that Cyprus wanted not aid but the support that a Canadian diplomatic mission would give it. Then, to my great surprise and to the consternation of Marcel Cadieux, Mr. Sharp undertook to have another look at the decision to close the High Commission.

After a very brief press conference, in which very little was said about the office, the two ministers walked to the aircraft. Although I had been instructed to avoid fanfare, I had arranged for a piper of the Black Watch—the regiment which then made up the Canadian contingent and was also about to be axed in the economy drive—to play a lament as Mitchell Sharp boarded the Cosmopolitan.

Fuad Sami, a prominent Turkish-Cypriot, visited me to convey his regret, "as an ordinary member" of his community, at our decision to close down. He declared that his community would greatly miss the Canadian voice because we were the most impartial diplomats in Cyprus and could understand the Turkish point of view better than others because we had two language groups in Canada. He said that he had wondered if we had decided to leave because of a tiff with the Greeks over the holding of a national day party on the Turkish side. This was a novel twist to me, for by celebrating Dominion Day on both sides of the Green Line, I and my two predecessors had demonstrated Canada's neutrality and our disregard for whatever the Greek-Cypriots might think of the practice. I told Mr. Sami about Mitchell Sharp's undertaking to Mr. Kyprianou to reconsider the decision and said that he could pass this on to Dr. Kuchuk. I added that if I were to pay a special visit to the Vice-President to convey this information, he might attach more significance to the undertaking than I felt was justified.

Although I had no illusions that Mr. Sharp's undertaking to the Cypriot Foreign Minister would make any difference, it was a disruptive factor for the remainder of the month. In the last week of November, I went to Ottawa for consultations and to learn about my own future. When I checked in at the hotel and phoned the young Cyprus desk officer, he exclaimed: "By the way, do you know why Nicosia is being closed? I don't!"

During the first morning of my rounds in the Department, it was said to me that the decision had been a purely departmental one. But all this was now becoming of only academic interest to me. I learned that the Minister had spoken to the Prime Minister "very briefly" about the closing of the post and that the answer was "no" to reconsideration. I had come to Ottawa with my own draft of a message to Foreign Minister Kyprianou conveying a negative response. A few days later, Ray Caldwell, the Acting High Commissioner in Nicosia, was instructed to see the Foreign Minister and tell him that, after a careful review, it had been concluded with great regret that it would be impossible to reverse the decision.

When I returned to Nicosia two weeks later, we proceeded quickly with the run-down of our operations. We stopped reporting on the political situation and ceased, on the diplomatic level, to concern ourselves with the problems of peacekeeping, and faced the problems of packing. Except for the Canadian Forces Adviser, the communicator and me, every Canadian in the office was being returned to Ottawa for duty. Happily, there were no rustications among us in consequence of the economy drive. The Cypriot staff were less fortunate: they were laid off with little to show for their service to Canada.

Orders came to send furniture from the office and residence to various embassies. Much of the residence furniture was to go to the newly appointed ambassador to the Vatican. When it arrived, it was cast off to staff quarters because a completely new set of furniture had been sent from hard-up External Affairs to the new ambassador. The official car in Nicosia was directed by Ottawa on a journey around the Cape of Good Hope and up to Kenya where it was wrecked by the local chauffeur within days of arrival. Its fate epitomized the wasteful side of the closing operation.

On the last day of 1969 I paid my farewell call on President Makarios. He was on the eve of a trip to Zambia and Tanzania and our conversation turned to Kaunda's doctrine of humanism and the question of Rhodesia. Africa was an appropriate subject on which to end the call—and the 1960s—which had begun for me on that continent.

I returned from the presidential palace to the High Commission where I invited the Canadian staff and Helen Pandelas, our local receptionist, into my office to thank them for their collaboration. I asked one of the security guards if, with all of us present, he would lower the Canadian flag that flew on the roof. When this was done, I wondered what we should do with the flag and someone suggested "Give it to Helen." So that is what we did and Helen, very moved, promised that when she was a grandmother she would still have the flag and think of it flying over 15A Heroes Street.

EPILOGUE

What was the Canadian diplomatic contribution in Cyprus to the events of 1969? Evidently small, for it is impossible to pinpoint any occasion when what we thought or said or did had a *decisive* impact on peacekeeping or peacemaking. Yet Canadian views were frequently sought by leaders of the two communities, by the UN Secretary-General's special representative, and by local diplomats of the Western countries most concerned for the future of the island. There were moments when the expression of these Canadian views by the High Commission gave pause for reflection.

The usefulness of the Canadian mission had been searchingly examined that year, particularly after we in Nicosia learned that the Department had decided to close the office. When all is said and done, the most important role that Canadian diplomats played during their five-year presence on the ground in this divided country was the preventive role. The tiny mission provided diplomatic support to the Canadian contingent in UNFICYP and to the efforts of the UN to make the contenders think twice before they caused trouble. On a day fifty-four months in the future—

after we were gone, when Canada had no direct, effective way of warning them—they failed to do that.

Turkey invaded Cyprus in the summer of 1974 and seized the entire northern half of the island for an independent Turkish-Cypriot regime. Though it has not received international recognition, its existence more than twenty years later suggests that the partition of Cyprus may be irreversible.

Perhaps our departure mattered.

NOTES

1. Bruce Thordarson, *Trudeau and Foreign Policy* (Toronto: Oxford University Press, 1972), 71.
2. For another account of the London meeting, see Arthur Andrew, *The Rise and Fall of Canadian Diplomacy* (Toronto: Lorimer, 1993), 86.
3. Canada. House of Commons. Standing Committee on External Affairs and National Defence, Evidence No. 50, March 8-22, 1969, 1779.
4. Telegram PST 53 of 17 October 1969 from External Affairs to Nicosia and other posts transmitting extracts relating to the Vatican and the "possible closing of posts" from Prime Minister Trudeau's press conference of 15 October.
5. The stopover in Cyprus by members and representatives of foreign governments travelling to Israel from an Arab country—or vice versa—had been standard procedure for many years to avoid requests for air clearances for direct flights to or from Israel which would have been refused by the Arabs. Double passports—one for Israel and the other for the rest of the world—were also employed by travellers in the area.

J.C. Gordon Brown served in the Canadian army in Canada and overseas. He joined External Affairs in 1947 and was posted to Berne, Pretoria and Moscow. From 1965-70 he was Ambassador to the Democratic Republic of the Congo (Leopoldville), then High Commissioner to Cyprus. In 1970 he studied for a year at the Imperial Defence College in London. On returning to Ottawa, Mr. Brown worked successively in African Affairs, as Director General of the Bureau of Administration and General Services, and as Inspector General of the Foreign Service. In 1976 he was named Consul General in Seattle.

5

PLAYING FOR TIME: SOUTH AFRICA, 1969-1972

HARRY H. CARTER

NOWADAYS MANY EYES are turned towards South Africa since there is a widespread belief that these years will be momentous for that country's future. The author of these notes is no expert on current events in South Africa. However, I hope that the reader of the experiences recorded below will find something of relevance to today. These experiences took place over twenty years ago but the racial problems of this beautiful and turbulent country have deep roots in time.

In the late summer of 1969 I was finishing a five-year assignment as Canadian Ambassador to Finland. Our Undersecretary came on a visit with the Minister. The former told me that my name was being put forward as Canada's next ambassador to South Africa. I was rather taken aback and said I had serious misgivings about accepting this posting since I had always considered myself to be a militant on civil rights, with a lifelong detestation of apartheid and all it stood for. To this he simply replied: "That's precisely why we're sending you there, Harry." End of discussion!

So we went. There was no time to return to Canada, even for a short holiday. We left northern Europe in early autumn and arrived in Pretoria about a week later, in early spring. "We" included my long-suffering wife, Pam, and our two daughters, then aged thirteen and seven.

Before we left Finland the Undersecretary had emphasized that a foreign policy review was under way in Ottawa which would of course include a study of our relations with South Africa. Among options to be considered would be the closing of our Embassy there or the less drastic step of recalling me and leaving the office under a chargé d'affaires. So our stay in South Africa might well be a brief one.

Another problem for us was the two-capital situation prevailing in South Africa. The practice of their government (i.e. the cabinet ministers) was to spend about seven months of each year in Pretoria (the executive capital) and five months in Cape Town (the legislative capital).

Obviously, envoys such as myself must accompany the ministers in order to do our jobs. This fact posed both housing and schooling problems for us. Canada owned a good residence in Pretoria but, like my predecessors, I was obliged to find and rent additional premises in Cape Town for our periods in that city. As to schooling, we were able to make an arrangement for our elder daughter (Vivien) to remain at the same school in Cape Town as a day girl when we were there and as a boarder when we had gone to Pretoria. The younger girl (Valerie), too small to be a boarder, was required to be a day girl at two different schools in two different cities.

When I caught my breath, after working out these details, I began to take stock of my situation. We had arrived in Pretoria in September 1969. Already the early spring weather was very pleasant, dry and stimulatingly warm by day and cool in the evening. At that time of the year Pretoria became the "Jacaranda City" as its sixty thousand jacaranda trees burst into bloom. (I was told that the jacaranda was not indigenous to South Africa but originally came from Brazil.) During the early evenings the streets of Pretoria were covered by an unforgettable mist of mauve, softening the angles of the office buildings and churches of the town. It was a quiet and dignified city at an altitude of about 4,500 feet—surely one of the highest capital cities in the world. In positions of dominance were the statue of Paul Kruger and the monument to the Voortrekkers. The pioneer history which they recalled was deeply embedded in the minds and hearts of this proud people.

So here I was, in the very heart of Afrikanerdom, as the accredited Canadian envoy. The presentation of my credentials to the State President, and my calls on ministers and other important people, had all gone smoothly enough. Yet, so far as I could understand my instructions, they amounted to my behaving as a sort of "Dire Warning" or "Resident Frown." I was meant to take every available opportunity to remind the South African government that its policy of apartheid was considered intolerable by my own government and that both time and patience were running out. This did not present any emotional problem for me since I regarded all this as the simple truth. However, I would not be achieving much if I were thrown out of South Africa within a month of arriving! So I decided that my best course was to try to learn as much as possible about the whole situation as quickly as I could and, of course, to contribute to the policy review going on in Ottawa as soon as I had something worth saying. I was well aware that Big Brother, i.e. THE DEPARTMENT, would react very impatiently if I started to sound off too loudly before I had spent a reasonable time in South Africa. There would be displeasure at such presumption. It would be considered "doubleplusungood."

However, in a more serious vein, the task of formulating Canadian policy towards South Africa was not an easy one. Our basic institutions had been built up on the principles of social justice for all (although we had often fallen short in carrying out those great principles). For many years Canadian spokesmen had denounced South Africa's policy of apartheid in strong terms. Increasingly, however, many of our most progressive citizens, in church and academic groups, were demanding more drastic action against South Africa. Canada was a major donor of aid to Black Africa and a prominent member of a Commonwealth based on multi-racial tolerance. On the other hand, Canadian governments had for many years made clear their belief in the value of international contacts in general and of trade and economic development in particular. So in sum, this seemed to argue for a policy of uncompromising adherence to social justice, but also an avoidance of precipitate unilateral action, which might damage the welfare of our own citizens as well as that of the people of Southern Africa, especially the Black majority.

All these factors were of course taken into account in the policy review of 1970 to which I tried to contribute from the field. The results of this review are briefly outlined later in this essay.[1]

During the years from 1969 to 1972 I travelled incessantly throughout South Africa and to the neighbouring Black-ruled countries of Botswana, Lesotho and Swaziland. In addition to being the Canadian envoy to South Africa I was also High Commissioner to these newly independent members of our mutual Commonwealth. During these years I paid about a dozen visits to their capitals: Gaberone, Maseru and Mbabane. All these countries were adjacent to South Africa, and Lesotho was indeed wholly encircled by the Republic. Usually I found these visits to be a tonic after the claustrophobic atmosphere of South Africa's apartheid. The Canadian government's interest in these three countries was essentially to try to lend a helping hand to their struggling economies. Our aid programs were in fact quite substantial and diversified. My role was a minor one, since most of the projects had already been planned between our CIDA and the representatives in Ottawa of the recipient countries. However, it was satisfying for me to be able to do anything at all of practical value.

My staff for these four assignments was a tiny one with only one other officer (later I had two). However, they were a good group and we all did what we could. In addition to our small Embassy (moving between Pretoria and Cape Town), Canada also maintained two other offices in Johannesburg and Cape Town for consular and trade purposes.

Naturally, besides all this travelling I did a great deal of reading and had conversations with anyone who seemed interesting—South Africans of all types and other diplomats. One of my best informants was my Black driver, a highly intelligent member of the Sotho people.

South African history attracted me a great deal. For example, I read several books about the Boer War and concluded that if I had been born in London around 1870 (instead of in Toronto in 1918) I would probably have been arrested at the turn of the century as a pro-Boer. I am far from being an admirer of the British imperialists of that era: Kitchener, Rhodes, Chamberlain and the rest; and my sympathies are all with the underdog Boers and their remarkably able leaders. For her part, Pam (a much better linguist than myself) became tolerably proficient in Afrikaans, being helped by her previous knowledge of Dutch.

However, nothing occurred which altered my strong dislike of the prevailing racial system. Indeed, my negative feelings were deepened and hardened by witnessing it in action.

By 1969 the South African government, long aware of the international opprobrium which its apartheid policies had caused, had attempted to defuse the situation somewhat by promoting the doctrine of "Separate Development" for the African ("Bantu") population and this doctrine was in fact the name-of-the-game during my period in South Africa. But essentially it was the same old game as before.

The figure I was given for the total South African population in 1970 was 21,282,000. Of these, 3,779,000 were classified as Whites; 1,996,000 as Coloureds; 614,000 as Asians; and 14,893,000 as Bantu (Blacks). This meant that the White population was about 17.8 percent of the total, while the Blacks amounted to just under 70 percent. (I am aware that in the past quarter of a century all these figures have substantially altered but my intention is to describe the situation when I was there.)

Within the nearly fifteen million Bantu population then living within the boundaries of South Africa—I was told that "Bantu" was a generic word meaning "people" in several of the indigenous African languages of the area—the main tribal groupings were the Xhosa, Zulu, North Sotho, South Sotho, Tswana, Tsonga-Shangaan, Swazi and Venda. It was the declared policy of the South African government to locate these various peoples (and the smaller tribal units) into about ten "Bantu Homelands."

While I was in South Africa this policy was being vigorously implemented, a process that continued for many years after I left. The idea was that the Bantu should "return" to these homelands, where they would enjoy citizenship and a degree of independence very different from their status in the so-called "White" areas, where more than half of them lived. I found it quite difficult to obtain precise figures for the breakdown between the Bantu then living in the homelands and those in the "White" areas, but the consensus I obtained from the South African Institute of Race Relations was that in 1970 about seven million Blacks lived in the homelands and approximately eight million in the "White" areas.

These so-called Bantu Homelands stretched in a great horseshoe around South Africa from the eastern Cape, the Transkei and the Ciskei, through Natal and the eastern Transvaal to the northern and western Transvaal and, finally, to the western and southern Cape. Briefly, these areas consisted of two main elements: scheduled areas declared as being occupied by Africans under the Natives Land Act of 1913; and additional land acquired by the South African Bantu Trust since it had been empowered in 1936 to buy land. I was informed that the total area of the homelands was merely 13 or 14 percent of the land area of South Africa. Furthermore, some of these parcels of land were divided into sections separated from each other by intervening "White" areas.

It was also evident to me that the homelands areas did not fully correspond to the areas traditionally occupied by the people concerned. For example, there were Tswana people living in both Botswana and in the relevant homeland area. The same applied to Lesotho and the Sotho homeland areas.

While some of the land in the Transkei and in the Zulu areas was quite fertile, much of the balance in the homeland territories was at best mediocre from the farming standpoint. Thus the theoretical position emerged that 70 percent of the people of South Africa were meant to live and work in less than one-seventh of the total land area, and that by no means the best one-seventh. Whatever merit there might have been to the "traditional" homelands argument this theory made no sense from the standpoint of economics, let alone simple justice. Overpopulation and underemployment in the homelands were rampant; and the South African government had had little success in persuading industry to move factories into or near the homelands, since there were extremely difficult practical problems involving lack of access to energy, transport and communications.

The result of all this was that more than half of the Black population (i.e. about eight million people in 1970) found it necessary for basic economic reasons to work in the so-called White areas in the mines, farms, factories, shops and so on. The greater part of them lived in adjacent townships such as Soweto, the huge Black dormitory near Johannesburg. It was the plight of these people which had, quite justifiably, caused so much international outrage down through the years, including stern condemnation by every Canadian government for over two decades. They had no vote, no citizenship rights and very limited job prospects. They were crammed together into rows of featureless boxes in their townships. Nearly all were poor, badly fed and with very limited education (although there were a few fortunate exceptions). "White" industry could not function without them but they were rigorously segregated from their White employers. They went to work on crowded buses or on bicycles or often on foot. Not only could they not vote but they were also subject to very strict pass laws. Their schools, hospitals and other facilities fell far short of those available to the Whites. The list of such flagrant injustices was a very long one.

Outside Soweto, 1971.

Despite my good intentions of waiting for awhile before passing on my policy views to THE DEPARTMENT, I did send a number of early reports making various arguments. These were precipitated by the considerations that time was pressing (the review would certainly be completed in 1970) and that, after all, I was the man on the spot. The attitude of Big Brother in Ottawa seemed to be that the review would proceed in stately fashion and that in due course I would be informed of Big Brother's decisions. But I was not prepared to play so passive a role. Very early in the game I came to the conclusion that for Canada to break off or diminish our relations with South Africa would be a serious mistake. Such a move would not help the Blacks and would dismay the liberal-minded White minority who were striving to build a more just society in very difficult circumstances. On the other hand, such a breach of relations by Canada would be greeted with contemptuous indifference by the reactionary elements who were now in control of South Africa. In short, it would simply make a bad situation worse. Admittedly, Canada had very little influence over events in South Africa but "very little" was still better than none at all.

During the next two and a half years (early 1970 to mid-1972) I pressed this argument as strongly as I could. Just before leaving South Africa (in July 1972) I summed up my views on this and many other points in my valedictory letter.[2] In 1971 and 1972 there was a doctrine regarding South Africa called "Selective Disengagement," which seemed to have some adherents in very high places in Ottawa. I considered this to be a load of self-righteous nonsense and I told THE DEPARTMENT so. I argued that it was quite unacceptable "to adopt the washing-of-hands attitude implied in the selective disengagement thesis. On the contrary, our point of departure, it seems to me, must be an attitude of compassionate concern for the South Africans of all race groups—Black, White, Coloured, Asian—whose lives have been caught up in one of the most prolonged and insoluble race situations in the world's history. We really cannot 'disengage' from this situation. It is too important and the world is too small. Contact must be maintained. Attention must be paid."[3] Time has in no way altered my views on this matter as they were stated in my 1972 letter.

During the latter portion of my posting in South Africa I occasionally gained the impression that THE DEPARTMENT was paying some attention to my views. However, this was *not* the case during my first six months there. In those days I thought there was a very real lack of communication. Rereading my letters to Ottawa of late 1969 and early 1970 vividly recalls my bitter feelings of frustration and futility.

So it was with some relief that in the summer of 1970, when the policy review had been completed, I noted that we would not be breaking relations with South Africa or withdrawing me. No trade boycott was to be imposed. However, the Canadian government would divest itself of any crown investments in South Africa (in fact these were very minor). More positively, our government would increase its aid commitments to the Black-ruled governments in Southern Africa in order to emphasize the theme of "Social Justice."

There was nothing in this with which I disagreed. It so happened that in the summer of 1970 my family took a belated home leave to Canada. This afforded me the opportunity of meeting the establishment of THE DEPARTMENT "made flesh." Indeed I had some useful talks with them. A meeting had also been scheduled with our Minister, Mitchell Sharp, but at the last moment it was cancelled because he had to cope with a crisis involving another country.

•

The Canadian foreign policy review of 1970 was, so far as South Africa was concerned, simply one more stage in a continuing process. Of course our government and its advisers continued afterwards to keep the whole question of our relations with South Africa under constant appraisal; from the field I often put in my two cents' worth for the next two years.

I argued against any softening of our opposition to apartheid and, indeed, my experience of it in action (as already mentioned) made me dislike it even more than I had before going to South Africa. I can best describe my reaction by quoting again from my valedictory letter of 1972: "It is immoral, politically dangerous and so obviously unChristian that it seems to me beneath the dignity of grown men to debate the point. Indeed there are times when one experiences a numbing feeling of despair, in contemplating so vast and well-organized an obscenity." [4]

During the periods when we were in Cape Town Pam and I enjoyed going on Saturday to the nearby race-tracks at Milnerton and Kenilworth to bet on the horses. There were two enclosures—one marked (in Afrikaans) for Whites and one for "Non-Whites." It was both depressing and instructive to see very similar Cape Coloureds going into these different enclosures. Some obviously had identification which established them as Whites, while others (the great majority) did not, although to my uneducated eyes their skin colours seemed exactly the same. I was told that in many cases the decision to provide the appropriate identity card often involved long, microscopic examinations of pigmentation, hair tissue and even finger nails.

The atmosphere of apartheid was, on the whole, more oppressive in Pretoria than in Cape Town. Nevertheless, one of my Black drivers was beaten up by White thugs just outside Cape Town. On another occasion, when we were in Pretoria, the same driver, a very intelligent and quiet man, got involved in an argument with the redneck superintendent of our chancery office building regarding the parking of our official car. This ended by the bullying superintendent calling my driver a "fucking Kaffir bastard." This was reported to me by my driver in a tone of weary resignation—he did not ask or expect me to *do* anything about it. But I had other ideas. I took my driver with me to confront this superintendent. I told the latter that there were international conventions protecting the staffs of embassies (including locally engaged employees) from harassment by citizens of the host country when such staff members were carrying out their official duties, as was the case in this instance. I added that these conventions were quite silent on whether the staff member's pigmentation should be White, Beige, Brown, Black or Emerald Green. So he would either apologize to my driver or I would raise the matter at a "very high level" with the Foreign Ministry. Fortunately the superintendent did apologize to my driver and this very distasteful episode ended. I was not bluffing, but obviously it was preferable to deal with the matter on the spot.

My Black cook was unfortunate enough to have his bicycle collide with a scout car driven by a member of BOSS (the Bureau of State Security). The cook spent the next six months having a portion of his small salary deducted to pay for the alleged damage to the scout car. He was told that he was very lucky not to be thrown into jail for damaging official property. Here I could not intervene, as my cook seemed to be technically at fault.

Shortly before I left South Africa I was in the vicinity of St. George's Cathedral near the centre of Cape Town, just before a very ugly scene developed. Several truck loads of BOSS operatives, complete with "attack-trained" police dogs, swarmed into the area. One of them grabbed a bullhorn and shouted at us (in Afrikaans of course) to disperse or face arrest. Rather reluctantly, I left. Later I learnt that baton-wielding members of BOSS, plus their dogs, then heavily attacked a group of students from the University of Cape Town, who fled for sanctuary into the Cathedral. (The students had been conducting an anti-apartheid demonstration quite peacefully.) The BOSS agents, with their dogs, pursued the students into the Cathedral and violently pulled them outside despite the vehement protests of at least one Anglican priest who was present.

By coincidence, that evening the Archbishop of Cape Town came to our residence for a game of bridge and dinner. I had never seen this mild-mannered prelate (Robert Selby Taylor) so angry. He was a tall, imposing man at 6 feet 4 inches and every one of those inches was quivering with fury! He said that not only had his church been violated, but the centuries-old traditions of sanctuary had been dragged in the mud. On the following day he issued a blistering statement to the same effect, which had a considerable impact even, so I was told, at high levels of the government. After all, the Archbishop was the Anglican Primate of South Africa, and he had long ago earned a reputation as a moderate and reasonable man. I considered this event quite significant and reported it in some detail to Ottawa.[5]

These and a half-dozen similar episodes completely confirmed my original view that South Africa in the period 1969-1972 was a thoroughly unjust society—dangerously so. However, in all honesty, I should add that despite my criticisms of their policies, I personally was never subjected to rudeness by South African ministers or officials. There were a number of awkward moments, inevitable when disagreement was so pronounced, but the amenities were observed.

However, the basic question on which I was paid to give advice was not whether South African society was unjust, but what Canada should *do* about this situation at the federal government level.

At this period, there were many people, including some distinguished observers, who likened South Africa to Nazi Germany. For my part, I had been a front-line soldier (an artillery officer) in the war against Hitler, though only after prolonged wrestling with my basic pacifist convictions. There were certainly ugly similarities between South Africa in 1970 and Nazi Germany thirty years earlier, but there were also striking differences. Most of the South African press was quite free, and a considerable portion of it (particularly the English-language press) was vocally anti-government. More important, the highest judiciary was quite independent of the government, and refused to be intimidated. I will give a dramatic example of this later on. So I concluded that arguments in favour of violent methods—such as we had been compelled to use against Nazi Germany—did not apply in this case. Not yet, anyway.

I also argued against a trade boycott of peaceful goods. Trade was good in itself and of course it helped all South Africans, not just the Whites. By the same token I advised against giving Canadian governmental assistance to the various "liberation movements" which advocated violence against the South African regime. I took the view that this was totally at odds with maintaining diplomatic relations with South Africa. If our government ever came to the conclusion that it must contribute directly to liberation movements then it should, in all honesty, take the prior step of breaking relations and recalling its envoy. And, as I had made clear several times, I did not think the time for that had yet arrived.

So what should we do? It seemed to me that our only possible course was to send out a series of slowly escalating warning signals to underline the point that we found South Africa's racial policies quite unacceptable. One such warning signal was, of course, an international boycott of segregated South African sports teams. While I disliked the notion of mixing sports and politics I strongly supported this particular sanction, which certainly had an impact on these very sports-minded people.

This was the gist of my policy recommendations to Ottawa in 1970-72. It will be apparent that I was clearer on what would not work than on what would. It is also evident that none of my views were original.

Fundamentally, my point of view was based on the notion that Western envoys such as myself were essentially playing for time. By advocating the avoidance of extreme measures I was saying implicitly that time was on the side of justice and moderation. I could not prove this and indeed, its evidence was not then apparent. 1971 and 1972 were *not* good years in South Africa's history. However, in the general gloom I sensed some hopeful signs. There were the independence of the high judiciary and the freedom of the press. There was the fact that, from personal observation, I had met many South Africans who were colour-blind in the best sense, people who were quietly working away in difficult circumstances to produce a more just society. There were indications that the younger generation of Afrikaners were more liberal, on the whole, than were their fathers or grandfathers, as evidenced by the lively debates taking place in such institutions as the University of Stellenbosch. And then there was the growing shortage of skilled White labour in an expanding economy. Thousands of jobs were being "dereserved." Blacks were increasingly being given skilled training. In time this might well produce a Black middle class with enough economic "clout" to negotiate political and economic changes without resort to extreme violence. These were the hopeful signs I sensed, but to express their concrete presence in 1970-72 was difficult indeed. Meanwhile, I hoped that our government would keep open our means of communication.

•

I suppose I was a rather outspoken envoy. Indeed it was clear to me that my government wanted me to speak out. However, this quite often led to embarrassing situations at official dinners. The South Africans are hospitable people by nature. On about a dozen occasions I was seated next to some South African lady (usually the wife of a cabinet minister or other prominent person) when, even before the soup plates were removed, she would burst out: "Why do you people hate us so much?" or some variant of this. I would reply that we did not hate the South Africans at all but that we found their government's racial policies quite unacceptable. Then I would be confronted by her with the latest stories from Canada showing, quite correctly, that we had our *own* problems. To this I would reply that our society certainly did have some faults and injustices. However, at least we had not developed an entire pyramid of legislation victimizing the majority of our residents from cradle to grave for something over which no human being had any control, namely the colour of his or her skin. This led to one of two results, either an icy silence for the balance of the dinner, or a weary remark to the effect that "you simply do not understand our problems."

On four occasions during these years I received long distance calls from reporters of the English-language press in Johannesburg asking whether it was true that I was about to be recalled to Ottawa. "Not so far as I know." These phone calls invariably followed some fierce anti-apartheid statement by one of our spokesmen in Ottawa or New York. Although I became bored with denying that I was about to be recalled, I did not mind these statements by our people since I basically agreed with their contents.

Yet while all this was going on I also found a number of very positive elements during our life in South Africa. For one thing, we made some valued friends among people who were simply trying to get on with their lives in a difficult environment. My best friend in Cape Town was an

Afrikaner, a Presbyterian minister (trained in Edinburgh) who had devoted his entire long life and his boundless energy to the service of the blind people of Cape Province: Coloured, White (as he was) or Black. It made no difference whatsoever to him. For many years he organized workshops, clinics and therapy for the blind, raised money for them, visited them tirelessly in hospitals or their homes and prayed for them. He was, in brief, everything that a Christian should be. As a result, he was one of the best-loved citizens of Cape Town and with him I visited places which were off the beaten track for diplomats.

Even among members of the government and its senior officials Pam and I had some friendly contacts (often I found the tennis court to be a good place to get to know people). While I never soft-pedalled my opinions about apartheid I did learn one valuable lesson, that it is possible to respect a person even when you strongly disagree with him.

Another positive feature was of course the sheer beauty of South Africa: its magnificent scenery, trees, flowers, shrubs, wild animals and birds. For someone like myself, whose hobby was photography, there were many wonderful moments.

In short I constantly felt, in my final year, that my senses were being bombarded by perceptions which alternately repelled and attracted me. I will never forget South Africa but I can only describe my reactions as if they were kaleidoscopic images in a child's toy. South Africa was the endless scrub land of the Karoo, the ridges of the Drakensberg mountains, the lovely (and segregated) beaches of the "Fairest Cape." It was the luxury of Bishopscourt or Houghton; also the squalor of Soweto or the ironic horror of the "Valley of Plenty." It was an attack-trained Pretoria police dog and the almost equally well trained personnel of the Bureau of State Security. But it was also the many daily acts of human kindness by ordinary people which transcended racial barriers. It was a group of basically weak men in high office trying to prove they were strong ones by executive bullying. It was a gallant woman, Helen Suzman, fighting her lonely battles for civil liberties in a hostile Assembly. It was the tufted head of a protea, the blaze of jacaranda in a Pretoria October, the scent of frangipani near Durban. South Africa was the spoor of an elephant, the swaying gait of a giraffe, the startled expectancy of a herd of springbok. No, I *won't* forget it.

•

In late 1971 I arranged a couple of dinners at our residence in Pretoria for several of the leading members of the Black community in Soweto: merchants, teachers and so on. Our guests were required to obtain permits from the Ministry of Bantu Affairs but these were forthcoming. In fact, although these dinners may have had some symbolic value, they did not give me many further insights into conditions within Soweto. Our Black guests were quite close-mouthed, even though we had been careful in selecting the sprinkling of White liberals present. Their caution was understanable. BOSS had many informers.

In August 1971 I attended the opening of the trial in Pretoria of the Very Rev. Gonville ffrench-Beytagh, the Anglican Dean of Johannesburg, who was facing charges under the Terrorism Act. I was vitally interested in this case both because of its intrinsic importance and because I happened to be a lay reader in the Anglican Communion. From all information available to me it was clearly absurd to think of this outspoken priest as being a terrorist of any kind, but the monstrous wording of the Terrorism Act was so broad that it could include almost anyone who agitated against the South African government's policies (definitely including myself, if I had been subject to their laws).

In any case, on November 1, 1971 the Dean was convicted in Pretoria on several counts under the Terrorism Act, e.g. that he had encouraged members of the Black Sash movement to break the law, and he was given the mandatory minimum sentence of five years. However, he was also granted the right to appeal. [6]

The option to appeal was exercised by the Dean's lawyers (led by Mr. Kentridge). On April 14, 1972 it was announced that the Court of Appeal in Bloemfontein, headed by the Chief Justice of South Africa (Ogilvie Thompson), had overturned the earlier decision convicting the Dean delivered by the Judge President of the Transvaal. In announcing the Appeal Court's decision to free the Dean, the Chief Justice made a lengthy statement, the gist of which was that the charges against ffrench-Beytagh had not been proven "beyond reasonable doubt." The Chief Justice's two colleagues on the Appeal Court concurred in his judgement.

By coincidence, my wife and I were guests for lunch at the residence of Chief Justice Ogilvie Thompson in Bloemfontein only an hour after he announced the Court's decision. I was able to have a private talk with him. I reported to Ottawa that "the Chief Justice is an impressive and commanding personality. He made very clear that his Court's decision was absolutely final." [7]

This proved to be the most positive development during my final period in South Africa. However, within two months it was followed by the disgraceful episode of the invasion of St. George's Cathedral in Cape Town by the men and dogs of BOSS, which has already been described. So, the roller-coaster continued.

•

My time in Cape Town came to an end. I returned to Pretoria to pack up and to pay my farewell calls in Botswana, Lesotho and Swaziland. In Pretoria the government behaved courteously. Both the Prime Minister (Mr. John Vorster) and the Foreign Minister (Dr. Hilgard Muller) called me in for interviews, in the latter case followed by an official luncheon. These two interviews followed almost identical patterns. Both ministers began by thanking me for increasing friendship between Canada and South Africa. In each case I thanked them, but said it had not been possible for me to do this. Even a better Canadian envoy than me, and there were scores of them, could not have done so. Friendship between Canada and South Africa would only be increased if the South African government radically changed its policies. Both men then asked me: "What would you advise us to do?" This gave me the opportunity to launch into my ideas for the gradual dismantling of apartheid. However, I had only proceeded for two or three minutes when both interviews were terminated, politely but firmly by Dr. Muller, more abruptly by the Prime Minister.

Well, I had fired my last cartridge and it had obviously bounced off a concrete wall! Again, I felt briefly a sense of failure and futility. However, a moment's reflection made it clear to me that it was most presumptuous of me to think in terms of "failure" or "success." I was only a very minor soldier in the army of those who were trying to play for time.

By now I quite literally had my air ticket in my pocket. But leaving South Africa would not in fact mean severing my relations with the problems of that country. For the next six years I would be looking at those same problems from the outside, as Director of the Anglophone Africa Division in Ottawa.

•

I am writing these notes at the beginning of 1994. Recently two good men from South Africa, one Black and one White, jointly shared the

Nobel Prize for Peace. Many of us rejoiced at this highly appropriate gesture. However, the problems at issue go far beyond two good men. Behind them, I am convinced, are hundreds of thousands of men and women of good will, from all races in South Africa, whose one ambition is to get on with their lives in an atmosphere of peace, tolerance and mutual respect. The problems they face are formidable and no one can predict the future, as South Africa enters these fateful years. It is the heartfelt prayer of one former resident that these people of good will may succeed.

NOTES

1. For more information see "Foreign Policy for Canadians," (1970). Booklet on United Nations, 17-20.
2. Pretoria Letter No. 190 of July 19, 1972. Department of External Affairs file no. 20-SAFR-1-2. (Reproduced and sent to all posts by Ottawa as Selected Despatch no. 13 of August 11, 1972).
3. Ibid.
4. Ibid.
5. My telegram no. 168 of June 5, 1972 from Cape Town to Ottawa. Department of External Affairs file no. 20-SAFR-1-4.
6. My telegrams nos. 449 and 450 of November 2, 1971 from Pretoria to Ottawa. Department of External Affairs file no. 20-SAFR-1-4.
7. My telegram no. 125 of April 17, 1972 from Cape Town to Ottawa. Department of External Affairs file no. 20-SAFR-1-4.

Harry Carter joined the Royal Canadian Artillery in 1940 and saw action in Normandy, Pas de Calais, Belgium and The Netherlands. Discharged with the rank of captain in 1945, he joined External Affairs the same year. After postings to New York, The Hague and New Delhi, he became Director of United States Division in 1961. Mr. Carter was Ambassador to Finland from 1964-69, then Ambassador to South Africa and (concurrently) High Commissioner to Botswana, Lesotho and Swaziland from 1969-72. He returned to Ottawa, became Director of Anglophone Africa Division at External Affairs from 1972-78, then worked as Director of Historical Division until 1983.

6

OTTAWA, ROME, BRUXELLES, 1972-1984 QUELS DÉFIS?

D'IBERVILLE FORTIER

« BIEN », ME SUIS-JE DIT, heureux d'avoir accepté de participer à ce florilège d'exploits diplomatiques, « quel raccourci pour la rédaction d'improbables mémoires! ». Irrésistible d'ailleurs ce thème proposé par David Reece: le rôle et l'influence des Chefs de mission diplomatique : le « To be or not to be » de notre confrérie. Blaise Pascal qui ne pensait même pas aux diplomates, trouvait « le moi haïssable ». Qu'il veuille bien nous excuser, du moins pour ces essais qui confondront du reste les premières personnes du singulier et du pluriel.

D'entrée de jeu, un paradoxe de taille : les décisions se prenant généralement dans les capitales par les ministres avec l'aide de leurs proches conseillers, comment les diplomates de carrière qui servent le plus souvent à l'étranger pourraient-il prétendre les influencer tant soit peu sérieusement ? Les chefs de mission diplomatique seraient-ils dès lors de simples figurants, qui auraient la fatuité de se prendre pour des acteurs dans la tragi-comédie des relations internationales? Tout dépend évidemment; la carrière, il ne faut pas l'oublier, est un écheveau d'affectations alternées entre la centrale et les capitales étrangères. Elle donne donc une vue syncopée de l'histoire, mais permet en principe un enrichissement continu. Comme chez les militaires, on y trouve des hommes et des femmes qui se sentent plus à l'aise à l'état-major et d'autres sur le terrain. En cas d'allergie à l'une ou à l'autre situation, mieux vaut s'abstenir, les rôles étant évidemment complémentaires.

Pour cette raison, et pour en marquer aussi les contrastes, j'ai choisi d'évoquer ici mes trois dernières affectations consécutives aux Affaires extérieures qui furent Ottawa, Rome et Bruxelles. Je m'arrêterai surtout pour l'Italie à la structuration de nos relations bilatérales, et pour la Belgique à certains effets de sa *régionalisation* sur ses rapports avec le Canada et le Québec ... [1]

À LA CENTRALE

J'occupai de 1972 à 1976 l'un des cinq postes de sous-secrétaire d'État adjoint aux Affaires extérieures existant à l'époque. Le sous-secrétaire A.E. Ritchie m'avait confié comme « zone d'intérêt » géopolitique une grande partie du tiers-monde, et des responsabilités fonctionnelles comme les relations fédérales provinciales, les institutions de la Francophonie et du Commonwealth, la culture et l'information. Il voulait un système hiérarchique souple. Les « patrons » du huitième étage de la maison Pearson devaient en particulier respecter les responsabilités des Directeurs généraux dont bon nombre avaient déjà eux-mêmes occupé des postes de CDM parfois de premier plan. Chaque portefeuille laissait à son titulaire une assez grande latitude sous réserve bien sûr de l'aval du Sous-secrétaire et du ministre.

Qu'il suffise d'illustrer ici, sans entrer dans les détails, des développements sur lesquels je pus exercer une certaine influence, voire même parfois une influence certaine. Par exemple en politique: à la suite de l'accession du Canada à titre d'observateur à l'Organisation des États Américains, resserrement des liens grâce à la première visite depuis 1960 d'un premier ministre canadien à trois pays de cette région; ouverture bilatérale à l'endroit de certains pays arabes desserrant ainsi l'étreinte israélienne sur la diplomatie canadienne; efforts soutenus pour donner des dents à notre politique *anti-apartheid* grâce à un code de conduite pour nos multinationales oeuvrant en Afrique du Sud. En coopération internationale : période d'expansion, reconnaissance de nouveaux domaines d'action dont un de mes fétiches, les communications sociales. (Au début personne ne savait même ce dont il s'agissait.) Tournée personnelle du Sahel pour y consolider nos efforts de coopération. En matière culturelle : élaboration presque terminée par mon prédécesseur au début de 1972, et lancement trois ans plus tard, du premier plan culturel quinquennal du ministère destiné à faciliter sa propre planification et celle de ses partenaires.

En francophonie internationale très active pendant cette période : création au sein de l'Agence de coopération culturelle et technique (ACCT) d'un Fond spécial et multilatéral de développement (FSD) permettant à ses membres de puiser aux ressources du Fond pour financer certains projets ; mise sur pied laborieuse mais réussie de la *Communauté internationale de radiodiffusion et télévision en langue française,* le CIRTEF, (encore un fétiche !) toujours présent à ce jour derrière les ondes de la francophonie. Dans le domaine des relations fédérales-provinciales un réseau d'informations diplomatiques sur les sujets d'intérêt commun et de fréquentes visites furent mis en oeuvre, à notre initiative, entre Ottawa et les provinces intéressées.

La collaboration avec le Québec, même sous le régime de Robert Bourassa, ne fut pas exempte de tensions. Une entente avait tout de même été conclue entre les deux capitales peu avant mon retour de Tunisie à Ottawa en 1972, donnant au Québec le statut inusité de *gouvernement participant* au sein de l'Agence de coopération culturelle et technique (ACCT). Il restait à en appliquer les termes ! À titre exceptionnel, une formule de direction politiquement indépendante des deux gouvernements fut retenue pour la réalisation du magnifique festival culturel de la Francophonie internationale *la Super francofête*, qui se déroula à Québec en 1975 précisément sous les auspices de l'ACCT. Survenant dans l'atmosphère surchauffée qui préluda à la victoire de René Lévesque et du PQ aux élections législatives de 1976, la formule ne suffit pas à éviter une *petite guerre des drapeaux* qui faillit, la veille même de son inauguration, faire échouer l'entreprise ... Pierre Trudeau qui était sur place n'entendait pas sacrifier les emblèmes du Nouveau-Brunswick et de l'Ontario. Mes fonctions me donnaient le rôle d'intermédiaire. On finit par s'entendre in extremis, comme dans bien d'autres cas généralement liés à des réunions internationales ou à des visites d'État dans la vieille capitale. Si cette digression peut sembler disproportionnée dans cette énumération sommaire des responsabilités d'un Sous-secrétaire d'État adjoint, on comprendra qu'elle est destinée à servir de toile de fond à notre troisième thème.

Quatre ans de travail intense et diversifié avec d'excellentes équipes de la maison Pearson ainsi qu'au niveau interministériel. Je ne prétends évidemment ni à plus ni à moins d'entreprises, de succès et d'échecs à ce poste que n'en connurent mes collègues. J'y éprouvai de grandes satisfactions ... mais pas au point cependant de refuser l'ambassade de Rome lorsqu'on voulut bien me l'offrir, et bien qu'elle présentât des horizons plus limités. C'était la réalisation d'un rêve!

LA PRÉSENCE CANADIENNE EN ITALIE, 1976-80

Ma dépêche d'adieu de Rome au ministère[2] me rappelle qu'au milieu des années 70, le *miracle italien* des années d'après-guerre était depuis longtemps mort et enterré; ce pays tant aimé vivait une autre période déchirante de son histoire. Aldo Moro, ancien président du Conseil, père de « *l'ouverture à gauche* » et président de la Démocratie chrétienne était enlevé et assassiné par les *Brigate Rosse* en 1978 ; une semaine avant notre départ, ces mêmes brigades abattaient le jeune militaire qui gardait l'édifice où nous visitions notre médecin de famille, et la veille même tentaient d'enlever nos voisins immédiats, à notre résidence de la via Camillucia.

La *révolte informelle* des étudiants en 1968, reprise par la classe ouvrière et la rue en 1969, avait ouvert la voie à la guérilla urbaine. La dégradation de la plupart des institutions et de l'économie nationales avait atteint un paroxysme exalté par l'ineptie du système politique et le laxisme de gouvernements qui n'avaient de stables que l'instabilité. On parlait de « l'ingouvernabilité de l'Italie » comme s'il s'agissait d'une maladie congénitale incurable et non du résultat de certains choix constitutionnels et politiques. Les élections anticipées de 1976 non seulement n'avaient rien réglé, mais ne semblaient avoir laissé pour toute issue que l'indéfinissable « compromesso storico » dont certains ne pouvaient s'empêcher de rêver, dans l'illusion d'acheter peut-être ainsi paix et stabilité. Le journaliste et politologue Alberto Ronchey écrivait en 1977 : « La Ière République est à bout de souffle.... La révolution que beaucoup attendent ou redoutent s'est déjà produite.... Le cas de l'Italie reste avant tout l'*autodéstabilisation* la plus anormale parmi les démocraties conflictuelles de notre temps ».[3]

Cet état de choses n'empêchait cependant pas le pays d'être l'un des grands partenaires du Canada sur plusieurs plans : histoire, peuplement, culture, commerce. Les hauts fonctionnaires d'Ottawa, les premiers ministres Robert Bourassa et Bill Davis avec lesquels j'avais pu avoir de substantiels entretiens selon l'usage avant mon départ d'Ottawa, n'en doutaient pas. La communauté italo-canadienne venait de signaler sa fidélité en contribuant massivement à la reconstruction du Frioul après le séisme qui avait ravagé la région en 1976. Les gens d'affaires et touristes canadiens continuaient à affluer. Mais l'Italie qui, malgré son inventivité et son dynamisme remarquable dans certains secteurs comme ses PME, était dans un état politiquement et économiquement moribond, ne faisait pas le poids aux yeux d'un grand nombre de nos compatriotes. Une attitude de *business as usual* pour l'Ambassade ne pouvait manifestement pas suffire à remédier à cet état de choses. C'est ainsi que, bien convaincus des possibilités qui s'offraient à nous, mes collègues et moi devînmes de véritables croisés du renforcement des relations canado-italiennes.

J'aimais résumer dans mes discours et écrits, chaque fois que l'occasion s'en présentait, les fondements de nos rapports dans un slogan percutant : « *Une alliance, un million d'italo-canadiens, un milliard de commerce annuel* ». Pourquoi n'avouerais-je pas de plus mon penchant pour des relations structurées, par la recherche et l'embrigadement de partenaires du pays qui viendraient contribuer chacun dans son secteur à l'œuvre commune, et démultiplier ainsi le rendement de nos efforts? La formule n'était pas nouvelle, mais tout le monde n'était pas d'accord là dessus. Je me rappelle en particulier la réticence de certains membres de notre section commerciale à faire trop de cas des Chambres de commerce, qui leur semblaient constituer un cheptel coûteux à nourrir et à abreuver matin et soir en vue de résultats aléatoires. Mais dans l'ensemble, Canadiens et Italiens se prêtèrent remarquablement au jeu qui s'ajoutait naturellement aux fonctions variées et exigeantes d'une grande ambassade secondée par un consulat général fort actif à Milan. (S'y trouvait également une délégation du Québec non moins active.)

Nous eûmes dans notre entreprise de puissants alliés, et un véritable chassé-croisé de visites ministérielles qui sont devenues indispensables à notre époque pour épauler les efforts des diplomates. L'Esprit-Saint nous aida aussi. Les dignitaires canadiens que nous amenèrent le décès de deux Papes, Paul VI et Jean-Paul Ier et l'installation de leur successeurs, étaient fort bien accueillis par notre ambassade auprès du Saint-Siège en conséquence de quoi nous les mettions aussi à contribution pour d'utiles rencontres avec les autorités italiennes.

À l'occasion de sa visite officielle au Canada en novembre 1977, le président du Conseil Giulio Andreotti et le PM Trudeau proclamaient à l'issue de leurs rencontres bien préparées un « *nuovo corso* » pour les relations entre les deux pays, dont ils énonçaient les grandes lignes. Il est sans doute vrai que les articles de journaux sont plus lisibles que les dépêches diplomatiques, mais les diplomates s'y entendent dans le rôle de souffleurs. Moins de trois ans plus tard, en juin 1980, dans une déclaration commune, à l'occasion cette fois de la visite à Rome de Pierre Trudeau, le président du Conseil, Francesco Cossiga et son invité se dirent « heureux de l'évolution positive sur tous les plans ... commerce en croissance rapide, accord de sécurité sociale ... accroissement de la présence canadienne en Italie au cours des dernières années » etc. Ils décidaient d'élargir le contenu du *nuovo corso* par la création d'un Comité ministériel mixte devant se réunir à la demande d' au moins l'une des parties, ainsi que l'échange de missions privées et publiques, la conclusion prochaine d'un traité d'extradition et d'une convention consulaire tous deux sur le métier, l'accroissement enfin des échanges culturels ainsi que l'amélioration de leur coordination. Ces constats et ces intentions annoncées au plus haut niveau attestaient des progrès accomplis. Que s'était-il passé?

J'emprunte essentiellement pour y répondre à la dépêche précitée, et tant pis si cela ressemble à un inventaire car c'en est un : création d'une Chambre de commerce italo-canadienne, avec siège à Rome et antennes à Milan et à Bologne, dotée de son propre périodique *Italia-Canada* ; diversification des activités de l'*Institut culturel canadien* (dont l'ambassadeur du Canada était président ex officio), qui permit de financer la création du *Centre académique canadien en Italie, ou CACI*[4]; création de l'*Association italienne des études canadiennes*, (section d'un remarquable programme créé par la centrale) ; lancement du périodique d'information générale haut de gamme *Canada Contemporaneo*. Un groupe parlementaire d'amitié italo-canadienne était mis sur pied à Rome, et les présidentes respectives de la Chambre des Communes canadienne Jeanne Sauvé et de la Chambre des députés italienne Nilde Jotti, convenaient de la formation d'une association bilatérale entre les deux parlements. La conclusion d'un nouvel accord culturel, vivement préconisé par notre ambassade, n'avait pas progressé malgré l'insistance italienne, en raison de l'opposition d'Ottawa à ce qui y alors considéré comme un danger de prolifération d'accords de ce genre ; mais on avait tout de même décidé d'accroître les échanges culturels avec l'Italie et de les mieux coordonner.

Voilà en gros ce que signifiait pour nous la « restructuration » ... que nous n'osions pas qualifier d'*aggiornamento*. La Direction du personnel reprocha au barreur son insistance, bien qu'il eût toujours pris soin de chercher à chaque étape d'obtenir l'aval d'Ottawa en usant, quand il le fallait, de la force du poignet. On en jugera aux deux exemples que voici. De nombreux universitaires canadiens, depuis les littéraires jusqu'aux archéologues, travaillaient en Italie. Ils devaient, ils en étaient convaincus et nous de même, s'organiser et se regrouper pour accroître l'efficacité de leurs recherches et leur influence dans les deux pays. Ils avaient besoin de l'ambassade pour le faire. Ils leur fallait aussi un toit pour leur secrétariat et leurs archives. Tout ceci fut expliqué à la centrale en long et en large. Nous avions des bureaux vacants sur la via Zara où se trouvaient notre consulat et nos services d'immigration. Ne pouvions-nous les prêter au Centre académique canadien en Italie, le CACI ? Après beaucoup de correspondance et de rappels, je lançai finalement un ultimatum à Ottawa : si je n'avais pas de réponse en deux mois, je déclarerais unilatéralement le CACI « d'intérêt public », et j'y installerais nos amis universitaires. Ce qui fut dit fut fait, sans peur et même ... sans reproche. C'est ainsi que le CACI pendit la crémaillère via Zara, à grand renfort d'*Asti Spumante*.

Deuxième exemple. Sur le front des relations interparlementaires, nous fondions de grands espoirs sur la visite attendue à Rome du président de la Chambre l'hon. James Jerome, prédécesseur de Mme Jeanne Sauvé. Il avait bien voulu m'autoriser à prendre rendez-vous au siège du parlement italien avec son homologue Signora Nilde Jotti, députée communiste et première femme à occuper ce poste. Je ne sus jamais si l'allégeance de la présidente italienne avait joué un rôle dans la décision de M. Jerome ... de prendre un avion pour Israël avant l'heure du rendez-vous. Il eut cependant la courtoisie de m'en informer ... le matin même. Le temps d'agir. Je lui présentai pour signature à l'aéroport deux heures plus tard, un projet de lettre bien sentie à Mme. Jotti, s'excusant de lui faire faux bond, et lui expliquant l' importance qu'il attachait à la création d'une association parlementaire italo-canadienne. Jerome eut la bonté d'apposer sa signature sur la missive que je m'empressai, toute affaire cessante, d'aller porter à la présidente. Nous venions d'avancer d'un grand pas dans le rapprochement de nos parlementaires. Les conversations passent mais les écrits restent. Le reste viendrait à son heure.

Mais combien de ces initiatives ont-elles survécues et existent-elles encore aujourd'hui une quinzaine d'années plus tard? s'interrogera légitimement le lecteur. C'est ce que je me demandai aussi en rédigeant ce texte. Je m'enquis donc auprès de mon ancien collègue aux affaires culturelles et ami Gilbert Reid, devenu depuis responsable des affaires publiques et de la culture à notre ambassade à Rome. Sa réponse est datée du 30 novembre 1993. Quel dommage de ne pouvoir la citer au complet! En bref, toutes les innovations ont survécu, bien qu'elles aient dû s'adapter aux contraintes financières. Le *CACI*, atteint de ce virus épidémique est à l'agonie, mais le professeur Egmont Lee de Calgary, ouvrier de la première heure, espère lui substituer une « *Académie canadienne* ». O merveille! Un accord culturel a fini par être conclu, et sa commission mixte va de l'avant. « L'accord risque de devenir encore plus pertinent, de suggérer Reid à titre d'opinion personnelle, car si le protectionnisme européen s'accroît, cet instrument sera indispensable pour nous éviter l'exclusion culturelle ». J'allais oublier de mentionner la création également après mon départ, du *Centro culturale canadese*. Reid, cet homme cultivé et parfait trilingue le dirige bien entendu!

In fine, on pourrait croire qu'en matière culturelle nous Canadiens étions essentiellement demandeurs. Pas toujours. Les oeuvres de Margaret Atwood, de Marshall McLuhan de Mordecai Richler et de plusieurs autres étaient bien connues des italiens cultivés. La visite de ces écrivains dans la péninsule, tout comme celle d'Anne Hébert et la présentation en italien des *Belles sœurs* de Michel Tremblay obtinrent de francs succès. L'*Institut culturel canadien* et l'*Ente pomeriggi musicali di Milano* présentaient dans cette ville le 24 avril 1977, en première européenne, l'opéra comique canadien *Colas et Colinette* de Joseph Quesnel qui fut créé à Montréal en ... 1799. Un opéra canadien à portée de voix de *La Scala*! Il y a quand même de très bons moments dans la vie d'un diplomate!

LA SOUVERAINETÉ DU CANADA MENACÉE EN BELGIQUE? 1989-84

Tout comme Rome, notre ambassade auprès du Roi à Bruxelles qui fut mon affectation suivante, constituait l'une de nos dix plus grandes missions diplomatiques dans le monde. Elle possédait huit sections soit politique et économique, commerce, immigration, consulaire, attaché militaire, GRC, attaché scientifique, information et son Centre culturel attenant, fort actif *intra* et *extra* muros. Le Québec y avait une Délégation générale, dirigé par le journaliste Jean-Marc Léger, puis par l'ancien ministre et futur maire de Québec, Jean-Paul L'Allier. Un bureau d'Ontario ayant pour chef Omer Deslauriers ancien enseignant, ouvrit ses portes pendant mon affectation. Je profite de l'occasion pour signaler que l'ambassade n'avait évidemment aucun mandat de surveillance à leur endroit, chaque mission s'occupant de ses propres affaires. C'était au Canada que devaient normalement se régler d'éventuels différends. Les Affaires étrangères belges traitaient pour leur part les représentants provinciaux avec courtoisie, sans plus. Nous entretenions par ailleurs d'excellents rapports personnels avec eux; l'ambassade rendait service de son mieux lorsqu'on le lui demandait. C'est ainsi que le Québec et l'Ontario purent jouir à Bruxelles, surtout grâce à nos interventions, d'un statu honorable inspiré de celui des bureaux provinciaux canadiens à Londres.

Les morts canadiens de la Deuxième grande guerre mondiale peuplent plusieurs cimetières belges, et leur souvenir est toujours présent à la pensée des Belges qu'ils soient flamands, wallons ou bruxellois. La Belgique est un de nos principaux partenaires francophones, et notre commerce bilatéral—y compris les marchandises en transit—venait au début des années 80 au quatrième rang en Europe. Avant la France, disions-nous non sans une certaine fierté. Ses universités ont contribué à la formation de plusieurs des nôtres, et beaucoup de nos touristes s'y rendent bon an mal an et vice-versa. Et puis les Wallons, les Flamands les Bruxellois, et sans doute les Belges germanophones, nous tiennent en reconnaissante estime et sont toujours intéressés à nos péripéties constitutionnelles. Une intimité évidente et beaucoup de pain sur la planche!

C'est du reste la conjoncture constitutionnelle dans les deux pays et donc, dans la perspective d'Ottawa tout au moins, la question de la « *souveraineté nationale* » qui devait s'imposer comme toile de fond dès notre arrivée à Bruxelles en septembre 1980, année référendaire au Québec, et pour une bonne partie de notre affectation de quatre ans. Rien là de surprenant dans le climat de susceptibilités et de concurrence où baignaient de nouveau les relations entre Ottawa et Québec surtout depuis l'accession au pouvoir de René Lévesque, et en présence du triangle Bruxelles-communauté flamande-communauté wallonne, soumis lui aussi à de sérieuses tensions par la réforme constitutionnelle belge. La doctrine québécoise du prolongement extérieur de ses compétences constitutionnelles intérieures était trop attrayante aux yeux des nouvelles entités politiques dont s'était dotée la Belgique, pour qu'elle puisse être esquivée.

Une première réforme en 1970 avait mis fin à la Belgique unitaire et l'avait engagée assez modestement dans la voie de la *communautarisation* et de la *régionalisation*. La loi belge du 8 août 1980 venait, peu avant

Le roi des Belges, Baudouin Ier, accueille le nouvel ambassadeur du Canada en septembre 1980. Trois mois plus tard ce sera le tour de René Lévesque, PM du Québec.

notre arrivée, de créer au nord et au sud deux Communautés culturelles et deux Régions économiques autonomes.[5] Le nord flamand eut tôt fait d'amalgamer les deux entités néerlandophones se donnant Bruxelles—très majoritairement francophone mais située en région flamande—pour capitale. Le sud wallon dut conserver sa Communauté et sa Région séparées, Bruxelles faisant partie de la Communauté francophone mais non de la Région wallonne. C'est tout simple n'est-ce pas? Il suffisait d'y penser.

La réforme communautarisait ou régionalisait donc, sans encore le transformer en fédération comme il l'est maintenant devenu, ce pays resté unitaire depuis sa création en 1830. À défaut d'accord entre les parties sur les compétences devant être dévolues aux nouvelles entités, les textes constituaient de petits chefs d'oeuvre d'ambiguïté. Ils allaient fournir ample matière à chicane. Même le Roi Baudouin admettrait plus tard qu'« il était difficile ... d'[y] reconnaître avec précision les attributions de chaque pouvoir ». Les fédéralistes pleuraient l'unité organique de l'État et tendaient à interpréter les nouvelles dispositions de façon restrictive. Les nationalistes et les ultras, estimant leur camp lésé, et les nouvelles administrations manquant de ressources, piaffaient devant ces entraves. Le combat pour une massive décentralisation qui rendrait chacun « *maître chez soi* » avait déjà débuté. Tout cela alors que les finances belges fort mal en point eussent requis la plus grande austérité. En théorie tout le monde était d'accord sur un point : « Les Belges vivaient au dessus de leurs moyens ». Ils n'étaient pas les seuls!

Il existait, au delà de diverses asymétries dans les compétences constitutionnelles internes de chaque pays, un relatif parallélisme entre les situations belge et canadienne. La grande différence était que le gouvernement de Bruxelles qui avait pour interlocuteurs des gouvernements nationalistes plutôt pragmatiques, mais non indépendantistes, estimait pouvoir se montrer relativement souple. Il ne pouvait par ailleurs compter ni chez les flamands, ni chez les wallons sur un groupe important et solide d'inconditionnels du nouveau statu quo. Beaucoup plus qu'Ottawa, il croyait donc, par tempérament comme par tactique, devoir composer et voir venir. Le flou artistique était de mise. Les Affaires étrangères ne s'engageaient naturellement pas, et quand il fallait absolument préciser, elles se contentaient de donner à l'interlocuteur diplomatique des « *non papers* » encore moins compromettants pour les autorités que les désavouables mais plus familiers « bouts de papier » diplomatiques.

Je me rendis compte de cet état d'âme dès ma première conversation avec le Ministre des Affaires étrangères Ferdinand Nothomb, quelques jours après mon arrivée à Bruxelles le 9 octobre 1980. L'un des plus épineux dossiers du moment dans nos deux capitales était le projet d'une conférence des ministres des affaires étrangères des pays francophones destinée à mettre au point les structures d'une Francophonie internationale au niveau des chefs de gouvernement. Le gouvernement canadien estimait pour sa part que dans une telle hypothèse, des représentants québécois pourraient faire partie d'une délégation canadienne, mais qu'ils ne jouiraient d'aucun statut particulier. L'entretien fut moins que concluant, Nothomb évitant de se prononcer sur les divers scénarios à l'étude. Comme on le sait, le projet de sommets francophones ne devait aboutir que des années plus tard, après l'arrivée au pouvoir à Ottawa en 1984 du gouvernement de Brian Mulroney. Le projet se heurtait aux réticences des gouvernements belge et canadien—surtout à celles de ce dernier—face aux revendications jugées exagérées du Québec et de la Communauté française de Belgique, souhaitant tous deux une participation à part entière à d'éventuels sommets francophones. Un lever de rideau prometteur de surprise pour un nouvel ambassadeur; le premier acte n'allait pas tarder.

J'appris le 14 novembre de Jean-Marc Léger, délégué général du Québec à Bruxelles, et ami de longue date, que le premier ministre René Lévesque arriverait en Belgique le 11 décembre pour une *visite semi-officielle* de trois jours impliquant le gouvernement belge, les communautés et les régions. Il allait s'agir pour moi d'établir en quelques semaines les meilleures relations possibles avec les dirigeants des trois ordres de gouvernement et des deux langues, pour éviter qu'on ignore mon existence le moment venu, excipant de conventions protocolaires. Il fallait aussi leur faire connaître les positions fondamentales d'Ottawa établies pour l'essentiel dans l'énoncé de politique *Le fédéralisme et les relations internationales* paru en 1968 soit l'indivisibilité de la politique et des relations étrangères, la volonté du gouvernement de servir tous les intérêts canadiens y compris bien sûr ceux du Québec et avec sa participation, le désir de travailler à l'épanouissement de nos relations avec la Belgique à tous les niveaux.

Ce dernier point important, car la situation était à certains égards l'inverse de celle qui s'était présentée dans les rapports du Québec avec la France et le Gabon. Cette fois il n'y avait pas à craindre que le gouvernement belge établisse lui-même des rapports que le gouvernement canadien jugerait irréguliers avec le Québec. Nous étions plutôt intéressés au précédent que pourrait créer la latitude que Bruxelles consentirait à ses propres entités. *Nous voulions aussi éviter d'être exclus de la scène francophone belge à chacun de ses paliers*, le développement de la francophonie s'inscrivant parmi les politiques prioritaires du Canada. Mon conseiller d'ambassade, Derek Fraser qui m'y avait précédé, connaissait bien la Belgique ainsi que toutes les nuances des relations fédérales provinciales et fut un précieux collaborateur.

Les pourparlers sur les aspects politiques et protocolaires de la visite durent être effectués en peu de temps, mais malgré certaines omissions, en bonne intelligence entre toutes les parties concernées auxquelles le protocole ou la ferme détermination d'établir des précédents, interdisaient pourtant de se rencontrer en séance plénière pour tenter de tirer les choses au clair. Pendant la visite, les règles non écrites de ce jeu furent généralement respectées. Le comportement du gouvernement belge fut exemplaire. Le PM Martens, qui aurait pu le faire selon les précédents, choisit même, sans aucune intervention de notre part, de ne pas recevoir René Lévesque. Le Roi l'accueillit en audience privée, ce qui était bien son droit, pendant que l'ambassadeur de Sa Majesté la Reine en droit du Canada faisait antichambre. Cela prépara bien ce dernier à être placé lors du dîner offert à Bruxelles par le président de la Communauté française, à une table excentrique, entouré de députés ... communistes belges. La Communauté culturelle et la Région françaises invitèrent l' ambassadeur à leurs réceptions mais à aucune séance travail et visites industrielles ou autres. « La présence fédérale aux festivités ... énerve les Québécois, mais rassure certains de nos hôtes en donnant une espèce de caution aux amourettes communautaires.... Dans les prises de position, on pratique l'art d'aller juste trop loin.... Manipulations et cachotteries de collégiens en mal d'émancipation » notâmes-nous dans un rapport à Ottawa, nous gardant bien d'exagérer les choses.

Pendant tout son séjour, le premier ministre Lévesque se montra courtois, parfois même cordial à mon endroit. Son épouse Corinne ne manquait cependant aucune occasion de s'écrier de Bruxelles à Namur, de Liège à Anvers et jusqu'au départ à l'aéroport de Zaventem : « Encore vous, Monsieur l'Ambassadeur ...? ». Les choses se gâtèrent cependant à l'occasion du discours prononcé par Lévesque à Liège dans un grand amphithéâtre archi-comble, devant un auditoire euphorique ... une espèce de libération provisoire des uns et des autres. Lévesque qui avait subi quelques mois plutôt un humiliant échec lors de son référendum sur la souveraineté-association, en avait gros sur le coeur et ne croyait manifestement pas qu'il suffit de « laver son linge sale en famille ». Il mit sa belle éloquence au service de sa hargne, et c'est au vitriol qu'il dénonça les infamies et l'oppression d'Ottawa. L'occasion nous paru discutable, le ton déplorable. Le lendemain, sous le ciel de Flandre il est vrai, « le jeu des fléchettes avait déjà remplacé le canon de Liège » pour René Lévesque sinon pour son flamboyant acolyte le ministre Bernard Landry.

Pour ce qui est du fond des choses, le Québec et la Communauté française s'étaient entendus pendant la visite sur une active coopération dans trois domaines : les relations culturelles (ce qui risquait de rendre caduc, au moins en partie, l'accord culturel belgo-canadien), les matières sociales dites en Belgique « personnalisables », réputées chez nous compétences partagées, et les conditions de leur participation respective aux futurs organes politiques de la francophonie internationale. La Communauté française ouvrirait de plus une délégation à Québec. L'apothéose de la visite de René Lévesque devait survenir sur les deux premiers points, deux ans plus tard, en novembre 1982, lors de la signature d'un important accord socio-culturel qui en était le fruit, entre le Québec et la Communauté. Les deux capitales nationales ayant été soigneusement tenues à l'écart, en ignoraient officiellement le contenu au préalable. Ottawa en accueillit plus tard la substance sinon la forme quasi souveraine sans broncher. En somme plus de peur que de mal.

Sur les questions de souveraineté, on comprendra qu'il ait fallu veiller au grain d'aussi près que nous le permettaient les circonstances, avant, pendant et après la visite. Je laisse aux historiens de départager les mérites des approches respectives de Pierre Trudeau, caractérisée par une méfiance assez naturelle à l'endroit d'un gouvernement québécois indépendantiste qui ne se convertit que tardivement « au beau risque » du fédéralisme, et de Brian Mulroney qui fut beaucoup plus libéral (!) avec les successeurs québécois, fédéralistes il est vrai. C'est en tout cas Mulroney qui déverrouilla pour tous les portes de la francophonie des sommets internationaux et les ouvrit spécialement au Québec, mais aussi au Nouveau-Brunswick, à l'Ontario et indirectement aux autres communautés francophones canadiennes, sans que ne s'écroulent les colonnes du temple.

Mais revenons au point de départ. J'écrivis ce qui suit dans un télégramme au ministère le 1er décembre 1980 : « Que faisons-nous pour notre part [en Belgique] au niveau politique en dehors d'un barrage nourri de mesures défensives? Fort peu, malgré les protestations et suggestions de l'Ambassade depuis des années.... Il faudrait être bien naïf pour croire qu'à long terme le fédéralisme canadien sera renforcé par une grande intimité Québec-Belgique dans un vide politique au niveau fédéral ».

La réforme institutionnelle belge, et le désir légitime du Québec et des communautés belges de renforcer leurs relations allaient, paradoxalement surtout avec la visite du PM québécois, modifier profondément et pour le mieux quant à la substance même des relations, la problématique des rapports belgo-canadiens. Une alliance de fait s'était formée entre le Québec et la communauté et la région francophone de Belgique, et à un moindre degré avec les institutions flamandes. Il n'y avait là rien d'anormal, me semblait-il, tant qu'il s'agissait pour des entités non souveraines de coopérer dans les domaines de leurs compétences. « Les efforts québécois peuvent constituer un atout pour l'ensemble de nos relations avec la Belgique », écrivions-nous encore à Ottawa, pourvu que soient respectées les règles du jeu. Elles ne l'étaient malheureusement pas toujours. Avec la politique québécoise des petits pas (excluant par définition les consultations avant l'événement) si bien exposée par l'ancien ministre Claude Morin dans son livre *L'art de l'impossible*, la forme comptait autant que le fond. Or c'était souvent la forme, le ton et les cachotteries qui avaient l'art d'exaspérer Ottawa, auquel le Québec et d'autres provinces reprochaient de leur côté de ne pas les tenir suffisamment informées et de ne pas les consulter suffisamment dans les domaines qui les intéressaient.

Sur le plan juridique, le bât blessait surtout en raison des prétentions des deux parties à l'accord entre le Québec et la Communauté française de posséder, sans aucun contrôle, le prolongement international de leurs compétences internes. Sur le plan politique, leur laisser le monopole de leurs rapports et se cantonner dans les questions de politique étrangère et le formalisme des relations interétatiques, eût vidé la diplomatie canadienne d'une grande partie de sa substance. C'est du moins ainsi que l'ambassade comprenait le problème et l'interprétait à l'intention d'Ottawa. Après avoir fait de nombreuses suggestions en vue d'échanges sectoriels, l'ambassade proposa le 24 mars 1981 une réorientation majeure des objectifs d'Ottawa dans ses relations avec la Belgique, assorti d'un plan d'action détaillé. Bien accueilli par la centrale, il fut suivi de résultats concrets dans presque tous les domaines. Notre attachement aux visites d'État, formelles ou informelles, et à l'institutionnalisation des relations par des activités diverses et la création, là ou cela pouvait être utile, de groupes belgo-canadiens de parlementaires, de tourisme, d'études canadiennes et de centres universitaires (naturellement intéressés aux études constitutionnelles) put se donner de nouveau libre cours dans le cadre d'une politique reconnue par Ottawa et acceptée par Bruxelles.

Voici quelques exemples de visites officielles survenues en quelques mois. L'initiative du PM Trudeau en faveur d'une relance des relations

Est-Ouest qui avaient atteint à cette époque un niveau particulièrement dangereux, l'amena à Bruxelles pour une brève visite en novembre 83. En février 84, Francis Fox, Ministre des communications y vint à son tour pour signer un accord sur la coproduction cinématographique et audio-visuelle. L'impasse persistante entre le gouvernement de Bruxelles et les Communautés française et flamande sur la régionalisation des relations internationales de Belgique empêcha, in extremis ces dernières d'y participer, non sans un grand suspense jusqu'au dernier moment. Puis ce fut le tour en mai de Monique Bégin, Ministre de la Santé, de nous rendre visite pour conclure un accord de sécurité sociale. Il ne fait aucun doute qu'à notre époque la présence et l'activité des diplomates dans des pays qui méritent une attention particulière doivent être renforcées par des contacts politiques de haut niveau. Les diplomates loin de s'en formaliser, le savent mieux que tout autre.

UN ÉPISODE COMMERCIAL *TOUT TERRAIN*

Dans un autre ordre d'idées, les tractations pour la conclusion d'un important marché à la toute fin de mon mandat à l'été 1984, prirent une tournure si épique qu'elles méritent d'être rappelées. La compagnie Bombardier voulait vendre au ministère de la défense belge 2 500 véhicules Iltis tout-terrain, et s'établir solidement en Europe. La narration détaillée de la saga mettrait en évidence l'imbrication des domaines commercial et politique, l'importance d'équilibrer les avantages consentis aux régions, des « compensations industrielles » devant selon l'usage être consenties en contrepartie du privilège d'être accepté comme fournisseur, la féroce concurrence que livra, avec ses appuis notamment en Flandre, la firme Mercédès, ouvertement soutenue par le Ministre de la défense Freddy Vreven. Combats de tranchées impliquant d'inlassables manoeuvres à tous les niveaux, sur tous les fronts, techniques, commerciaux et politiques ; appui constant à Bombardier pendant des mois par notre section commerciale, représentations à coup de notes diplomatiques et en personne par l'ambassadeur auprès de divers ministres dont Vreven, celui des Affaires étrangères Léo Tindemans, et pour finir le PM Wilfrid Martens. Bombardier alla même jusqu'à troquer, pour plus d'effet à l'occasion de certaines visites, la Chevrolet de l'ambassadeur pour la Rolls Royce de son concessionnaire bruxellois!

Nous ne laissâmes que le Roi Baudouin hors du coup! Et en fin de course, Bombardier et nous, gagnâmes. La diplomatie commerciale, forcément mal connue du public, restera toujours une grande branche de la diplomatie tout court, et un des premiers objectifs de la politique étrangère.

Mentionnons avant de conclure qu'un de mes prédécesseurs à Bruxelles, Jules Léger, qui avait quitté ce poste pour devenir Gouverneur général du Canada, m'écrivit en août 1980 une lettre mémorable. Elle suggérait, avec l'habituel humour de son auteur, « une coopération entre les trois sages canadiens de Bruxelles pour que la *troisième option* soit étudiée de nouveau à fond, pour forcer le ministre d'abord, ensuite et surtout, peut-être, le successeur de Trudeau, de reprendre le thème [de la recherche d'un meilleur équilibre de nos relations économiques entre les ÉUA, l'Europe et le Japon] qui est essentiel à la survie d'une mentalité canadienne ». Oubliée cette lettre? Que non! C'est exactement ce que mes collègues ambassadeurs du Canada à Bruxelles accrédités auprès de l'OTAN et de la CÉE—coauteurs du présent ouvrage—et moi, fîmes au printemps 84 en trois dépêches écrites dans l'optique de nos fonctions respectives, mais parlant à l'unisson. L'engouement canadien bien justifié pour les promesses économiques de la région du Pacifique, risquait en effet de faire oublier la pérennité, et le caractère presque familial, de nos liens avec les pays de l'Europe. Je rentrai au Canada peu après pour me consacrer à un autre aspect de l'identité canadienne. Mon départ m'empêcha de mesurer l'impact, s'il en fut, de notre épître à trois voix sur la politique étrangère canadienne.

•

Chacun réagira à sa manière à nos témoignages. Les uns intrigués diront : « mais pourquoi connaissions-nous si mal le rôle de nos diplomates à l'étranger? ». D'autres, les blasés, y trouveront sans doute la confirmation de leurs préjugés. C'était un risque à prendre. Personnellement je crois, que les circonstances de temps et de lieu aidant, un ambassadeur peut exercer, dans un rôle bilatéral ou multilatéral, une influence importante. Il s'agit au fond d'avoir de bonnes idées au bon moment, et beaucoup de persévérance pour en convaincre un pouvoir tantôt à portée de main tantôt fort éloigné. Il y a aussi le facteur chance.

En général les affectations à la centrale sont naturellement propices à se faire voir et entendre. A l'étranger, selon la Loi organique de 1983, « le chef de mission assure la direction et la gestion du poste ... et [y] contrôle l'activité officielle des ministères et organismes fédéraux ». Un point c'est tout sur les Chefs de mission! La vieille notion qu'un ambassadeur est d'abord chargé de représenter son pays à l'étranger—sans doute jugée surannée—et d'y mettre en oeuvre la politique étrangère de son pays semble s'être tout simplement évaporée. Qu'on se le dise! À l'ère des gestionnaires, on ne « représente plus » ; cela ferait *trop mondain*. Lorsque je fis remarquer cette omission dans la nouvelle loi à notre sous-secrétaire d'État Marcel Massé, maintenant devenu ministre au sein du gouvernement de Jean Chrétien, au cours d'une réunion annuelle de CDM tenue à Bruxelles, je crus le voir pâlir. Était-il possible que les rédacteurs ait oublié ce petit détail?

Ces réunions, comme celles des CDM à Ottawa en cours d'affectation, sont et resteront indispensables. Ni les télex ni les futures autoroutes électroniques ne suffiront à maintenir le contact humain. Quand il était sous-secrétaire, Allan Gotlieb en était si convaincu qu'il avait créé au début des années 80 le « Groupe des conseillers en politique étrangère», auquel j'eus le privilège d'appartenir. Il était composé de huit CDM rappelés à Ottawa une fois l'an pour s'entretenir d'un grand thème avec la direction, le ministre, et même en 1982, le premier ministre. C'était une bonne idée … au moins pour les participants! Pour le reste, on ne saurait évaluer sa propre influence. C'est aux autres qu'il faut poser la question. Et puis, qu'est-ce que la politique étrangère? Un fleuve qui s'alimente à cent affluents et infléchit son cours selon la volonté populaire, ou un ruisseau qui canalise les idées et les intérêts de quelques-uns? Cela dépend beaucoup il me semble des caprices de l'histoire, de ceux du ministre et … du patron du ministre.

NOTES

1. Sources : En général collection privée de l'auteur des lettres et télégrammes envoyés pour la plupart au MAE, documents officiels, coupures de presse; rapports annuels du MAE.
2. Rome à Ottawa, 14 juillet 1980, no. 228, « Perspectives italiennes : *Italia fara da se?* »
3. *Accade in Italia, (C'est arrivé en Italie) 1960-1977*, Alberto Ronchey, Alberto Garzini Editore, ed. Arthème Fayard, 1977.
4. Le CACI dont Hamilton Southam fut le premier président, se joint subséquemment aux centres canadiens d'Athènes et du Caire, pour constituer sous sa présidence l'*Institut canadien de la Méditerannée*.
5. La Belgique est devenue une fédération de par une quatrième réforme de l'État survenue en 1993. Sa nouvelle constitution qualifiée de *bipolaire et centrifuge* est d'une extrême complexité. Elle reconnaît aux Communautés et Régions une compétence internationale dans leurs domaines de compétence interne, sans qu'en soient encore définies toutes les modalités. De même les compétences dites *résiduelles* appartiendront à ces entités plutôt qu'au gouvernement central. Le professeur

belge Francis Delpérée rendant compte de l'extrême décentralisation explique que «pour les uns, la révision est le point d'aboutissement [et que] pour d'autres ce n'est qu'une étape sur la voie de la dislocation d'une société politique ... une question revient d'une manière lancinante. Les Belges ont-ils la volonté de vivre ensemble? ». Textes et documents, *La Belgique fédérale après la quatrième réforme de l'État de 1993*, par les Prof. André Alen et Rusen Ergec, publiés par le Ministère des Affaires étrangères, du Commerce extérieur et de la Coopération au développement, Bruxelles, mars 1994 F/94/1. Aussi Delpérée, F., *La Belgique est un État fédéral*, Journal des Tribunaux, 1993 pp. 637-46.

D'Iberville Fortier, D.Sc.Econ., fut admis au Ministère des Affaires Extérieures en 1952. En 1953 il a servi comme troisième et deuxième secrétaire à Washington jusqu'à 1956, quand il est devenu conseiller des commissaires canadiens à la Commission Internationale de Surveillance et de Contrôle (CISC) en Indochine. Après un séjour à Ottawa en 1958, il servit aux Affaires économiques, M. Fortier est retourné en Indochine en 1959 comme Commissaire sup. à la CISC au Cambodge. De 1961 à 1963, il est détaché auprès du Secrétariat de l'OTAN à titre de chef du service de presse, puis est nommé Directeur du service de presse et liaison du MAE. En 1968 M. Fortier fut Président du Groupe de travail du Bureau du Conseil privé sur l'information gouvernmentale. L'anneé suivante, il est nommé ambassadeur en Tunisie et en Libye, un poste qu'il conserva jusqu'en 1972, quand il fut nommé Sous-secrétaire d'État adjoint MAE. De 1976 à 1984, M. Fortier fut ambassadeur en Italie et Haut Commissaire à Malte, puis ambassadeur en Belgique et au Luxembourg. De 1984 à 1991 il servit comme Commissaire aux Langues Officielles. M. Fortier est Commandeur de l'Ordre des Chevaliers de Malte et Officier de l'Ordre international de la Pléiade.

7

LES OTAGES DE STANLEYVILLE

INTERVIEW DE M. MICHEL GAUVIN
PAR M. D'IBERVILLE FORTIER

Ce qui suit est un extrait de l'interview de l'ex-ambassadeur Michel Gauvin pour le programme d'histoire orale de la Bibliothèque du Parlement et des Archives nationales fait par d'Iberville Fortier en 1992.

M. Fortier : Cela nous amène en 1961, au début de ce qu'on pourrait appeler vos missions spéciales. Ce que l'on remarque, c'est que vous avez été chef de mission diplomatique pendant 20 ans. Sauf pour la Grèce, où vous avez passé cinq ans, et la Chine, où vous avez passé quatre ans, on a l'impression qu'on a besoin de vous un peu partout et qu'on vous confie toujours des missions spéciales.

Nous allons les voir ensemble. C'est même au coeur du sujet, parce que c'est cela qui fait que vous êtes vraiment un diplomate pas comme les autres, auquel on a confié des missions spécifiques au lieu de l'envoyer tout simplement défendre des intérêts pendant une période normale de quatre ou cinq ans.

Le premier épisode, c'est la mission qu'on vous a confiée au Congo, durant la rébellion de Stanleyville. Pourriez-vous nous parler des divers aspects de cette mission? Pourquoi cette mission? Qu'est-ce que vous alliez y faire? Comment est-ce que cela s'est passé?

M. Gauvin : C'est une longue histoire. J'essaierai d'être aussi bref que possible. Premièrement, le ministère a décidé de m'envoyer au Congo six mois après l'indépendance. C'était un poste considéré intéressant parce que le Canada avait aux Nations Unies un détachement de 1 000 signaleurs. De fait, si on avait eu une guerre à ce moment-là, je ne sais pas ce que le Canada aurait pu faire, parce que la majorité de nos signaleurs étaient au service des Nations Unies. Avant l'indépendance le Congo avait été pour le Canada un poste essentiellement d'intérêt commercial.

En arrivant au Congo, j'ai vu les Nations Unies opérer sous la direction du secrétaire général Dag Hammarskjöld. On peut dire qu'il a été un secrétaire général activiste. Il rêvait que les Nations Unies deviennent l'instrument du maintien de la paix et de l'ordre dans le monde. Il avait eu beaucoup de succès lors de l'intervention des Nations Unies au canal de Suez, où d'ailleurs M. Pearson, notre premier ministre, qui était à ce moment-là ministre des Affaires étrangères, avait joué un rôle déterminant qui lui a valu le Prix Nobel de la Paix.

Le Canada avait intérêt à avoir sur place quelqu'un qui puisse rapporter à Ottawa les conditions politiques et autres qui y prévalaient. Au Congo, il y avait une grande division entre Kasavubu qui était président, et Lumumba, premier ministre. Kasavubu était l'homme sur qui on comptait pour faire une transition pacifique entre l'ancien et le nouveau régime. Au moment des cérémonies de l'indépendance, Lumumba a fait un discours attaquant la Belgique et le roi des Belges s'est fait enlever son sabre alors qu'il était dans sa voiture. La gendarmerie congolaise s'est révoltée, appuyée par Lumumba. Il y a énormément de Blancs qui ont été tués. À ce moment-là, les Belges étaient prêts à rétablir l'ordre, mais les Nations Unies s'y opposaient. C'est ainsi que les Nations Unies sont venues au Congo, appuyées par la plupart des pays occidentaux, alors que les Russes s'y opposaient. La France trouvait aussi que c'était une intervention internationale injustifiée. Je parle de De Gaulle. C'était son attitude. Il aurait préféré que la Belgique rétablisse l'ordre plutôt que les Nations Unies.

Les Nations Unies, c'était un peu la Tour de Babel avec des contingents de tous les coins du monde. Le représentant du secrétaire général était Dayal, un indien dont les sympathies et préférences allaient à Lumumba. C'était la division, non seulement entre les pays de gauche et les pays occidentaux, mais aussi entre les pays pauvres, les pays sous-développés, et les pays riches. Ceci a conduit à une guerre intestine au Congo, où le Katanga, avec Tschombé, probablement le plus intelligent et le mieux éduqué des Congolais, était appuyé par les Belges dont les intérêts économiques étaient considérables. C'est ainsi qu'est arrivée la tentative de sécession du Katanga et que les troupes indiennes des Nations Unies sont intervenues.

L'unité nationale du Congo s'était faite grâce aux Belges. Il n'y avait jamais eu d'unité avant eux. Il ne faut pas oublier qu'au Congo, beaucoup de gens ne savaient même pas qui habitait à quelques kilomètres avant les Belges. D'ailleurs avant l'arrivée des Belges, le Congo était connu comme *the darkest part of Africa*. Lorsque le Congo avait été accordé aux Belges en 1905 par le Traité de Berlin, personne n'en voulait. On l'a donné de fait au roi. Le roi Léopold n'avait pas suffisamment d'argent pour maintenir le Congo, et le gouvernement belge a pris la succession du roi après un long débat au Parlement et beaucoup de réticence.

M. Fortier : Voilà donc un pays qui a une vaste population et beaucoup de ressources naturelles, mais qui n'est pas tout à fait un pays et qui a des problèmes très graves, et il y a une intervention des Nations Unies. Quel est l'objet de cette intervention?

M. Gauvin : Premièrement, c'est de s'assurer que le Congo ne devienne pas un pays.... Dans le contexte international, on s'inquiétait que le Congo, avec ses richesses naturelles, puisse tomber sous contrôle communiste. Lumumba était d'ailleurs appuyé par beaucoup de pays communistes ou d'orientation marxiste. D'un autre côté, les Occidentaux donnaient l'impression d'être d'anciens colonisateurs qui voulaient revenir au Congo pour s'accaparer les richesses.

C'est ainsi que, lors de la sécession du Katanga, les Nations Unies se sont trouvées dans une situation d'intervention, alors qu'en réalité les Nations Unies n'avaient pas le mandat de devenir l'instrument du gouvernement central, qui était à Léopoldville, pour préserver l'unité du pays. C'est ainsi que les Nations Unies, se sont embarquées dans une « guerre sainte » contre le Katanga. Hammarskjöld a dû intervenir personnellement et se rendre au Katanga pour rencontrer Tschombé et tenter de trouver une solution pacifique. C'est à ce moment-là qu'il a été tué dans un accident d'avion. On a prétendu que son avion avait été victime des forces prokatangaises, mais cela n'a jamais été prouvé. Je crois que c'est purement un accident.

Les Nations Unies sont restées au Congo, mais avec le temps les gens s'en désintéressaient. Financièrement, cela coûtait énormément cher. Les Nations Unies étaient divisées et ne pouvaient plus remplir leur rôle original de maintien de la paix. Éventuellement la gauche a formé un gouvernement à Stanleyville, composé de gens qui avaient appuyé Lumumba. Lumumba avait été tué à ce moment-là, mais il y avait encore ses partisans. Gizenga, par exemple, en était le chef. C'était un ancien ministre dans le gouvernement du Président Kasavubu.

En 1964, le Congo était de nouveau divisé et les forces de Stanleyville avaient pénétré un peu partout dans la province orientale au nord de Léopoldville ; elles s'étendaient et menaçaient Léopoldville. C'est à ce moment-là que sous l'influence du général Mobutu, le président Kasavubu a invité Tschombé à Léopoldville comme premier ministre, pour remplacer le premier ministre Adoula qui s'avérait incapable.

M. Fortier : Donc, voici les ennemis réconciliés et une tentative amorcée pour rétablir la situation et empêcher la croissance de l'influence de la gauche. Vous, personnellement, où en êtes-vous à ce moment-là? Est-ce que vous êtes toujours sur le théâtre, comme on dit, ou si vous êtes rentré à Ottawa? À quel moment s'est située votre mission spéciale?

M. Gauvin : J'ai quitté le Congo en 1963. Je suis retourné au Ministère et, à ce moment-là, la situation que j'ai décrite continuait de se détériorer. Le gouvernement de Tschombé, avec l'appui de Mobutu, a décidé d'employer les mercenaires pour repousser ce qu'on appelait dans le temps les révolutionnaires de gauche. Donc, les forces de Stanleyville décidèrent de prendre les missionnaires en otages pour empêcher les forces de Mobutu d'attaquer Stanleyville.

Parmi ces missionnaires une trentaine étaient des canadiens. Il y avait au Canada un débat à la Chambre des communes. L'opposition demandait : mais, qu'est-ce qu'on fait là-bas? C'est une affaire qui concerne les Belges et les Américains. Nous ne sommes pas mêlés à ce conflit civil. Comme j'avais connu beaucoup des révolutionnaires de Stanleyville alors qu'ils étaient à Léopoldville, on avait eu l'idée que je pourrais aller plaider leur libération arguant que les Canadiens n'avaient rien à voir dans ce conflit.

M. Fortier : Nous arrivons donc à votre première mission spéciale. On vous donne un mandat. Est-ce que vous pouvez nous en rappeler les termes?

M. Gauvin : Le mandat était simplement d'essayer de libérer les otages canadiens à Stanleyville. Je suis d'abord allé à Washington pour m'informer de la position américaine, parce que les Américains appuyaient le gouvernement de Léopoldville et se préparaient peut-être à intervenir avec les Belges sur une base humanitaire et à employer la force pour le faire. Ensuite, je suis allé aux Nations Unies pour avoir leur version des faits. De là, je suis passé à Bruxelles. Les Belges ne m'ont pas dit grand-chose, parce que l'intervention américaine et belge était encore secrète. De là, je suis passé à Genève pour voir la Croix-Rouge. Je voulais essayer de pénétrer à Stanleyville avec les avions de la Croix-Rouge et de plaider auprès des autorités pour qu'elles relâchent les missionnaires canadiens. Je devais partir pour me rendre au Congo et trouver moi-même un moyen de pénétrer à Stanleyville, peut-être en nolisant un avion, parce qu'il était évident que la Croix-Rouge ne voulait pas que quelqu'un autre que la Croix-Rouge fasse partie de l'équipage de son avion.

M. Fortier : Est-ce que cette attitude de la part de la Croix-Rouge était destinée à se conserver tout le mérite de ce qui pourrait se produire, ou si c'était pour des raisons légitimes de bon fonctionnement de ce processus humanitaire? Ce qu'on vous avait confié comme mission, c'était humanitaire et la Croix-Rouge avait aussi une mission humanitaire. Pourquoi n'aimait-on pas amener des corps étrangers, si l'on peut dire?

M. Gauvin : La Croix-Rouge avait déjà pénétré à Stanleyville, mais avait été forcée de revenir bredouille. C'était assez délicat, parce que les autorités de Stanleyville soupçonnaient la Croix-Rouge de favoriser le monde occidental. La Croix-Rouge n'avait pas réellement la confiance des révolutionnaires. Ma présence à bord d'un de leurs avions aurait probablement servi d'excuse aux révolutionnaires pour dire : Vous nous amenez un homme d'un pays adversaire, qui est avec les Américains et les Belges. La Croix-Rouge aurait pu perdre le peu de crédit qu'elle avait.

Alors que j'étais encore à Genève, j'ai reçu un téléphone d'Ottawa, en plein milieu de la nuit. On m'a dit : Vos plans sont changés; vous n'allez plus à Léopoldville, vous irez au Kenya rencontrer M. Robert Thompson, Chef du parti du Crédit social, qui était en Afrique de l'Ouest.

À ce moment-là, le gouvernement Pearson était un gouvernement minoritaire qui se maintenait au pouvoir avec l'appui des Créditistes. On critiquait le gouvernement en disant: Qu'est-ce que M. Thompson fait en Afrique? Est-ce qu'il se promène parce qu'il a aidé le gouvernement minoritaire à se maintenir au pouvoir? Est-ce une récompense, alors qu'il y a des gens qui sont maintenus en captivité par des rebelles à Stanleyville? Quelqu'un a eu la bonne idée d'utiliser Thompson, de l'associer à la mission qui m'avait été confiée. On se rappelait qu'il avait été missionnaire en Éthiopie et qu'il s'occupait des petits-enfants de l'Empereur qui étudiaient ici, à Ottawa. Je me suis donc rendu au Kenya pour y rencontrer Thompson qui venait, je crois, du Ghana. Ne l'ayant jamais rencontré avant, je ne le connaissais pas. Parmi un groupe de gens qui sortaient de l'avion, j'ai vu un monsieur qui m'a paru être Canadien. Je me suis approché et j'ai dit : *Doctor Thompson, I presume?* Tout comme Stanley, lorsqu'il était à la recherche de Livingstone. C'était bien lui. J'ai donc amené Thompson à l'Hôtel Stanley à Nairobi. Là, en descendant pour dîner, nous avons rencontré le ministre des Affaires étrangères d'Éthiopie, Ketema Yifru, qui était à l'hôtel avec le secrétaire général de l'Organisation de l'unité africaine, un Guinéen très près du Président Sékou Touré. Il y avait aussi le général Yassu, chef d'état-major des forces éthiopiennes, que j'avais connu au Congo alors qu'il était chef du contingent éthiopien aux Nations Unies. Ketema Yifru avait été un élève de Thompson lorsque ce dernier avait servi comme éducateur en Éthiopie. Ketema Yifru a demandé : Mais qu'est-ce que vous faites ici, monsieur Thompson? Thompson lui a expliqué que nous allions voir l'Empereur pour lui demander d'intervenir auprès des forces de Stanleyville afin qu'elles libèrent les otages.

M. Fortier : Il s'agit de l'Empereur d'Éthiopie, Hailé Sélassié, qui était à ce moment-là président de l'Organisation des États africains, ou à quel titre?

M. Gauvin : Hailé Sélassié était connu comme le père de l'Afrique et jouissait encore d'un certain prestige en Afrique. On le respectait beaucoup. Nous avions pensé que s'il faisait un appel à titre de père de l'Afrique, les autorités de Stanleyville libéreraient peut-être les otages. Quand Thompson a dit ceci à Yifru, sa première réaction a été : Mais qu'est ce que l'Empereur a à voir là-dedans? Il y a un comité ad hoc responsable de la crise de Stanleyville dont le président est Kenyatta; nous n'avons rien à voir là-dedans. Le secrétaire général de l'Organisation de l'unité africaine abondait dans le même sens.

Le lendemain nous avons quitté Nairobi et nous somme arrivés à Addis-Abéba où Thompson a pris contact avec le Palais impérial. On nous a dit que l'Empereur recevrait M. Thompson à son palais de Debrezeit à quelque 50 kilomètres au sud d'Addis-Abéba. Addis-Abéba est une ville à près de 3 000 mètres, et c'était la pratique pour les gens d'un certain âge de se retirer à une plus basse altitude. D'ailleurs les missionnaires canadiens qui étaient là le faisaient toutes les fins de semaines. L'Empereur a laissé entendre à M. Thompson qu'il considérait la possibilité d'intervenir—nous l'avons vu un samedi soir—et qu'il nous recevrait le lundi matin à 10 heures pour nous dire exactement ce qu'il ferait et quel émissaire il enverrait à Stanleyville en son nom.

Ayant rencontré Ketema Yifru, je savais qu'il s'opposerait à ce que l'Empereur intervienne, parce que ce dernier était quand même vulnérable.

En 1966, l'empereur Hailé Sélassié visite le pavillon canadien à une kermesse au bénéfice de la Croix Rouge éthiopienne, accompagné par l'ambassadeur Gauvin.

L'empereur, réellement, devait éviter de paraître comme le défenseur des Occidentaux, ce qui pouvait être le cas s'il intervenait directement et ignorait le comité ad hoc de Kenyatta.

M. Fortier : Incidemment, M. Gauvin, vous n'étiez pas en train de faire votre mission par quelqu'un d'autre en suggérant l'empereur?

M. Gauvin : Ma mission à moi était de servir le Canada et ce dernier trouvait, avec raison, qu'utiliser l'influence de Thompson sur l'empereur avait ses mérites.

D'ailleurs, j'ai immédiatement envoyé un télégramme à M. Pearson en lui disant : Nous allons voir l'empereur lundi, et il est important que Thompson ait un message de votre part le remerciant d'intervenir, parce que je crains que Ketema Yifru, qui va rentrer à Addis-Abéba lundi, ne dissuade l'empereur d'intervenir. J'ai envoyé ce message par l'ambassade des États-Unis parce que c'était le moyen le plus rapide de rejoindre le premier ministre du Canada en fin de semaine. Nous avons attendu à l'ambassade des États-Unis la réponse du premier ministre qui n'est jamais venue. Le lundi matin, nous avons reçu un message du palais nous disant que l'empereur ne nous recevrait pas à 10 h mais en fin d'après-midi, vers 17 h.

À ce moment-là, nous avions appris des Américains que Ketema Yifru et le secrétaire de l'Organisation de l'unité africaine étaient arrivés de Nairobi vers 10 h le matin. Autrement dit, ce qu'on soupçonnait allait arriver. De fait, lorsque nous sommes allés voir l'empereur.... Je dois dire premièrement que, sachant ceci, j'avais préparé un aide-mémoire pour l'empereur, en français parce qu'il était de culture française, bien qu'il parlait un petit peu l'anglais, dans lequel je le remerciais de nous avoir reçus la première fois et surtout de nous avoir dit qu'il interviendrait et que le premier ministre du Canada l'en remerciait, cela pour l'obliger à ne pas revenir sur l'engagement qu'il avait pris auprès de nous le samedi soir.

Ketema Yifru, qui était présent, a dit : Écoutez, il n'est pas question que l'empereur se mêle de cette affaire; il y a le comité ad hoc qui s'en occupe et l'Empereur ne peut pas intervenir.

Le pauvre Thompson était très déçu que notre mission ait failli. Pour tirer le meilleur parti de la situation j'ai préparé un communiqué que Thompson allait émettre à la presse à l'effet qu'il avait reçu de l'empereur la conviction que les otages seraient épargnés. Thompson est retourné au Canada. À moi, on a dit : Dans ce cas, retournez à Nairobi, prenez contact avec le comité ad hoc et voyez ce que vous pouvez faire pour retourner au Congo, peut-être en avion. Pendant que j'étais à Nairobi, les négociations se terminaient, et les Belges et les Américains allaient intervenir à Stanleyville; c'est-à-dire que les Américains allaient fournir des avions pour transporter les troupes que les Belges allaient parachuter.

M. Fortier : Quel aurait été le poids d'une intervention de l'empereur auprès d'autorités de gauche qui n'étaient pas favorables à ajouter au prestige impérial? Je pense que c'est un point assez intéressant. S'il était vraiment intervenu, est-ce qu'il aurait pu être influent?

M. Gauvin : Cela est discutable. Son intervention aurait probablement influencé le comité ad hoc et Kenyatta à prendre une attitude plus positive sur la question des otages. Tout le temps, le comité ad hoc assurait les intéressés, ceux qui avaient des otages là-bas, qu'ils avaient des garanties des gens de Stanleyville que rien n'arriverait aux otages. Mais il était évident que la chaleur montait, que les gens de Stanleyville se sentaient encerclés et qu'une attaque viendrait. Le cas échéant ils disaient qu'ils exécuteraient les otages. On était dans une situation désespérée, en ce sens que la décision avait été prise par la Belgique, avec l'aide américaine, d'intervenir par la force. De fait à Nairobi, les Américains et les Belges m'annoncèrent que l'opération devait avoir lieu le lendemain. À ce moment-là, il n'était plus question pour mois d'essayer d'aller à Stanleyville. C'était déjà trop tard. La façon qui me paraissait la plus logique et la plus efficace, c'était de pénétrer à Stanleyville immédiatement après le parachutage. Je suis parti avec un avion anglais qui transportait des médecins et des brancardiers de Nairobi. Nous sommes allés pendant la nuit à Kampala pour faire le plein d'essence et sommes arrivés à Stanleyville le lendemain du parachutage. La bataille continuait. Les parachutistes avaient capturé l'aéroport, mais les alentours étaient encore entre les mains des rebelles. Nous avons dû survoler le champ d'aviation pendant environ une heure avant d'avoir la permission de descendre. En arrivant à l'aéroport, j'ai demandé où était le quartier général de Mobutu. On m'avait dit qu'il serait là. Il y avait un mercenaire avec un jeep qui m'a dit : Venez, je vous y amène. Le gardien à la porte du quartier général où étaient les mercenaires et Mobutu—c'étaient des mercenaires en grande majorité qui étaient là—m'a demandé : Qu'est-ce que vous venez faire ici? J'ai dit : Je veux voir le général Mobutu. Dites-lui que je suis l'ancien chargé d'affaire du Canada; il va savoir qui je suis; mon nom est Gauvin.

Lors de mon séjour à Léopoldville comme chargé d'affaires, j'avais très bien connu Mobutu, j'avais même été un des seuls Blancs à être invité au baptême de l'une de ses filles. Il me connaissait très bien. D'ailleurs, par la suite, chaque fois que quelqu'un présentait ses lettres de créance comme ambassadeur, la première chose qu'il disait était celle-ci : Et l'ambassadeur Gauvin, où est-il? Notre ambassadeur ne revoyait Mobutu le plus souvent qu'à la fin de son séjour au Congo pour prendre congé. La question revenait encore : Et l'ambassadeur Gauvin, où est-il? C'est pour vous dire que j'avais maintenu avec lui de très bonnes relations. Tout cela était aussi dû au fait que, dans le contingent canadien aux Nations Unies il y avait des officiers du 22ᵉ Régiment qui, parce qu'ils parlaient français, avaient été affectés au quartier général de Mobutu. Ce sont eux qui m'ont introduit au colonel Mobutu dès mon arrivée au Congo en 1961.

Toujours est-il que Mobutu arrive. Il dit : Qu'est-ce que vous faites ici? Je lui réponds en blaguant : J'ai entendu dire que vous aviez des problèmes et je viens vous aider. Mais qu'est-ce que je pouvais faire? Je n'avais pas la liste des otages canadiens et ne savais pas où ils se trouvaient exactement. J'ai dû me rendre à Léopoldville pour obtenir cette information.

Les mercenaires ont très bien travaillé à ce moment-là. Leur chef Michael Hoare, un Sud-Africain, était un officier qui avait servi avec les forces britanniques pendant la dernière guerre en Asie et au Moyen-Orient. Il était très efficace. On allait chercher les otages dans les fermes avoisinantes de Stanleyville. On mettait une jeep avec une mitrailleuse en avant, un camion sur lequel on avait mis des matelas venait derrière, et une autre jeep suivait avec une mitrailleuse. On circulait à grande vitesse sur des routes de terre pour atteindre les fermes et les endroits où on croyait qu'on détenait encore des otages et on les ramenait à Stanleyville sous la protection des forces congolaises et des mercenaires. C'est ainsi qu'une religieuse canadienne avait été libérée par ce chef des mercenaires. Elle était tellement heureuse d'être libérée qu'elle l'a pris par le cou et l'a embrassé. Puis elle a dit : Oh! excusez-moi, je n'ai jamais embrassé un homme. Il lui a répondu : Do not worry, madam, I have not been kissed by a nun for a long time.

Après les premières opérations de sauvetage des mercenaires, j'ai pensé que la chose la plus utile pour moi serait d'aller à Léopoldville et d'obtenir la liste des missionnaires que nous avions dans cette région, ce que j'ai fait. Je suis retourné à Stanleyville, et finalement on a libéré le reste des Canadiens.

M. Fortier : C'était une libération des Canadiens. Est-ce que cela s'est passé jusqu'à la fin de la manière que vous mentionniez, avec des jeeps et des mitrailleuses, ou est-ce que votre mission a pu arriver à des méthodes un peu plus diplomatiques et moins militaires?

M. Gauvin : Mon rôle était essentiellement de m'assurer que tous les Canadiens qui avaient été détenus en otage, dont le nombre se situait entre 35 et 40, recevraient l'assistance nécessaire pour rentrer à Léopoldville. C'est ce qui est arrivé. À ce moment-là, je suis retourné à Léopoldville pour faire rapport au chargé d'affaires du temps, et l'ambassade les a pris en charge. Pour ma part, je suis rentré au Canada, ma mission étant à ce moment-là terminée.

M. Fortier : Est-ce qu'on a su par la suite si tous les otages avaient été rendus vivants? Quelle était la situation?

M. Gauvin : Je crois que deux ou trois d'entre eux ont été victimes. Ils ont été tué par les Simbas, comme on les appelait « Simba » veut dire « lion ». C'étaient des jeunes révolutionnaires indisciplinées qui tiraient à gauche et à droite et qui tuaient les Blancs qu'ils rencontraient. Mais, en grande partie, ils ont été libéré sains et saufs.

M. Fortier : Est-ce qu'on peut dire, en jugeant plus tard de cette mission, que vous aviez fait tout ce que vous aviez pu et que donc cette mission valait la peine d'avoir été entreprise, même si les événements ne s'étaient pas déroulés comme on aurait pu le prévoir?

M. Gauvin : Je crois que sur le plan politique, c'était utile parce que dans le débat à la Chambre, le gouvernement était pressé par l'opposition de faire quelque chose pour tenter de libérer les otages canadiens. C'était naturellement leur libération qui importait, mais c'était aussi efficace pour faire taire l'opposition qui était assez critique du gouvernement.

M. Fortier : Sur le plan personnel, vous aviez déployé beaucoup d'imagination, me semble-t-il, dans la manière dont vous aviez fait les choses. Est-ce qu'il y a quelque chose d'autre que vous auriez pu faire, en y repensant plusieurs années plus tard?

M. Gauvin : Je pense que je ne l'aurais peut-être pas fait exactement de la même façon. Je n'aurais pas pris, par exemple, la responsabilité de dire à l'empereur que je le remerciais au nom de M. Pearson. D'ailleurs, bien des années plus tard, M. Pearson est venu en Grèce au moment où j'étais ambassadeur. Il était venu chez moi avec son épouse. J'avais beaucoup de respect pour M. Pearson et j'avais mis mon chauffeur à son service pour ses visites touristiques. Il ne demeurait pas à la résidence mais il y passait souvent. Il aimait bien prendre son verre au bord de la piscine et causer. Nous sommes devenus assez intimes. D'ailleurs, je l'avais connu auparavant. À ce moment-là, j'ai osé lui poser la question : Pourquoi ne m'avez-vous jamais envoyé une réponse à mon télégramme? Vous l'avez bien reçu, ce télégramme? Il m'a dit : Ah! oui, mais on s'est dit que, de toute façon, Gauvin allait le faire. L'avantage pour lui était tout à fait clair. Si les choses vont mal par la suite, on critique et on dit : On n'a jamais fait cela; c'est Gauvin qui l'a fait de sa propre initiative. J'acceptais cela. Ce qui m'intéressait était d'avoir la confirmation qu'il avait bien reçu mon télégramme. C'était assez amusant.

M. Fortier : C'était une aventure qui complétait votre séjour diplomatique en Afrique d'une façon assez extraordinaire. Est-ce que cela a été votre dernier contact avec l'Afrique comme diplomate?

M. Gauvin : À la suite de cette mission, j'avais fait un rapport dans lequel j'avais signalé qu'Addis-Abéba, où nous n'avions pas de représentation diplomatique, était le siège de l'Organisation de l'unité africaine et que tous les pays de l'Afrique et bien d'autres avaient une représentation là. Il y avait aussi une autre raison. Je dois dire premièrement que les Jésuites avaient été expulsés d'Abyssinie, au siècle dernier par l'empereur Ménélik. Assez renard et astucieux, profitant de ce que les Italiens avaient perdu la guerre et ayant besoin d'éducateurs pour moderniser le pays et éduquer les gens, Haïlé Sélaissié s'était adressé au Pape en lui proposant que les Jésuites pourraient revenir si on lui envoyait des éducateurs à la condition que ces éducateurs soient de langues anglaise et française. Où est-ce qu'on trouve des gens qui sont à la fois anglophones et francophones ailleurs que dans la province canadienne? Ce sont les Jésuites canadiens qui sont allés en Éthiopie immédiatement à la fin de la guerre pour établir un système d'éducation. Ils ont eu une très grande influence en particulier le supérieur, le Père Matte qui avait l'oreille de l'Empereur. Ils étaient toujours là. Parmi eux, j'ai trouvé d'anciens professeurs lorsque j'étais chez les Jésuites et aussi des confrères de classe, Pion, Savard, Laurendeau etc. ... Ils m'ont convaincu qu'il serait dans l'intérêt du Canada d'avoir une représentation à Addis. Un an après mon retour au Canada, Marcel Cadieux, qui était le sous-secrétaire, m'a appelé un jour pour me dire : Dans ton rapport sur l'Éthiopie, tu as recommandé qu'on ouvre une mission ; eh bien, on l'ouvre, et c'est toi qui vas y aller. C'est ainsi que je suis devenu ambassadeur en Éthiopie.

Michel Gauvin, CVO, OC, DSO, Chevalier de la Légion d'honneur, participe au débarquement de Normandie et termine la guerre en Allemagne au rang de major. Il entre au MAE en 1947 et est détaché auprès du bureau du Premier ministre jusqu'en 1950 à titre de secrétaire de langue française. En 1951 il est nommé en Turquie et ensuite au Portugal. Il passe une année au Vietnam à la Commission internationale en 1955 pour ensuite suivre les cours du Collège de la défense nationale à Kingston. En 1957 il part pour ensuite Venezuela et pour l'Argentine. En 1961 il est nommé chargé d'affaires au Congo ex-belge. De 1964 à 1966 il est directeur adjoint des affaires de l'Amérique latine. En 1966, il est ambassadeur en Éthiopie avec accréditation à Madagascar et en Somalie. En 1969, il est ambassadeur au Portugal et ensuite en Grèce. En 1976-77 il est secrétaire canadien de Sa Majesté et coordonnateur des visites royales ainsi que Consul général à Strasbourg. De 1978 à 1980 il est ambassadeur au Maroc, et de 1980 à 1984 en Chine. Au cours de sa carrière il a été envoyé en missions spéciales pendant la guerre civile au Congo (1964), ainsi qu'à Saint-Domingue (1965), et au Vietnam (1973).

8

EN AMBASSADE AU MOYEN-ORIENT DE 1970 À 1974

JACQUES GIGNAC[1]

QUAND JE SUIS ARRIVÉ À BEYROUTH, en janvier 1970, pour y représenter le Canada au Liban, en Syrie, et en Jordanie, je ne me faisais guère d'illusion sur l'importance accordée à cette région par notre administration qui la plaçait décidément en queue de liste de nos priorités. L'Ambassade dont je prenais charge venait d'ailleurs d'échapper de justesse à la série de fermetures décidées en 1969 en réponse à une première campagne d'austérité budgétaire engagée par le gouvernement. Le ministre du commerce de l'époque, l'honorable Jean-Luc Pepin, avait fait prévaloir les impératifs commerciaux de son ministère sur les recommandations de son collègue des Affaires extérieures. Nos services commerciaux de Beyrouth ayant la charge de couvrir tout le Moyen-Orient arabe à l'est du canal de Suez, monsieur Pepin ne pouvait accepter, comme alternative réaliste et pratique, un transfert des responsabilités commerciales de Beyrouth vers l'un des autres postes du proche ou lointain voisinage (Téhéran, Le Caire, ou Ankara). Le Cabinet avait donc rejeté la recommandation des Affaires extérieures, mais cet épisode en disait long sur les objectifs de la politique étrangère canadienne d'alors à l'égard du monde arabe.

Vu ce contexte, ma nomination n'avait été confirmée, en novembre 1969, qu'après de longs mois de tergiversation et d'attente qui valurent au poste de rester sans titulaire pendant la meilleure partie de cette année-là. D'une brève tournée de rencontres à Ottawa pour me préparer à ma nouvelle charge, j'avais tiré la conclusion que notre administration considérait nos intérêts comme très limités dans cette partie du monde. Dans le domaine politique, on ne s'attendait pas à ce que je sois plus qu'un observateur de la conjoncture et un porte-parole de notre politique multilatérale dite « d'équilibre », relativement au conflit israélo-arabe. Bref, il s'agissait d'adopter une approche plutôt passive. Dans le domaine commercial, on se disait pleinement satisfait du travail de notre ambassade et l'on escomptait de moi, essentiellement, un rôle d'appui.

Après une année de voyages, de contacts et d'observation dans mes trois pays d'accréditation, j'en vins à la conclusion qu'autant la région offrait un énorme potentiel aux intérêts économiques du Canada, autant nous manquions d'une politique adéquate pour en tirer parti. Ce jugement était conforté par l'expérience de mes collaborateurs des services commerciaux, qui ne manquaient pas de venir me faire part de leurs résultats et de leurs observations au retour des périples entrepris dans le territoire de leur ressort, plus vaste encore que le mien. Le conflit israélo-arabe et ses incidences sur notre diplomatie d'après-guerre pouvaient peut-être expliquer cette inadéquation de nos moyens. Mais depuis, l'évolution des choses avait forcément entraîné des changements de perspectives, mettant en lumière toute une gamme d'intérêts (économiques, commerciaux, mais également politiques et même stratégiques comme il s'avérera relativement au pétrole), qui échappaient à la dimension multilatérale de notre diplomatie. Car celle-ci, axée sur la Question du Moyen-Orient, couvrait jusqu'alors l'essentiel de nos relations avec les pays arabes. Au-delà d'une politique où tout était filtré à travers le prisme du conflit israélo-arabe, une autre approche s'imposait pour répondre adéquatement à de nouveaux besoins de nature essentiellement bilatérale. Le défi était de taille, mais j'étais déterminé à y faire face au mieux de mes capacités.

Depuis mon arrivée à Beyrouth, j'avais acquis la ferme conviction qu'il était possible de développer des relations bilatérales actives et substantielles avec les pays arabes, au bénéfice notamment de nos intérêts économiques et commerciaux, sans rien compromettre de notre diplomatie à l'égard d'Israël ou de nos principes et de notre position dans le conflit israélo-arabe. Je m'étais d'ailleurs vite rendu compte à travers mes divers contacts, et c'était pour moi inattendu, que notre « politique d'équilibre » dans le dossier israélo-arabe, malgré les réserves qu'elle pouvait soulever chez mes interlocuteurs, suscitait néanmoins de leur part un respect et une crédibilité dont nous n'avions jamais vraiment tiré avantage dans nos relations avec eux. La facilité avec laquelle j'avais accès partout, la courtoisie avec laquelle on me recevait, l'intérêt que l'on me manifestait, comme les propos que l'on me tenait, me révélaient des dispositions favorables à un rapprochement avec notre pays, un désir d'œuvrer en ce sens, d'établir des rapports plus suivis et d'avoir des échanges plus substantiels.

Il en était bien autrement du côté canadien où prévalait, tant au sein de la fonction publique que de la classe politique, une tradition de réserve et de méfiance à l'égard d'un monde arabe toujours ouvertement hostile à Israël. Un tel environnement ne pouvait, a priori, que favoriser des politiques timorées, sinon négatives, envers les pays concernés et rendait particulièrement difficile tout effort de rapprochement avec eux. Dans les circonstances, il s'agissait de modifier un climat et d'inciter à un changement d'attitude plus conforme à nos intérêts. À cette fin, la voie de l'argumentation théorique me paraissait illusoire. En revanche, celle d'une approche pragmatique me semblait mieux convenir pour établir, dans les faits et par des résultats tangibles, le réalisme, la rentabilité et le besoin d'une politique axée sur le bilatéralisme au Moyen-Orient, conformément à la sagesse de l'adage anglais : « the proof of the pudding is in the eating ». Au préalable, la définition d'objectifs bien ciblés s'imposait ainsi que l'identification de créneaux précis, ouverts à la compétition de nos services et produits. Ceci fait, une stratégie d'interventions ponctuelles auprès des gouvernements intéressés devenait possible, à l'appui de nos efforts pour trouver de nouveaux débouchés. Elle s'imposait dans des pays comme le Liban ou la Syrie où l'État, de façon courante, jouait un rôle déterminant dans l'adjudication des marchés. Elle paraissait pertinente pour amorcer, comme je le recherchais, un processus d'échanges commerciaux substantiels au bénéfice de nos exportations, qui serait appelé à déboucher tôt ou tard sur des relations bilatérales plus générales. Il s'agissait de favoriser ainsi une évolution des esprits et une ouverture de notre politique, plus en harmonie avec la réalité de nos intérêts. Tel fut, à partir du printemps 1971, l'objectif principal de mon action.

Déjà en Syrie, dès mai 1970, peu de temps après mon accréditation, j'avais signé, au nom du gouvernement, un substantiel accord de fourniture de blé portant sur trois ans dont le financement était assuré par des crédits canadiens. C'était une première entre les deux pays dont était très conscient celui qui était, à l'époque, le ministre syrien du commerce, Abdel Khaddam, avec lequel je transigeais. Personnage influent du Baath, le parti unique du régime, Khaddam (qui devint ministre des Affaires étrangères après le coup d'État qui porta Hafiz Al-Assad au pouvoir, et qui fut nommé quelques années plus tard, vice-président de la République, fonction qu'il occupe toujours), me fit part, dès notre première rencontre, de son souhait de voir se développer les échanges économiques et commerciaux de part et d'autre, à partir de l'entente sur le blé que nous nous apprêtions à conclure. Il était conscient de ce qui pouvait nous séparer sur la Question du Moyen-Orient, mais nous considérait comme un interlocuteur honnête et respectable avec lequel un dialogue constructif et des relations mutuellement avantageuses pouvaient se développer. Il m'encourageait à explorer avec lui la possibilité d'étendre à d'autres secteurs le champ de notre coopération. Je lui répondis que, sans avoir d'instructions spécifiques, je pouvais tout de même l'assurer de la convergence de nos vues là-dessus et de ma détermination à œuvrer en ce sens au cours de mon mandat. A la suite de ces premiers contacts très cordiaux et très ouverts, je pris l'habitude d'aller lui rendre visite, ainsi qu'à son successeur, aussi souvent que les circonstances le permettaient. Mes collaborateurs en faisaient autant à leur niveau. Cette action commença à trouver un écho : l'accord sur le blé fut prolongé et élargi, les produits canadiens furent en plus grande demande (y compris nos voitures qui furent l'objet d'importants contrats d'État), des projets de coopération en matière agro-alimentaire ou de forage pétrolier s'amorcèrent, la perspective de l'ouverture d'une ambassade syrienne à Ottawa fut envisagée. En somme, dans un pays aussi éloigné de notre politique étrangère que la Syrie, où nos exportations jusqu'alors étaient à peu près au point mort, nous commencions à avoir l'indice qu'une politique bilatérale active pouvait s'avérer rentable pour nos intérêts, tout en se conjuguant avec notre politique multilatérale d'équilibre sur la Question Israélo-arabe. Je ne manquais pas une occasion de le faire valoir, par écrit ou autrement, à mes interlocuteurs de toute provenance au Canada.

•

Cette approche, je la mis encore à l'épreuve au Liban, mais de façon plus systématique et plus concertée. Ainsi, lorsque je rendis une visite de courtoisie au Président de la République, M. Soleiman Frangié, peu après son investiture à l'automne 1970, je saisis l'occasion pour lui parler entre autres de l'état des relations bilatérales entre nos deux pays. Nous fûmes vite convenus qu'elles manquaient de substance. Leur avenir n'était guère encourageant si rien n'était fait pour les stimuler. L'intensification des échanges commerciaux lui paraissait, comme à moi, une approche réaliste pour y parvenir. Pour lancer le processus, il accepta d'explorer avec son gouvernement la possibilité de se procurer, au Canada, une partie du blé que le Liban devait importer chaque année. L'affaire n'était pas simple, car les Américains et les Australiens occupaient déjà ce marché qu'ils considéraient comme une chasse-gardée. Avant mon départ d'Ottawa, on m'avait d'ailleurs indiqué que je perdrais mon temps à essayer de changer cette situation. Le conseil m'avait paru mal avisé : n'avions-nous pas du blé à vendre, n'étions-nous pas concurrentiels et les Libanais n'étaient-ils pas importateurs de produits céréaliers? Du côté libanais, le gouvernement en place n'était pas plus encourageant. M. Frangié lui-même, alors ministre du Commerce sous l'administration du Président Hélou auquel il allait succéder, m'avait exprimé ses doutes, à l'occasion d'une visite de courtoisie que je lui faisais, sur la possibilité de changer cette situation. C'était pourtant un homme particulièrement bien disposé à l'endroit de notre pays. En le quittant, je lui avais indiqué mon souhait de revenir lui parler à ce sujet, puis, le prenant de court, je lui avais souhaité bonne chance dans ses entreprises politiques prochaines. Or ses ambitions présidentielles, dont j'avais été confidentiellement informé, étaient jusqu'alors encore secrètes. Mais il avait très bien saisi l'allusion. Et lorque je lui fis ma première visite dans ses nouvelles fonctions, le souvenir de ce souhait paraissait lui être resté en mémoire, à en juger par l'empressement et la qualité de l'accueil qui me fut réservé et les résultats qui sortirent de cette rencontre.

Notre entretien, en effet, amena le Président à donner un accord de principe à l'inclusion de sociétés canadiennes parmi les firmes intéressées aux appels d'offre et de service pour les grands projets et les marchés du ressort du gouvernement libanais. Pour marquer ce tournant, il décida sur-le-champ d'envoyer son directeur de l'Office des Céréales du Liban en mission exploratoire à Winnipeg. Celui-ci en revint très satisfait et avec un premier ordre d'achat de quelques milliers de tonnes. Quelques mois plus tard, le directeur de l'Office du Blé du Canada, M. Vogel, en voyage d'information autour du monde, s'arrêta à Beyrouth. Je saisis l'occasion pour faire avancer nos pions sur l'échiquier de la région. Je l'amenai chez le Président Frangié discuter les problèmes économiques et alimentaires de la région qui l'intéressaient. Celui-ci en profita pour lui dire sa satisfaction des premiers rapports établis entre les deux pays au niveau des Offices du Blé respectifs. De la discussion émergea un accord de principe de trois ans pour l'achat annuel de 50 000 tonnes de blé canadien par le Liban. Ces premiers succès allaient déboucher, au cours des années suivantes, sur d'autres ventes, plus importantes encore, qui finiront par mettre le Canada au premier rang des fournisseurs de céréales du Liban. Ils nous donnaient un clair signal des débouchés qui s'offraient à nos produits dans cette partie du monde, jusqu'alors négligée par nous, si tant est que nous nous donnions la peine de nous y intéresser et de la cultiver.

Les divers grands travaux d'infrastructures envisagés en début de mandat du Président Frangié me parurent également offrir d'intéressantes perspectives à nos exportations. Certains projets, comme l'agrandissement du port de Beyrouth ou l'irrigation de terres agricoles, furent portés à l'attention d'entreprises canadiennes. Nos meilleures chances toutefois apparurent dans le domaine de l'éducation. Pour des raisons d'intégration et d'unité nationale, le gouvernement libanais, en effet, souhaitait établir, à travers le pays, un réseau d'écoles publiques[2] de niveau scolaire comparable à celui des écoles privées, sinon supérieur. Pour cela, il fallait construire une série de bâtiments pour y accueillir, en un même lieu, des élèves jusqu'alors dispersés par petits groupes, le plus souvent chez des particuliers au hasard des locations disponibles. Encore là, assurée de l'appui des services canadiens intéressés, une action soutenue à tous les niveaux de l'administration libanaise, jusqu'à celui du Président de la République, eut pour résultat d'intéresser le Liban à l'expérience canadienne et de l'ouvrir à notre coopération dans ce dossier. Dans ce contexte, la Société de Sidérurgie du Québec (Sidbec) fut invitée à construire une école pilote avec la possibilité, en cas de réussite, d'obtenir le contrat pour une partie sinon l'ensemble du projet, soit 125 écoles, dont le budget devait dépasser les trente millions de dollars. L'école pilote fut construite, avec grand succès d'ailleurs, mais le projet malheureusement devait tomber victime des jalousies et rivalités intercommunautaires libanaises. Certains craignaient, du côté des chrétiens maronites comme celui des musulmans sunnites, que le succès de l'opération ne devienne une menace à la survie et à l'influence de leur système scolaire communautaire respectif.

En 1973, après trois ans d'efforts assidus et patients de ce genre, nous constations que nos exportations au Liban étaient passées de 4,5 millions $ (niveau où certains experts les disaient condamnées à plafonner) à plus de 20 millions $. Il s'agissait d'une augmentation de plus de 400 pour cent. Si de tels résultats pouvaient être atteints au Liban, pays aux ressources très limités, que ne fallait-il pas attendre des voisins autrement puissants?

Aussi mes agents des services commerciaux, avec l'appui de quelques gens d'affaires canadiens concernés, commençaient à réclamer cette approche auprès des autres pays de leur ressort, particulièrement ceux qui disposaient de richesses pétrolières.

L'Iraq était de ceux-là. Ottawa m'en avait transféré la responsabilité au cours de 1973. Le gouvernement canadien répondait ainsi à la suggestion pressante de Bagdad qui s'objectait désormais à l'accréditation d'un ambassadeur résidant en Iran, pays avec lequel ses relations étaient tendues. La célérité mise par les Irakiens à organiser la présentation de mes lettres de créance et la cordialité de leur accueil, lors de ma première visite en novembre 1972, traduisaient peut-être des illusions de leur part sur le sens que nous donnions nous-mêmes à ce changement. Pour nous, il ne s'agissait guère plus que d'un ajustement technique, de nature à nous faciliter les contacts et à nous donner de meilleures chances d'accès à ce marché. Pour eux, ils y voyaient peut-être l'indication d'une disposition, de notre part, à l'établissement de relations plus étroites et substantielles en réponse à leurs attentes. Car à l'époque, déçus par les faiblesses et les carences de la technologie et de la coopération des pays de l'Est, ils recherchaient de nouveaux partenaires à l'Ouest pour mettre en œuvre leur ambitieux programme de développement économique. Ils avaient déjà mis leur dévolu sur des pays comme l'Autriche, l'Italie et l'Espagne, et étaient en voie de régler avec la France le contentieux de l'IPC (Irak Petroleum Company) de façon à reprendre leurs relations avec elle. Mais ils souhaitaient également un accès à la technologie et au savoir-faire nord-américain. En rupture de relations avec les États-Unis depuis un certain temps, ils en venaient néanmoins à traiter avec des firmes américaines de réputation internationale, comme Bechtel, auxquelles ils n'hésitaient pas à confier certains de leurs plus importants projets quand ces compagnies étaient les plus compétentes et les plus compétitives. Mais politiquement, cette situation ne pouvait les satisfaire. Aux yeux de mes interlocuteurs irakiens, le Canada pouvait donc apparaître comme une option intéressante à cet égard, par la richesse de ses moyens, l'avancement de sa technologie et l'indépendance de sa politique étrangère. C'est peut-être ce qui les conduisit à ouvrir dès 1972 une ambassade à Ottawa.

Le climat était donc propice pour discuter avec eux des possibilités énormes que pouvaient offrir à nos entrepreneurs la mise en oeuvre de leur ambitieux plan national de développement et d'équipement. Il s'agissait d'un marché annuel de plusieurs milliards de dollars qui s'ouvrait progressivement et dont nous risquions d'être absents. Les perspectives étaient d'autant plus encourageantes qu'on se montrait partout très sympathique et ouvert aux démarches de mes collaborateurs et aux miennes. Toutefois, je compris rapidement que pour mes interlocuteurs, rien de très ambitieux ne pourrait aboutir sans la mise en place d'un accord-cadre, comme instrument essentiel pour régler les modalités de la coopération entre nos deux pays. Ainsi en avait-il été pour les quelques pays européens avec lesquels ils entretenaient des liens privilégiés. Compte tenu du caractère particulier des Irakiens et de leur régime politique, ce souci de vouloir définir, au préalable, les paramètres d'une coopération avec un éventuel partenaire comme le Canada, pays qu'ils connaissaient très peu, n'avait rien de très surprenant dans les circonstances. Mais une telle approche ne correspondait pas à la nôtre. Il fallait donc laisser la situation mûrir.

Entre-temps, on apprendrait à mieux se connaître de part et d'autre; on ferait acte de présence auprès des ministres et de leurs hauts fonctionnaires pour les familiariser avec le Canada ; on chercherait à stimuler nos exportations par quelques initiatives pragmatiques dans des secteurs intéressants pour nos produits et services et à renforcer ce faisant notre crédibilité de partenaire sérieux, concurrentiel et fiable. Encore là, le blé nous offrit la meilleure porte d'entrée. Aucun accord ne nous liait aux Irakiens dans ce domaine, même s'ils nous achetaient chaque année de substantielles quantités qu'ils nous payaient comptant. Cette absence d'instrument prévisionnel les mettaient à la merci d'aléas de toutes sortes. Profitant d'une situation de gêne du côté irakien, par suite d'une pénurie sur le marché mondial, je pris sur moi d'inviter le directeur de leur Office du Blé à se rendre à Winnipeg, pour y explorer sur place les possibilités de convenir d'arrangements plus satisfaisants. Il en revint avec un accord à long terme pour de très importantes quantités, nous plaçant dès lors en tête de liste de leurs fournisseurs avant les Australiens et les Américains, nos compétiteurs immédiats. Dans un deuxième temps, les Iraqiens mirent à l'étude la construction, avec notre coopération, d'une série de silos pour stocker les céréales à travers le pays, un projet d'une soixantaine de millions de dollars. Parmi d'autre contrats importants, ils procédèrent encore à l'achat de 30 locomotives canadiennes. Les résultats de nos premières démarches étaient donc prometteurs, malgré l'absence de tout instrument de coopération intergouvernemental. Les chiffres demeuraient certes modestes par rapport au marché potentiel, mais avec des exportations qui étaient passées de 1 million $ à 100 millions $ en un an, nous étions sur la bonne voie et pouvions attendre la suite sans trop nous inquiéter.

•

Avec l'Arabie Saoudite, nous n'avions jamais eu jusqu'en 1973 d'autres relations que commerciales, dont les services de mon Ambassade, avaient la responsabilité. Ceux-ci multipliaient les efforts pour obtenir, en faveur des fournisseurs canadiens, une part des marchés relevant de la compétence du gouvernement. Les résultats étaient toutefois décevants. En l'absence d'un ambassadeur accrédité auprès du Roi, la porte des ministres et hauts fonctionnaires restait fermée à nos représentants commerciaux, qui déploraient cette situation et souhaitaient voir notre gouvernement y remédier.

Je pris l'initiative, début 1972, de porter la question à l'attention des Affaires extérieures à Ottawa. Il y avait urgence d'agir rapidement dans ce dossier pour obtenir du gouvernement l'établissement de relations diplomatiques avec l'Arabie Saoudite par l'accréditation latérale d'un ambassadeur de la région. Il y allait, selon moi, de nos intérêts économiques et commerciaux, comme de nos intérêts politiques, vu l'émergence rapide de l'Arabie Saoudite parmi les principaux acteurs sur la scène du Moyen-Orient.

Ottawa mit plus de six mois à réagir. Était-ce l'urgence de la chose qui échappait, était-ce la réaction de certains milieux qu'on craignait, je ne saurais le dire. La réponse finit par venir et heureusement elle était positive. À mon corps défendant, on me confiait même la responsabilité d'être le premier ambassadeur à représenter le Canada auprès du roi d'Arabie Saoudite. Avec le soutien de mon collègue saoudien de Beyrouth, mon agrément fut obtenu en un temps record et les lettres de créance présentées au roi Fayçal en juin 1973. Dès lors les portes de l'administration saoudienne commencèrent à s'ouvrir à nos représentants commerciaux et leurs démarches à y être reçues avec sympathie par leurs interlocuteurs respectifs. De mon côté, l'empressement, la cordialité et l'intérêt que le Roi m'avait manifestés, dès notre première rencontre, se répercuta à tous les niveaux de la hiérarchie du Royaume. J'y découvris partout une disposition à la coopération et aux échanges avec le Canada dans la perspective des grands travaux d'infrastructure déjà en cours, grâce au financement des revenus pétroliers, déjà considérables dès cette époque. L'horizon qui s'offrait à nous dès le départ était donc très prometteur. Cependant pour en tirer tout le profit, l'évidence s'imposa à moi que nous devions, sans attendre, ouvrir une ambassade sur place à Djeddah qui était alors la capitale diplomatique du Royaume. J'en fis donc la recommandation, peu après la présentation de mes lettres de créance. Pour des raisons identiques, je fis de même pour l'Iraq. Je ne pouvais m'attendre à une réaction rapide de la part de notre administration alors que notre politique à l'égard du monde arabe oscillait encore entre les pôles de l'indifférence et de la méfiance. Les priorités allaient à d'autres régions que le Moyen-Orient. Il s'agissait du moins d'un autre élément apporté à un dossier dont, pouvait-on espérer, l'importance sans cesse croissante finirait par s'imposer.

Trois mois plus tard, en septembre 1973, je me retrouvais à Ottawa, en consultations. Je n'y étais pas venu depuis deux ans. Entre-temps, les pays arabes du Moyen-Orient s'étaient lancés dans des programmes de rattrapage et de modernisation économique dont le Canada restait à l'écart. Je comptais profiter de ma visite pour tenter de sensibiliser ministres et hauts fonctionnaires intéressés aux dossiers de mon ambassade et obtenir notamment l'organisation de visites de haut niveau, politiques et commerciales, pour relever le profil du Canada et attirer l'attention de nos milieux responsables sur l'énorme potentiel qui s'offrait à nous dans la région. Mes efforts pour rencontrer le ministre du Commerce de l'époque, l'honorable Alastair Gillespie, furent infructueux. Son sous-ministre me reçut, certes, avec beaucoup de gentillesse et non sans curiosité, mais il ne se laissa pas convaincre par mon plaidoyer. Son ministère n'envisageait pas dans l'immédiat l'envoi d'une mission commerciale au Moyen-Orient, tout en acceptant le principe d'une telle démarche à moyen terme. Il excluait une visite par son ministre dont le calendrier, de toute façon, était rempli pour les douze prochains mois. Les priorités étaient ailleurs.

Aux Affaires extérieures, on était généralement sympathique à mes efforts, mais on n'y voyait pas l'urgence du message que j'avais à transmettre, et encore moins l'à-propos pour moi de le transmettre personnellement au Ministre, Mitchell Sharp, ou au Sous-Secrétaire d'État, Ed Ritchie, comme je le souhaitais. Dans les circonstances, je pris sur moi de demander rendez-vous directement à ceux-ci. M. Sharp, rencontré par hasard dans un couloir de l'Édifice Pearson, accepta aimablement de me recevoir deux semaines plus tard. Malheureusement, quand vint la date de la rencontre, la guerre du « Yom Kippour » venait d'éclater, précipitant mon retour à Beyrouth. M'excusant de ce contretemps qui m'empêchait de le voir, je fis savoir à M. Sharp que les événements qui me ramenaient à mon poste illustreraient, mieux que mes propos, l'importance du monde arabe pour nos intérêts et l'urgence que nous avions d'y prêter attention. M. Ritchie, pour sa part, me reçut sans délai. L'entrevue, m'avait-on prévenu, ne devait pas dépasser les dix minutes. M. Ritchie me retint, en fait, plus d'une heure. En réponse à une série de questions, plus pertinentes les unes que les autres, qu'il me posa sur les pays de mon ressort, je lui fis part de mon analyse de la situation et de mes recommandations dans les circonstances. Manifestement il prêtait beaucoup d'intérêt au travail que j'y avais accompli. Il en avait eu rapport directement par certains de ses contacts, dont M. Vogel, directeur de l'Office canadien du Blé que j'avais reçu à Beyrouth. La question du pétrole le préoccupait particulièrement. À deux semaines de la guerre du « Yom Kippour », il devait être l'un des rares hauts fonctionnaires à Ottawa dans ce cas. Chaleureux, il me félicita de mes efforts en faveur du commerce canadien au Moyen-Orient, dont il mesurait l'importance pour l'avenir de nos intérêts économiques et commerciaux. Aussi acceptait-il ma recommandation d'ouvrir sans tarder une ambassade en Arabie Saoudite. Pour Bagdad, où je lui demandais de faire de même, il trouvait plus sage d'attendre encore quelque temps, pour éviter de braquer certains secteurs de notre opinion publique. Je ressortis de cet entretien particulièrement réconforté. J'avais trouvé un allié de taille, écouté par ses pairs et les membres du gouvernement pour sa clairvoyance, son jugement et sa sagesse. Effectivement, suite à cette rencontre, M. Ritchie fit inscrire Djeddah sur la liste prioritaire des ambassades à ouvrir l'année suivante, contrariant ainsi les recommandations du Ministère. Moins d'un an après, le nouveau poste était en opération et le premier ambassadeur résident, Michael Shenstone, avait été nommé.

La guerre de « Yom Kippour » qui me surprit au Canada, hâta mon retour à Beyrouth, début octobre 1973. Comme beaucoup d'autres, je m'interrogeais sur les conséquences de cet événement pour le Proche-Orient et le reste du monde. Je m'inquiétais aussi de son impact sur l'évolution de notre rapprochement avec les pays arabes, auquel je travaillais, depuis bientôt quatre ans, à la tête de mon Ambassade. Jetant un coup d'oeil en arrière sur le chemin parcouru depuis mon arrivée, en janvier 1970, je pouvais regarder les progrès réalisés avec satisfaction. Notre attitude à l'égard des pays de la région devenait moins frileuse. La décision d'ouvrir une ambassade en Arabie Saoudite en était le plus récent indice. Nos intérêts bilatéraux avaient gagné en visibilité dans chacun de mes pays d'accréditation. Il deviendrait de moins en moins possible de les ignorer ou de les minimiser, à mesure que nos milieux d'affaires les découvriraient pour leur compte, ce qui était inévitable. Bref, les jalons posés depuis 1970 constituaient un acquis non négligeable pour faciliter, comme je le souhaitais, l'émergence d'une dimension bilatérale beaucoup plus ouverte, ambitieuse et percutante, dans notre politique à l'égard de cette partie du monde.

Restait à espérer que le nouveau conflit qui venait d'éclater ne compromettrait pas le processus engagé. Or, contre toute attente, il allait avoir l'effet inverse, du fait de la crise du pétrole née dans son sillage. Avec celle-ci, le Canada découvrait brutalement qu'il pouvait être directement affecté, sinon menacé, dans ses intérêts vitaux, par des pays qu'il avait à peu près ignorés jusque-là. C'est ainsi qu'en Arabie Saoudite, avec laquelle nous venions à peine d'établir des relations diplomatiques, la rumeur courait que le Canada serait placé sur sa « Liste Noire » des pays soumis à un embargo du pétrole. Dans l'ignorance de nos réalités géopolitiques et dans l'illusion de notre autosuffisance statistique en matière de production pétrolière, certains saoudiens espéraient resserrer ainsi l'étau autour des États-Unis, principalement visés par ces mesures, sans que nous ayions à en souffrir vraiment. Les choses étaient évidemment moins simples. En l'absence d'un oléoduc pour les relier aux puits de l'Ouest canadien, nos provinces de l'Est devaient satisfaire leurs besoins pétroliers par des importations, dont une partie provenait de l'Arabie Saoudite. Des mesures d'embargo contre nous, de la part de cette dernière, risquaient donc de nous gêner sérieusement.

•

Je reçus comme instructions de m'assurer que le Canada ne serait pas inscrit sur la « Liste Noire ». Pour m'en acquitter, j'eus à me rendre deux fois en Arabie Saoudite pendant les dernières semaines de 1973. Au cours d'une première rencontre à Djeddah, le secrétaire général des Affaires étrangères Massoud m'informa que son gouvernement, n'ayant rien à nous reprocher à propos du nouveau conflit israélo-arabe, ne nous soumettrait pas au boycott pétrolier. Comme pays neutre, nous devions toutefois subir le régime des coupures graduelles de livraison imposées à tous les pays neutres. Pour échapper à toute mesure, comme pays ami, il nous faudrait formuler une déclaration de soutien, en trois points, de la résolution de la Question israélo-arabe et palestinienne. En réponse à cette dernière exigence, je pus remettre le jour même une note écrite aux Affaires étrangères saoudiennes, grâce à l'obligeance de l'ambassade britannique locale qui me permit d'obtenir à cet effet le feu vert immédiat d'Ottawa.

Satisfait des résultats de ma rencontre et des assurances obtenues, je m'apprêtais à reprendre le chemin de Beyrouth quand on me fit savoir, le lendemain, que le ministre des Affaires étrangères, Omar Al Saqqaf, demandait à me voir d'urgence. C'était pour m'annoncer que les engagements de la veille donnés par M. Massoud ne tenaient plus. Un réexamen de la situation avait conduit son gouvernement à conclure qu'il n'avait d'autre choix que de nous inclure dans la listes des pays boycottés, vu notre rôle d'important fournisseur pétrolier des États-Unis. Surpris par ce brusque renversement, je me permis de réagir sur-le-champ pour tenter d'éviter le pire. En termes déférents mais fermes, je fis valoir au ministre l'ignorance du Canada, de sa politique et de sa géographie que son pays manifestait en adoptant cette décision, et les effets désastreux que celle-ci pourrait avoir pour l'avenir des relations toutes nouvelles entre nos deux pays. Dans les circonstances, l'annulation de la mesure proposée était dans le meilleur intérêt des deux parties. En réponse, Saqqaf se déclara impressionné par mon plaidoyer et, soucieux de donner toutes les chances à nos liens naissants, prit sur lui de renverser la décision sur-le-champ ; j'avais sa parole, nous ne serions pas soumis à l'embargo. À ma grande satisfaction, l'argument des bonnes relations bilatérales avait prévalu. Une fois de plus, il me fallut déchanter. Les milieux pétroliers continuaient de maintenir que le Canada figurait toujours sur la « Liste Noire », en dépit de mes représentations et des engagements d'Omar Saqqaf. Je reçus à nouveau instruction d'obtenir des éclaircissements du gouvernement saoudien. Je retournai donc chez ce dernier, début décembre 1973. Il me reçut, cette fois, dans un bureau du Palais royal à Riyad. Très embarrassé, il dut m'avouer qu'il avait perdu la bataille livrée en notre faveur ; à son grand regret, il n'était plus en mesure de tenir l'engagement qu'il m'avait donné. En réponse, je lui fis part de ma profonde déception. Je ne pouvais que réserver la réaction de mon gouvernement, n'excluant pas que celui-ci considère avoir été abusé. J'allais donc faire rapport et aviser.

En sortant de chez le ministre, inspiré peut-être par le lieu où je me trouvais, je décidai que l'affaire était assez grave pour justifier un appel direct au Roi. À l'époque, il était exclu de téléphoner à l'extérieur du pays à moins d'un préavis de quatre ou cinq jours et la nature délicate du dossier excluait le recours habituel aux services de communications des Ambassades britannique ou américaine sur place. Je ne pouvais donc pas consulter Ottawa sur la suite de mes démarches, à moins de retourner à Beyrouth et encourir un délai d'une semaine et plus. Il me parut plus sage d'agir, sans plus attendre, selon les voies et moyens qui m'offraient les meilleures possibilités de remplir mes instructions. C'est ce que je fis le lendemain, après une nuit de réflexion, en demandant à voir le Roi le jour même. Avec deux chefs d'État en visite à Riyad au même moment, je n'étais pas optimiste sur la réponse qu'on me ferait. J'avais du moins l'espoir que ma requête sensibiliserait le Roi personnellement au sérieux de nos préoccupations.

Agréablement surpris, je reçus dans l'heure suivante une première réaction encourageante par l'intermédiaire du chef du Protocole royal. Il me fit savoir que Sa Majesté avait bien reçu ma demande et lui accorderait une attention personnelle; entre-temps, elle l'avait prié de me transmettre ses cordiales salutations et de s'assurer de ma disponibilité au cours de la journée. Le Palais reprit contact avec moi en fin d'après-midi pour me faire savoir que le Roi avait revu le dossier qui m'intéressait et donné de nouvelles instructions à son ministre des Affaires étrangères à ce sujet, le priant de me recevoir de nouveau le jour même. On m'envoya donc à l'hôtel un fonctionnaire du palais pour m'accompagner à mon rendez-vous. Il s'agissait d'un jeune homme d'à peine trente ans. En se présentant, il me demanda, d'entrée de jeu, si j'étais du Québec. Lui ayant confirmé ce qu'il paraissait savoir déjà, il poursuivit en s'informant de l'évolution de la question constitutionnelle au Canada. De toute évidence, j'avais devant moi une des rares personnes dans cette partie du monde à être familière avec la politique contemporaine de notre pays. Je lui dis mon étonnement. Il me répondit qu'il avait fait son Ph.D. à Princeton sur les relations américano-canadiennes. Je compris le message que m'apportait la présence de ce jeune inconnu à mes côtés. Ce dernier avait eu pour tâche de documenter le Roi et son gouvernement sur le Canada et les particularités de ses relations avec les U.S.A. et de confirmer l'information que je m'efforçais de leur transmettre depuis mon accréditation. Je sentis que j'avais gagné la partie et que le Canada avait du coup acquis une place bien à lui dans la diplomatie saoudienne. Tel fut le sens de mon nouvel entretien avec Omar Saqqaf qui me reçut, cette fois, avec une cordialité et une jovialité que je ne lui connaissais pas. Me remerciant chaudement de mon intervention auprès du Roi, il me révéla qu'elle avait forcé la réouverture du dossier et, avec l'aval du Roi, entraîné le renversement de la décision qui avait été prise à notre encontre sous l'influence d'un groupe de jeunes technocrates au sein de leur administration. C'était donc pour lui une douce revanche, prise avec l'appui du Roi, et il s'en réjouissait ouvertement. Pour ma part, je ne pouvais que me féliciter de cette crise qui avait mis en lumière la vraie nature du Canada au plus haut niveau du pouvoir et nous avait, du coup, gagné sympathie et traitement favorable. Des perspectives les plus sombres du matin, je passais le soir aux plus prometteuses. C'est donc très satisfait de la tournure des choses que je fis rapport de cette journée à Ottawa.

•

Peu de temps après cet épisode, j'apprenais la venue à Beyrouth au début de février 1974, à titre privé, de l'honorable Jean Chrétien, alors ministre des Affaires Indiennes et du Nord. Il profitait de la présence de son neveu, Raymond, à l'Ambassade, pour venir se reposer chez lui. Conformément à ses désirs, aucun accueil particulier, aucune rencontre, y compris avec moi, ne furent prévus. Pourtant, je ne fus pas étonné de recevoir un coup de fil, dans l'heure suivant son arrivée, pour me demander s'il pouvait passer me voir chez moi. C'est ce qu'il fit aussitôt. Il souhaitait connaître, me dit-il, le fruit de mes quatre années d'expérience au Moyen-Orient et les conclusions que j'en tirais. Comme il désirait placer cet échange sur un plan personnel, je suggérai à cet effet la formule d'une conversation à bâtons rompus, dans le cadre tranquille d'une station de ski de la montagne libanaise, à Faraya, à trente minutes de Beyrouth. Le lieu était propice pour échapper au brouhaha de Beyrouth et j'y louais un châlet pour la saison d'hiver. C'est là qu'alliant l'utile à l'agréable, dans le cadre grandiose de la montagne libanaise, sous un soleil éclatant, dominant une mer d'azur, j'eus l'occasion pour la première fois depuis mon arrivée à Beyrouth, de communiquer de vive voix, à un membre du gouvernement canadien, le fruit de mon expérience et de mes observations au Moyen-Orient et l'essentiel des conclusions que j'en tirais.

Monsieur Chrétien parut intéressé par mes propos et sensible à mes arguments en faveur d'une politique canadienne beaucoup plus active dans la région. Il se laissa même convaincre de rendre visite le lendemain au Président Frangié et recueillir directement les vues de cet homme politique d'expérience et avisé. Il reçut confirmation auprès de lui de l'urgence pour le Canada d'agir de façon à ne pas être laissé pour compte dans une région du globe qui commençait à sortir de sa léthargie pour entreprendre son développement économique, grâce aux énormes moyens que lui procuraient soudainement les revenus du pétrole. Il quitta toutefois Beyrouth sans dire quel usage il comptait faire de ce qu'il y avait entendu et observé.

Je devais apprendre, par la suite, que dès son retour à Ottawa, M. Chrétien avait pris sur lui de soulever sans préavis, en réunion de cabinet, la question de notre politique à l'égard des pays du Moyen-Orient. Il y aurait préconisé l'adoption d'urgence d'une approche beaucoup plus positive et dynamique envers eux, fondée sur les intérêts bilatéraux respectifs. Pour marquer ce nouveau départ, il aurait suggérer l'envoi sans délai dans la région, sous la conduite d'un ministre, de la mission ministérielle économique et commerciale qui était sous considération depuis déjà quelque temps au Ministère du Commerce. Son intervention produisit ses fruits sur-le-champ et fut, selon moi, le coup de pouce qui mena enfin le gouvernement à poursuivre une diplomatie beaucoup plus ouverte et active à l'endroit des pays concernés, sur la base des intérêts réciproques bien compris.

•

Dès mars 1974, l'honorable Donald Macdonald, alors ministre de l'Énergie et des Ressources naturelles, reprenant un projet déjà à l'étude se rendait en voyage officiel au Liban et en Arabie Saoudite. C'était une première dans ce dernier pays qui n'avait encore jamais reçu un membre du gouvernement canadien. Le succès fut incontesté, avec accueil au plus haut niveau de l'État et des égards qui marquaient bien la qualité spéciale des relations qu'on cherchait à établir avec le Canada. Le message reçu à cette occasion était clair. La coopération économique du Canada était manifestement souhaitée et recherchée.

Cette visite fut immédiatement suivie d'une autre, en avril 1974, par le ministre du Commerce, l'honorable Alastair Gillespie, à la tête d'un important groupe d'hommes d'affaires qu'on avait réussi à rassembler, malgré un très court préavis. Le périple cette fois incluait également l'Iraq. Les perspectives d'exportations de biens et services, découvertes par la délégation, confirmèrent et dépassèrent tout ce que nous avions cherché à faire connaître, jusqu'alors, depuis Beyrouth. Ce fut particulièrement le cas en Iraq. M. Gillespie s'était laissé persuader par son collègue Donald Macdonald, auprès de qui j'étais personnellement intervenu à cet effet, de s'y rendre après son séjour au Liban et en Arabie Saoudite. Le potentiel d'affaires qu'il y découvrit avec les membres de sa délégation l'impressionna au point que l'installation d'une ambassade résidente lui parut une urgence aussi grande qu'en Arabie Saoudite. Homme de décision, il voulut l'annoncer sur-le-champ, au terme de sa visite, comme une des conclusions qui en ressortaient. M'ayant demandé mon avis à ce sujet, je lui fis remarquer qu'une telle initiative relevait du domaine du Secrétaire d'État aux Affaires extérieures, son collègue M. Sharp avec qui il lui revenait donc de la soulever; pour ma part, je ne pourrais que m'en réjouir puisqu'elle correspondait à ce que je recommandais depuis quelque temps. Sur ce, M. Gillespie procéda de lui-même et informa les Irakiens et la presse de l'ouverture prochaine de la nouvelle ambassade avant de quitter Bagdad pour s'en expliquer ensuite avec M. Sharp, non sans succès puisque la décision fut mise en œuvre l'année suivante. On imagine mal ce genre de choses aujourd'hui! Au bilan de cette mission, on enregistrait l'identification de marchés précis à conclure et le principe convenu de la conclusion d'accords cadres économiques et de l'établissement de commissions mixtes conjointes.

La visite du Roi Hussein de Jordanie au Canada, en août 1974, fut le dernier jalon posé, avant la fin de mon mandat, sur la voie d'un rapprochement avec les pays arabes du Moyen-Orient. Déjà en 1971, le

Roi m'avait exprimé le souhait d'entreprendre une telle visite quand le moment favorable se présenterait. J'avais plaidé en faveur d'un tel projet et en avait fait accepter le principe par Ottawa dès 1972. Sa réalisation était toutefois remise *sine die*. Les arguments pourtant ne manquaient pas pour justifier une telle initiative. Il y avait un déséquilibre flagrant dans la politique canadienne en matière de visites en provenance du Moyen-Orient. On ne comptait plus les hautes personnalités israéliennes qui avaient été accueillies dans notre pays. Par contre, à ma connaissance, jamais chef d'État ou de Gouvernement ou même ministre des Affaires étrangères en provenance des pays de cette région n'y était venu. Hussein s'imposait comme le candidat idéal pour entreprendre un redressement de ce côté. Chef d'État d'un pays qui ne menaçait plus Israël, personnalité de haut profil, il représentait par ses qualités de modération et de réalisme le meilleur espoir du côté arabe d'une évolution vers un règlement négocié du conflit israélo-arabe.

L'occasion de faire aboutir la chose se présenta soudainement, en mai 1974, quand le Roi Hussein me demanda de venir le voir à Amman. Il m'informa alors qu'il avait reçu une invitation à participer au cours de l'été au Festival aérien international d'Abbotsford, en Colombie-Britannique. Vu son vif intérêt pour l'aviation et ses titres de pilote amateur, il était tenté de l'accepter, d'autant qu'à la même époque il devait se rendre à Seattle, tout à côté, pour y rencontrer les autorités de la Compagnie Boeing. Avant d'y donner suite, il souhaitait savoir si les autorités canadiennes verraient quelque inconvénient à son projet. L'assurant à l'avance d'un excellent accueil s'il entreprenait le voyage, je pris sur moi de lui dire qu'il me paraissait difficile de le réaliser sans faire escale d'abord à Ottawa, où il ne s'était jamais rendu, pour y être reçu par le Gouverneur Général et le gouvernement canadien. Je fis rapport aussitôt de cette démarche en l'accompagnant de ma recommandation favorable la plus instante aux Affaires extérieures. La perspective d'élections en juin 1973 n'était pas de nature à faciliter l'entreprise. Cependant, la réélection du Gouvernement était tenue pour probable. Le premier ministre Trudeau pour sa part, à qui le caractère inusité de la demande et la personnalité hors du commun de son auteur n'était pas fait pour déplaire, assura en fait la réalisation de la visite par son intervention rapide. Il y donna, en effet, le feu vert à cette visite sans attendre la réaction de monsieur Sharp qui s'apprêtait en fait à lui donner un avis négatif à ce sujet en raison des élections ainsi que des problèmes touchant la sécurité du Roi. On peut penser que, sensible à l'évolution positive de l'opinion publique au Canada sur le Moyen-

Orient, et intéressé à faire la connaissance d'une personnalité de la stature du Roi Hussein, il vit là une occasion de confirmer son ouverture vers les pays arabes de la région. La visite eut donc lieu. Elle permit certes l'établissement de liens personnels et amicaux entre Hussein et Trudeau, qui venait d'être réélu, mais contribua surtout à confirmer l'évolution de la politique canadienne vers un bilatéralisme rentable avec les pays arabes.

Deux semaines après ce voyage, à la fin du mois d'août 1974, je quittais définitivement Beyrouth. Ma mission prenait fin après quatre ans et huit mois. Au terme d'un séjour aussi long, ce départ marquait certes un arrachement à une région à laquelle ma famille et moi étions devenus très attachés ; mais il suscitait surtout chez moi un sentiment de satisfaction d'un mandat bien accompli. L'objectif que je m'étais fixé à mon arrivée avait été atteint : le Moyen-Orient arabe était devenu partie intégrante de la politique étrangère bilatérale du Canada. Dans l'année suivant mon départ, trois ambassadeurs résidents allaient prendre ma relève à Beyrouth, Djeddah et Bagdad, nos échanges économiques et commerciaux avec les pays de la région connaîtraient une rapide progression, les visites de toutes sortes se multiplieraient. Bref, nous aurions désormais des relations sans complexe avec le monde arabe et nos intérêts pourraient y trouver leur compte. Le bilan ne pouvait être plus positif ou mieux illustrer ce que pouvait accomplir un ambassadeur du Canada, faisant son métier avec détermination, lorsque les circonstances s'y prêtaient.

NOTES

1. L'auteur a rédigé le présent article sur la base de ses souvenirs personnels sans avoir recours aux archives du Ministère des Affaires extérieures.
2. Les écoles publiques libanaises étaient jusqu'alors le parent pauvre du Système d'Enseignement libanais qui favorisait à leur détriment l'Enseignement privé placé sous le contrôle des diverses communautés religieuses qui dominaient la politique du pays.

Jacques Gignac entre au MAE en 1958. Il a d'abord reçu diverses affectations à Boston, Paris et Ottawa. Il fut ambassadeur au Liban de 1970 à 1974. Depuis Beyrouth il était également accrédité en Syrie et en Jordanie, et plus tard en Iraq (1972) et en Arabe Saoudite (1973). En 1974 on lui confie l'Ambassade de Tunis. Revenu à Ottawa en 1977, il y assume diverses responsabilités comme sous-secrétaire d'État adjoint, puis comme sous-ministre adjoint au MAE. De 1982 à 1986, il dirige, à titre d'ambassadeur, la Représentation du Canada près les Communautés économiques européennes (Bruxelles) et, en 1986-87, notre Délégation auprès des organisations des Nations-unies à Vienne où il siège de plus comme gouverneur canadien à l'Agence atomique internationale. De 1987 à 1992, il est ambassadeur aux Pays-Bas.

9

ASSIGNMENT IN CHINA: 1984-1987

RICHARD V. GORHAM

IN CONTRAST TO THE EXPERIENCE of most of my colleagues in the Department of External Affairs, who had a variety of assignments in various parts of the world, my foreign assignments during my 39 years in the Department were all in Asia: twice in Japan for a total of eleven years, three years in India, two years in Cambodia and, finally, three years as Ambassador to the People's Republic of China, from September 1984 to October 1987.

My assignments in Japan, India and Cambodia had made me very much aware of China's important position and influence in Asia, highlighted by much publicized events such as its intervention in the Korean War, its military threat to the offshore islands of Quemoy and Matsu in the mid-1950s, its armed attack on India in the early 1960s, and its support of North Vietnamese political and territorial aspirations in Indo-China throughout the period of the Vietnam War. However, I had no direct contact with, or experience of China until 1972, when I first visited that country, accompanying the delegation of the then Secretary of State for External Affairs, the Hon. Mitchell Sharp, who made the first foreign minister level contact between Canada and China.

This was during the period of the Cultural Revolution and our visits to the cities of Guangzhou, Beijing, Shijiazhuang (the burial place of Norman Bethune), Shanghai and Hangzhou were cursory, controlled and carefully managed. My main recollections of that visit are of a country of drabness, whose people were all dressed in blue unisex garb, ever-present political slogans, and a suspicious hostility on the part of almost all passers-by which contrasted sharply with the official professions of friendship with "foreign guests" by our official Chinese interlocutors.

Praises of Norman Bethune, the Canadian doctor who served and died with Mao Zedong's forces during the war with Japan, were on everyone's lips, and the hotels and guest houses in which we stayed were all well stocked with Mao Zedong's "little red book" of essays, translated into many languages of the world. Indeed, one of three such essays decreed for compulsory reading and memorization by the Chinese masses concerned Norman Bethune, whose unselfish contribution to China was seen by Mao as living proof of the strength and vitality of international socialism. It also had the effect of making Canada known in very flattering terms to every Chinese citizen—an advertising coup for Canada which would have made Madison Avenue green with envy!

Questions asked of any Chinese at that time about the nature and direction of China's communist society were invariably answered by endless repetitions of politically correct stock answers and explanations to the extent that one began to wonder—and many foreign visitors came to believe it—that the Middle Kingdom, which had at one time led the world in culture and discovery, had perhaps once again achieved pre-eminence, this time by creating a new species of communized mankind totally content with its collectivized lot. It became abundantly clear later that all that had been achieved was an impressive degree of mass obedience to a political dogma which was based on the fear of guaranteed, immediate and brutal social, mental and physical punishment for any and all who strayed from the politically sanctioned path. The unanimity of expressions of complete satisfaction by all our interlocutors represented nothing more than desperate acts of self protection.

One other memorable highlight of that visit was a long meeting between Mr. Sharp and members of his delegation and the man who was then Premier of China, Zhou Enlai. After a long wait in the guest house, pending confirmation of the meeting, we were all ushered into the Premier's presence, and greeted courteously in English and French, and we posed for the traditional group photograph. The first part of the meeting was a long, incredibly detailed monologue by the Premier about the difficulties that China had experienced in its relations with the Soviet Union. This concluded, he suddenly turned the discussion to China's relations with Canada and, much to the surprise of all, recalled that the previous regime in China had purchased some river boats from Canada but had never paid for them and that this outstanding debt should be paid as quickly as possible.

The matter of this debt had been a bone of contention in Ottawa between the Department of Finance, which never forgets an unpaid bill, and the Department of External Affairs, which was certain that the People's Republic would not acknowledge the debts of the despised Nationalist regime of Chiang Kaishek. After much discussion between the two Departments, prior to the visit, it was agreed that the troublesome matter would not be raised during the happy occasion of the first foreign minister level visit but would be deferred to a later time when such difficult questions could be raised without spoiling an otherwise positive atmosphere. In the event, following Zhou Enlai's initiative, officials of the two governments resolved the matter to their mutual satisfaction within three to four weeks!

Zhou Enlai's action regarding this matter made a very lasting impression on me regarding his statesmanship and the fact that China could be counted on to live up to its obligations. Years later, when I was Ambassador to China, I visited the Min Sung shipping company, which had acquired the river boats, and took pleasure in recounting the story and stating that the company's credit rating with Canada had been restored and that we would be pleased to entertain any proposals they might wish to make concerning a possible purchase of new ships. Unfortunately, no such proposals were made, but perhaps sometime in the future—who knows?

My arrival in China fourteen years later, in September 1984, brought me to a remarkably changed and rapidly changing country which had emerged from the trauma and famine of the "Great Leap Forward," the awful persecutions of the Cultural Revolution and the attempted coup by the "Gang of Four." It was a China with a new leadership who were, themselves, personal survivors of punishment, imprisonment and ostracism by their own regime, but who were determined to rectify many of the past wrongs and develop the nation's economy and social welfare. They were also anxious to restore popular support for the Communist Party, in order to enable it to maintain its power and its ability to control and lead a unified, modernized nation of a billion people and provide for China a proper and respected place in the community of nations.

By 1984 the "responsibility system," begun in the rural areas in 1979-80 to encourage agricultural production, had proved immensely successful; the sterile and non-productive rural communes had been abolished and farmers could now produce crops more freely and for personal profit.

Free markets flourished in every village, town and city, and political slogans in praise of the "Four Modernizations" were emblazoned on billboards more extensively than classical political slogans in praise of Marxism, Leninism and Mao Zedong Thought. (In the course of my time in China these, too, changed to billboards displaying the praises of

Sony, Hitachi, Mitsubishi, Nissan and Toyota and admonitions regarding traffic safety.)

Trees were more evident on the streets, as a result of vigorous tree planting policies, and construction of office buildings, hotels and apartments abounded everywhere. Shortly after my arrival some Toronto entrepreneurs opened their new "Toronto-Beijing Hotel" with an appropriate grand flourish. Other luxury hotels soon followed, some owned by Chinese official institutions such as the police or the armed forces, which viewed them as sure-fire money makers.

The suspicious hostility toward foreigners, so palpable in 1972, had become virtually non-existent in 1984 and, in Beijing at least, foreigners from whatever country were not given even a second glance by passers-by. All were now described as "foreign friends," not "foreign spies," although restrictions were still maintained to regulate all personal contact between citizens and "foreign friends" to those situations which were officially sanctioned as being within the authorized limits of friendship. Thus all embassies and diplomatic living compounds were permanently guarded by armed military personnel, ostensibly for the foreigners' protection, but in reality to prevent any unauthorized contact between the "foreign friends" and the Chinese masses, for no Chinese could enter these compounds without an official Chinese authorization.

Shortly after my arrival, China celebrated, on October 1, 1984, the 35th anniversary of the Communist Revolution, with a profusion of flowers, parades, fireworks, mass dancing on Tiananmen Square and personal celebrations throughout the land. Wherever one looked there was ample evidence that Deng Xiaoping's October 1st announcement that the people of China were "happy and full of hope" was based on factual reality; it was clear to all that over the previous four or five years much social, political and economic progress had been made and that, in response to rising expectations, there was more to come.

Prior to undertaking my assignment to China the Department had proposed that I spend a few months of intensive study of Mandarin Chinese. Traditionally, such courses of study had been followed in Hong Kong but I opted for a course of study at Cornell University in Ithaca, New York. I made this choice on the advice of my former Japanese language teacher, Mrs. Eleanor Jordan, who maintained that learning a foreign language could best be done initially in one's own cultural environment, with concentrated study on grammar and pronunciation, aided by all the modern and sophisticated teaching methods and language labs;

it would be followed later by concentration on vocabulary building and fluency practice in the relevant foreign language environment. I knew that Mrs. Jordan was currently managing a concentrated Japanese language program at Cornell and at my request she put me in touch with Dr. John McCoy, the Director of a similar Mandarin program at the same university, who undertook to set up a special intensive course for me and a less intensive one for my wife.

From September 1983 to May 1984 I spent my days listening to language tapes and studying Chinese with Dr. McCoy, his Hong Kong born wife, Stella, and a group of young Chinese students at Cornell as my special tutors. It was my firm intention to present my credentials as Ambassador in Chinese and prior to my arrival in Beijing I requested the Embassy to draft an appropriate brief text with the Chinese version both in characters and the "pinyin" Roman syllabary, so that I could practice it during the summer weeks before departure from Canada. Unfortunately, this part of my study plan was frustrated by advice from the Embassy that the credentials ceremony did not involve any speeches but rather a friendly half-hour chat, something it would not be feasible to prepare for. However, on arrival and only a few hours before the credentials ceremony, I learned that I would be expected to say a few words about the good relations between Canada and China, how pleased I was to be in China and how much I looked forward to my responsibilities, and so forth—exactly the type of remarks that I had originally intended to make. Therefore, on a rush basis, and with the help of our local interpreters, I prepared a brief text in Mandarin, practiced it diligently over the few hours before the ceremony and fulfilled my pledge to deliver it in Chinese to the Vice-President Ulan Hu, to whom I presented my credentials on September 5, 1984. (I wished that I had more time to prepare and perfect my presentation, because I fear that the Vice-President may not of been certain whether I was speaking Chinese or some other tongue!)

During my language study I had concentrated on reading ability but discovered, after my arrival, that I should have concentrated on making appropriate remarks and short speeches at the many official banquet dinners my wife and I would have to attend when accompanying visiting dignitaries and supporting Canadian companies attempting to obtain export contracts in China. In this regard I received much help from Mr. Jean Duval, a superbly competent interpreter, employed by the Secretary of State Department, who often accompanied official Canadian delegations to China and who would coach and encourage me in my after-dinner presentations. Eventually I became reasonably competent and, in order to add a bit of humour to the occasion, developed an opening gambit of saying in Chinese, "I would like to make a few remarks in Chinese and will provide my own English interpretation. I know that my Chinese is not very good, but I think you will agree that my English interpretation is not bad!" This usually produced a good laugh, except from Embassy staff members who were tired of hearing it; it earned a comment in the *Vancouver Sun*, whose reporter was covering a banquet in Shanghai celebrating the beginning of Canada China air service by Canadian Pacific Airlines, that "the Canadian Ambassador is a stand-up comedian of Pacific Rim-like girth!"

It also backfired on me on the occasion of the visit to China of the Premier of Ontario, David Petersen, a man with a great sense of humour, during whose visit I had used my opening speech gambit on a number of occasions. On the last evening of the visit I was pleased and impressed when the Premier, obviously with the coaching of Jean Duval, who had accompanied him as interpreter, began to make a few after-dinner remarks in Chinese. Suddenly, much to my surprise—my wife later said my face showed absolute consternation—I heard the premier making the same opening gambit, concluding that he thought that his Chinese and his English interpretation was as good as, if not better than, mine. In response, all I could say was that he had, literally, rendered me speechless!

The Embassy at that time consisted of a staff of 29 locally engaged and 37 Canada-based employees and operated on a budget of approximately $1.1 million. It was located in the former Pakistani Embassy compound in the San Li Tun diplomatic area and was rented from the Diplomatic Service Bureau of the Ministry of Foreign Affairs, the Chinese landlord for all of our personal and official accommodation and the employer of all of our locally engaged staff. The Embassy office space was much too small for our needs, with one officer forced to use a converted washroom as an office, but it did have a garage with a Department of National Defence mechanic to keep our vehicles in order, and a small medical clinic to help keep us healthy. It also had a tennis court, a swimming pool and a small "Maple Leaf Club," which were a godsend for recreational activity and staff morale, because Beijing and China at that time offered the foreigner very few social or recreational amenities and life outside working hours could become depressingly dull.

In Shanghai there was one welcome exception to the dullness of social life for the foreigner in China: the tea room of the Peace Hotel (the former Cathay Hotel, where, it is said, Noel Coward completed his play "Private Lives"). In the evenings the tea room boasted a delightful jazz band of sexagenarian Chinese musicians who had played in the old days and who had survived the Cultural Revolution, hiding themselves and their instruments from Red Guard vigilance and punishment. It was a decidedly fun place for resident and visiting foreigners and my wife and I enjoyed it very much on our visits to Shanghai, where we were in the process of reopening a Canadian consular and trade promotion office.

The band was described in a full page article in the May 18, 1987 edition of *Time Magazine*, which noted that the 64-year old band leader was sporting on his lapel "a tiny maple leaf pin, a gift from the Canadian Ambassador in Peking." During the visit to Shanghai of Governor General Jeanne Sauvé in 1987, she and her party, my wife and I, and the accompanying Chinese protocol and security personnel all enjoyed dancing to the band's music. At the conclusion of the evening I was delighted to hear the Governor General admonish her military Aide-de-Camp, who was busily trying to sort out and verify dozens of flimsy paper receipts for refreshments consumed, by saying "Oh, go ahead and pay it. I have had a wonderful time!" Some time later I discovered that I had been immortalized in a Shanghai City tourist brochure advertising amusement opportunities by a photo of me dancing to the band of the Peace Hotel!

In my retirement, I was very pleased to learn that in November, 1994, on the occasion of Prime Minister Chrétien's "Team Canada" visit to China, eight of the accompanying provincial premiers danced the night away to the sounds of the same jazz band, minus the trombonist, who had died. I am reliably informed that on this occasion Premier Rae of Ontario sang a jazz number and that Raymond Chan, the Secretary of State Asia-Pacific, was a "furiously good jiver." It is good to know that traditions live on!

As our Embassy staff increased over the subsequent months it was necessary to move the Commercial Section to new nearby premises, but much time, effort and expense was required to negotiate satisfactory arrangements with the Diplomatic Service Bureau. Eventually, a team of carpenters, electricians and builders from Public Works Canada had to be brought in to complete the premises to an adequate standard.

The Official Residence where my wife and I lived and did our official entertaining was created from two apartments on the top ninth floor of what was once the only high rise building in the San Li Tun area and serviced by two very temperamental elevators. The furnishings and the equipment of the Residence had suffered much from general financial austerity measures and neglect of upkeep and were a far cry from the photographs we had been shown in Ottawa, which prompted my wife, on her first morning, to make the accusation that "I have been deceived!" However, after several weeks of much personal effort on her part and lengthy negotiations with the Department in Ottawa and the Diplomatic Service Bureau in Beijing the Residence was made to function effectively.

Plans for a new Canadian Embassy and Official Residence had been under discussion over the past several years between the Department in Ottawa and the Chinese authorities in Beijing and seemed to continue on interminably. Indeed, when Mr. Arthur Menzies, who had been Canada's Ambassador to China several years before my time, asked me, during a visit to China, how the new Embassy project was coming along, I asked him how he answered such questions during his time as Ambassador. He replied that he usually expressed hope that the project would start within the following year, to which I responded that I was giving enquirers the same response!

During the preparations for the visit to China by Brian Mulroney, I suggested to the members of the advance party that the Prime Minister might like to turn the first shovel but was firmly admonished that only city mayors shovelled and that such an activity would not be appropriate for the Prime Minister!

Eventually, however, construction was started in 1986 (the first shovel having been turned by the Minister of International Trade, the Hon. James Kelleher, during his visit to China) but immediately ran into innumerable problems caused by confusion over different construction standards, availability of necessary equipment, materials and qualified technicians. At the time of my departure from Beijing in 1987 the project had made very little visible progress and final completion and occupancy would not occur until several years later.

My official letter of instructions from the government did not reach me until April 1985, almost eight months after my arrival, a delay attributed to the fact that the Department was in the process of reviving the worthwhile practice, which had fallen into disuse, of providing ambassadors with a specific mandate. Nevertheless, it was clear from the very beginning of my assignment that our major tasks were to keep the Department informed about the fast moving political and economic developments taking place in China during the reform process, to discover and exploit opportunities for increasing Canadian exports to China and to implement a small, but significant Canadian development assistance program focused on human resource development in China.

The trade promotion activity of the Embassy demanded much time and attention and involved a good deal of travel throughout China by myself and members of the Embassy Commercial Section for the purpose of discovering and assessing the interests of the provinces and the major cities in the area of economic development, and identifying opportunities for Canadian companies in this regard.

Our major trade files covered coal and oil development in the northeast, hydroelectric projects on the Yangtze River (the much publicized Three Gorges Project), the promotion of aircraft sales by Canadair and de Havilland, telecommunications projects throughout the country and efforts to increase the sale of Canadian wheat, potash and other resource products. At the same time efforts were made to enable China to sell more of its traditional exports to Canada.

To cope with the increasing work pressure, more staff were assigned to the Commercial Section, which had to be relocated in more functional premises. Moreover, in 1986, a Canadian presence was revived in Shanghai with the re-establishment of a Canadian Consulate-General in that great commercial metropolis, a task which involved much haggling with the Chinese authorities to obtain suitable premises.

In 1983 Canada-China two-way trade exceeded $1.8 billion, of which $1.6 billion represented Canadian exports, primarily of wheat, aluminium, copper, wood pulp and fertilizers. Our trade promotion efforts not only ensured that Canada continued to enjoy a large share of China's market for these products but also changed the composition of our exports to include a very substantial increase in manufactured end products, comprising high technology items such as aircraft, thermal power boilers, telecommunications equipment and oil drilling equipment. The successful conclusion of animal and plant quarantine agreements opened the way for substantial sales of live animals and of semen and embryos.

Trade promotion efforts in a country where political and economic systems are substantially different from those of one's own land often reach a successful conclusion only after several months or even years of discussion and negotiation. This was certainly true in the case of China. During my assignment much energy was devoted was devoted by the government of Canada, the Embassy and company representatives to sell Canadair Challenger aircraft, an effort which eventually paid off with a firm contract and delivery in August of 1986. Similar activity in regard to de Havilland Dash 7 aircraft paid off some months after my departure.

Many of the government's Team Canada achievements—commercial contracts concluded during the Prime Minister's visit to China in the autumn of 1994—were the results of work begun almost a decade earlier. For example, Canadian companies which eventually concluded contracts in 1994 for projects in China's Liao He oil fields first visited the area with Embassy commercial officers in 1986. China's current interests in CANDU nuclear technology, most recently expressed during Premier Li Peng's 1995 visit to Canada, began in 1985 when he was visibly impressed by the explanation he received from the Hon. Pat Carney, then Canadian Minister of Energy, concerning the extent of CANDU nuclear power generation in Canada.

During the period of my assignment a great variety of other important agreements were concluded with China, covering such diverse areas as double taxation, financial credits, telecommunications, agriculture, forestry, science and technology and sports exchanges, and these provided a firm basis for developing further contacts of mutual benefit.

Arrangements were also established for periodic consultations between Canadian and Chinese officials on international affairs, disarmament and United Nations affairs, which would offer excellent opportunities to explain Canada's viewpoint on these issues and to influence, at least to a small degree, Chinese policy formulation.

Indeed, at the conclusion of my assignment, the Chinese Foreign Vice-Minister noted that "more has been accomplished in the past three years than in any other similar period since diplomatic relations were established."

The steady improvement of our bilateral relations with China was greatly assisted by high-level political visits by Prime Minister Mulroney, Governor General Sauvé, the Premiers of Quebec, Newfoundland and Ontario and the Federal Ministers Carney (Energy), Jellinek (Sports) and Kelleher (Trade); equally helpful were the visits to Canada by the President of China, the Chairman of the Military Commission of China and various Chinese ministers and senior officials.

High-level political visits from Canada to a foreign country always put a great deal of pressure on the Canadian Embassy in that country. The diplomatic personnel are expected to help develop a meaningful program and to ensure that all goes well and that the visitor concerned and, more importantly, his or her staff members are satisfied that the Embassy has done everything possible—and sometimes even the impossible—to make the visit a success. Misunderstandings and difficulties often arise between the Embassy, the host government and the officials who arrive in advance of the visitor to work out precise details of the visit.

The host government usually has its own procedures and style for the reception of visitors. The advance team often has conflicting desires regarding logistics, schedules, media exposure, the visitor's personal attitudes and wishes, and so forth, and the Embassy finds itself caught in the middle, trying to explain to the host government the special desires of the visitor's team and to explain to that team the limitations on the abilities or willingness of the host government to accommodate to those desires.

This phenomenon is present to some degree every time VIPs visit and it could was certainly be observed during the visit to China of Prime Minister Mulroney. His advance team imposed many demands of a logistic and scheduling nature, deemed necessary in light of their experience of a Canadian environment, but perhaps not customary in China; the host government found them difficult to understand and, at times, was reluctant, if not unwilling, to meet them.

One memorable example was the last minute insistence of the advance party that a couple of chairs be placed on the dais in front of the Great Hall of the People on which the Prime Minister would stand to take the welcoming salute and the playing of national anthems. The reason given for this request was the concern that the Prime Minister who, it seems, occasionally suffered from a mild case of vertigo, would have something to hold on to and use to steady himself in case of need. The Chinese Chief of Protocol, to whom I conveyed this last-minute request, was somewhat puzzled, noting that there had never before been such a request and that the presence of chairs on the dais might appear strange and occasion some comment. Nevertheless, in view of my insistence, he undertook to do whatever was possible and I was pleased to see the next day, at the arrival ceremony, the chairs were in place as desired, that no problems had developed, and that there was no media comment.

Some months later, on the occasion of the visit of the Governor General, I was surprised to note, at the similar arrival ceremony, that the dais was now graced permanently with brass stanchions, which could serve as support for any visitor in need of it. When I made my farewell call on the Chief of Protocol he chuckled with pleasure at my observation that Canada seemed to have established a permanent feature of Chinese protocol procedures for the purpose of ensuring the stability of visiting dignitaries taking the salute on the welcoming dais!

The most interesting—indeed fascinating—aspect of my assignment to China was observing the day-to-day effects of the economic and political reform process. In the months following my arrival, positive policy changes were almost as rapid and extensive as the negative ones that had occurred in the first decades of the revolution, and they presented a fascinating spectrum of changes and developments at all levels of Chinese society.

Beginning in 1979-80 the Chinese Communist Party and government authorized the abolition of the system of rural communes, which had proved sterile and non-productive, and replaced it with the "responsibility system," which permitted farmers much more freedom of choice in the growing and marketing of agricultural produce. In 1984 the Party officially endorsed the policy of extending the successful rural "responsibility system" to the urban industrial sector, with the goal of "building socialism according to Chinese characteristics" and developing an industrial economy "more responsive to market forces." Urban industrial enterprise workers were promised more pay to provide them with improvements in the standard of living similar to those now enjoyed by the rural population, which was experiencing prosperity unprecedented in China's long history. The establishment of service enterprises—previously deemed anathema by communist societies—was encouraged, and the Party decreed that "intellectuals," who had at one time been denounced, denigrated, harried and harassed as the "number nine stinking class," should now be respected and even allowed to occupy positions of influence in the Party and the government.

Top Party leaders suddenly announced that there was really nothing anti-revolutionary about Chinese women wearing pretty clothes and using cosmetics and that the former Party-decreed ascetic dress style of keeping clothes for nine years in accordance with the slogan "three years new; three years old; three years patched" should be replaced by purchases of new clothing whenever desired, if for no other reason than to support the textile industry. Premier Zhao ZiYang ostentatiously appeared everywhere in western business suits and, although many other leaders continued to where the traditional Sun YatSen style of tunic (the so-called Mao jacket), that revolutionary style of apparel became less and less common.

One pleasing result was an increasingly amount of clothing that was colourful and stylish; women of all ages began to appear again in attractive dresses, with stylish coiffures and decorative cosmetics and jewellery. During the state banquet given by Queen Elizabeth on the Royal Yacht

Britannia in Shanghai Harbour, in October 1986, the usual British pomp and glitter was matched by the invited Chinese ladies decked out in a variety of attractive Chinese or western costumes and wearing jewellery, which one senior lady confided to my wife she had not dared to display for the past thirty years!

In the autumn of 1986 Beijing was the site of a Pierre Cardin fashion show, and in the Chinese exhibit at the Canadian National Exhibition in Toronto, in August 1987, Canadian girls of Chinese origin were hired to model displays of stylish Chinese-made Western dresses and other ladies' clothing. In September 1987 the Chinese press proudly announced that China would participate in a Paris fashion show, and a "Candid Camera" section in the local newspapers began showing pictures of Chinese girls in Shanghai and Guangzhou dressed in attractive costumes of varying style and design.

In late 1984 we foreigners in China were surprised to learn that senior Party leaders were now declaring that disco dancing was not at all anti-revolutionary or lascivious, but was rather a healthy and desirable form of exercise which could also provide the occasion for men and women in the 30-40 age bracket to meet and marry and make up for such opportunities that were lost during the turmoil of the Cultural Revolution. Dance halls sprang up all over the country and, in 1985, the authorities commissioned a group of amateur musicians, including one Canadian, to tour the major cities of China to demonstrate the techniques of disco dancing.

In October 1985 during my visit to the southern Chinese city of Nanning, a determined lady official who was our mentor and guide surprised us with an invitation to visit a dance hall (one of three in the city that operated every night), equipped with a live orchestra, a bar service, and couples of all ages on the dance floor. When asked to dance, our guide confessed that she had never done so, but indicated a willingness to try, which she did with gusto! A senior cadre at our table, when asked why he and his wife were there, explained that it was only because dancing was "good exercise," but he did not disagree that it was also good fun.

In the northeastern city of Shenyang (formerly Mukden) the local people established a special morning disco that was open from 7 to 10 in the morning, especially for persons over 40 years of age and, according to the press, the place was packed every day!

In October 1986, in a landmark development, Walt Disney Productions contracted to show some 100 performances of Mickey Mouse and

Ambassador Gorham and Li Xiannien, President of China, 1985.

Donald Duck on Chinese TV (which by that time served 300,000,000 viewers). Less than a year later Colonel Sanders Kentucky Fried Chicken became established just off Tiananmen Square!

In a remarkable personal interview with me in 1985 the man who was then President of China, the late Li Xiannian, who had the reputation of a "hard line" member of the Communist Party and was a veteran of the famous Long March, explained that during the pre-revolutionary period of military resistance to the Japanese and, later, the nationalist forces of Chiang Kaishek, the Chinese Red Army forces relied heavily on the peasants for refuge, information and support. When the Communist forces achieved power they sought to reward the peasants by eliminating the landlord class and giving land to the peasants. He went on to explain that, inspired by socialist zeal and copying the Soviet system, the Party took the decision to collectivize and, later, communize the countryside, in the belief that this would harness the productive forces of the masses to achieve great results. Unfortunately, he said, this policy proved to have been a mistake, for labour productivity declined and, rather than work, peasants "would lie about with the sun shining on their backsides." Hence, he explained, the current reform process, noting that "the idea that all persons are equal is a great theory but it doesn't work." He agreed that equal opportunity for all was an acceptable objective and acknowledged that under the new reform system some would prosper more than others, but according to him, the regime was determined that "no one would be allowed to become too rich or to become too poor." I could not resist commenting that he sounded like the government of Canada!

The serious business of political and social reform also had its share of amusing situations. In 1986 Party officials in Shanghai, after a few days of public hesitation, authorized a local art studio to hire nude models. According to the press, over a thousand candidates, male and female applied, with one father, who accompanied his teenage daughter declaring that since the Party had approved, it must be all right! In November of the same year the press reported that China, which had recently become a member of the International Bodybuilding Association, was organizing a local competition in the south of the country to select candidates for the following year's international competition. There was a heated controversy, well reported in the press, over the decision of the local Physical Culture and Sports Commission that the female contestants should wear bikini costumes "so that their muscles can be displayed fully to the judges." Critics asserted that this would "offend public decency and corrupt public morality," while reformists argued that society should "take a more tolerant attitude toward change." The view of the Commission eventually prevailed and some 600 news reporters flocked to cover the event, even though, encountering a new form of Chinese moneymaking, they were themselves required to pay a substantial admission fee!

By the end of 1986, within the short space of two years, the evidence of significant progress could be seen in all aspects of Chinese life. During the period of my assignment I visited 18 provinces and 28 cities and everywhere, except in Tibet, I saw people well fed, healthy, well clothed and clean—remarkably so considering the difficult living conditions that often prevailed. There was also a total absence of beggars. Of course, areas of considerable poverty existed and the authorities began to admit openly that some 250 million Chinese were dependent on foreign aid—so described—provided by Canada and other countries under the World Food Program. Nevertheless, it was clear that active steps were being taken to improve these adverse conditions which, of course, were nothing compared to the misery of pre-revolutionary times or the deprivation that I have witnessed in other parts of Asia or in Latin America.

In the commercial and industrial sectors every Chinese city and province was anxiously attempting to generate foreign exchange to pay for modernization of outdated machinery and the introduction of new facilities and modern technology. Enterprises, scientists, technicians and engineers were being lured from all countries to participate in China's modernization in a wide variety of formats: straight sales, leases, coproductions, joint ventures, payments in cash or kind. Chinese students were flocking to western countries to develop skills in all fields: in 1986 Canada alone received over 2,000!

Special economic zones and "open cities" were being established to entice foreign enterprises with special arrangements for tax remissions and repatriation of profits; such measures placed the Chinese in the happy position of being able to pick and choose among world competitors on the basis of the best product for the lowest price and the lowest interest rate. Further, to encourage foreign investment, the Chinese authorities began working to put in place patent and copyright laws and even established a bankruptcy law, something unheard of in a communist society!

In the early years after the 1949 Revolution the Chinese Communist Party and government had obviously copied much from the Soviet Union in terms of political, economic and social policy. Relations began to cool after the death of Stalin and Khrushchev's revelations of the excesses of the Stalinist regime. They reached a low point in the late 1960s as a result of frontier clashes and the Soviet decision to withdraw all of its technical assistance projects. When the Chinese responded by withdrawing all locally engaged Chinese employees from the Soviet Embassy in Beijing, the Embassy from that time onwards—and certainly until the time my assignment ended—employed no Chinese staff and provided all local services by means of personnel brought in from the Soviet Union.

It is therefore not surprising that the Chinese were not impressed by the Gorbachev's "glasnost" and "perestroika" reforms, which concentrated on political reforms first and economic reforms later. The Chinese, in contrast, promoted economic reforms first and approached the more difficult problem of political reform much more slowly and with much more caution. They were confident that their method would be more successful than Gorbachev's and there was no desire to emulate the Soviet model. In fact, at least one Eastern European country, Hungary, was openly discussing with the Chinese the best way of adopting Chinese-style reforms.

The Chinese authorities were, of course, fully aware that the social and economic changes taking place would inevitably increase popular demands for political reforms and they began to respond in a positive, albeit cautious, fashion. Efforts were being made to put in place the rule of law so that citizens and institutions would no longer be at the mercy of the whims and dogmas of those currently enjoying political office and power. Regulations restricting internal travel were gradually being relaxed and Chinese citizens were allowed to travel abroad or even emigrate with much greater freedom than before.

Even the all-dominant Communist Party of China, with its 44 million membership and its impressive organization down to the grass-roots level throughout the country, began to undergo modernization and reform. Party dogma now admitted that Mao Zedong had made mistakes and that even Marx and Lenin, as prescient and far-seeing as they may have been, could not possibly have predicted the situation of the world and of China in the 1980s.

Old-line and aged cadres were being gracefully retired and gently put out to pension and ultra-radicals recruited during the Cultural Revolution were being disciplined, sometimes severely, for bureaucratic and autocratic abuses of power. Education was becoming a more requisite criterion for membership in the Party than peasant or worker ancestry, as the Party leadership endeavoured to refurbish the popular base of the Party, so badly tarnished during the Cultural Revolution and the period of the "Gang of Four."

The immediate objective of the regime was to double the national income by the end of the century and to double it again over the subsequent 50 years! The longer-term objective—supported by all Chinese, who are proud of their historical greatness and have smarted under the humiliation of a century of domination by foreign powers, from the Opium Wars to the expulsion of the Japanese—was that China should once again become a great power and a true "Middle Kingdom."

Deng Xiaoping and his colleagues, good pragmatists all, knew that the long-term objective would indeed be just that, and they acknowledged that the achievement of a 200 percent increase in national income by the middle of the next century would require decades of political stability and economic and social progress. They also recognized that even fulfilment of this purpose would give the Chinese masses a per capita income of only $1,500—extremely modest by European or North American standards—but would nevertheless be an achievement of epic proportions, giving the people the highest standard of living in their history.

The success of the economic reforms inevitably meant that certain segments of the population would become financially richer and able to enjoy a higher standard of living, while others would remain at, or even be reduced to, a lower standard. It was a course fraught with political risks and the regime realized that it must proceed warily.

In 1983-84 concerns of the ultra-conservatives within the Communist Party about the growth of "spiritual pollution" in China, caused by the "evil winds" from the Western industrialized world, resulted in a partial crackdown reminiscent of the Cultural Revolution. This was sufficiently disturbing to the general populace and the younger Party members to produce an almost immediate reversal of the "spiritual pollution" campaign, and the slow but steady progress toward social and political modernization continued almost unabated, but with caution. Some Party elders were removed from office but the more ambitious plans for "Party rectification," which would have removed the ultra-radicals from the Party, were not very successful.

The best indication I ever received of the serious intention of the regime to institute effective political and economic reform process came in 1986 from the lips of Zhao Ziyang, at that time Premier, on the occasion of a small intimate dinner he hosted for our former Prime Minister, Pierre Trudeau. During the discussion I had asked the Premier why, in the recently announced national budget plans, no amounts had been earmarked for the development of the Three Gorges hydroelectric project on the Yangtze River. He gave as the reason the continued concerns and divided views within the Party and the Government on the desirability of proceeding with the project or abandoning it. Mr. Trudeau asked whether, amid such a conflict of views, it would be the role of the Premier of China to make the final decision. Zhao Ziyang answered, "No, we will not have any more one-man decisions in this country. We must establish a consensus!" My reaction to this statement was twofold: it was the best expression of opinion I had ever heard in favour of the democratic process in China and that it would be a long time before the Three Gorges project would finally be approved.

In 1986 the new buzzwords of "political reform," or more precisely "reform of the political structure," became the subject of a good deal of surprisingly frank, even provocative, debate and discussion in Chinese newspapers and publications, a debate which was alleged to have been the motivating factor in a series of large-scale student demonstrations organized in December in several of China's major cities and prestigious academic institutions to demand more "democracy."

These student demonstrations clearly sharpened the debate within the Party about political reforms and revealed the strength of the conservative elements to be much stronger than expected. Deng Xiaoping and the other reformists were quick to respond by joining the chorus of denunciations of "bourgeois liberalism" (i.e. criticism of the supremacy of the Communist Party) and stressing the sanctity of the "Four Cardinal Principles" (i.e. proletarian dictatorship; Marxism, Leninism and Mao Zedong Thought; primacy of the Communist Party; and adherence to the "socialist road") as the fundamental basis of "socialism in accordance with Chinese characteristics."

The popular Party General Secretary, Hu Yaobang, was forced to resign and a few outspoken professors and writers were disciplined and/or expelled from the Party. Writers and authors were sharply reminded of their "responsibility" to provide correct guidance in their artistic creations and new measures of control over publications were instituted.

Despite the shock of the December disturbances, however, the progress of reforming the political structure continued, albeit at a much slower pace. To mark the 60th anniversary of the Chinese Communist Party on July 1, 1987 the Chinese media made a special point of publishing again the text of a remarkable speech given by Deng Xiaoping to an enlarged Politburo meeting on August 18, 1980. In this speech the venerable leader had emphasized the critical need to implement political reforms and to overcome the Party's major problems of "bureaucracy, over-concentration of power, patriarchal methods, life tenures in leading posts, and privileges of various kinds," which were inhibiting China's modernization—problems which he went on to document in scathing detail. The Party Plenum in October, 1987 endorsed the reformers' program, but insisted that it be implemented at a slower and more measured pace.

As in every society, the key to China's future rests heavily on the younger generation which, in terms of its numbers and political awareness, is a formidable force, much better educated than any previous generation and aware of national and world events through transistor radios, television, fax machines, contacts with foreigners and overseas Chinese and their own study and travels abroad, undertaken by very large numbers. It is a generation no longer satisfied with Party propaganda or willing to accept the word of Party officials, neighbourhood association leaders and so forth as the gospel truth, a generation destined to represent a very serious challenge to the Chinese Communist Party and its retention of power in China.

At the conclusion of my assignment in China in October 1987 I prepared some personal reflections summarizing various observations of the changing scene which I had been privileged to witness at first hand. In regard to the process of political reform in China I wrote as follows:

Whatever the nature and degree of political reform the Party is prepared to accept or adopt, foreign observers should not be deluded into thinking that China will emerge as some sort of mirror image of Western European or North American style of democracy with full freedom of political expression, a fully free press, or a full respect for individual rights and liberties.

The Communist Party of China, which has achieved its position of power after decades of bloody struggle and sacrifice and which, despite all of its social and political vicissitudes, has given a billion Chinese people a better lifestyle than any previous regime or system of government, is determined to retain its power and it will not willingly give up its control. Inside the velvet glove of economic and political reform the Party still has an iron hand and will probably be prepared to use it if it feels pressured in self-preservation to do so.

China has always had authoritarian regimes and likely always will and probably that is an inevitable requirement for governing a nation of a billion people. Whatever the reforms, the Chinese state will continue to be an authoritarian one, with attributes that would be unacceptable in Canada or other democratic societies. We all want a China that has political, economic and social stability, but we will have to accept that such stability will be the result of a high degree of authoritarianism and strict limitations on individual liberty.

The most unfortunate and shocking setback to the reform process of the Tiananmen massacre in 1988 seems to have proved my forecast to have been terribly correct!

I ended my reflections on China on a personal note about what it was like to live and work in China as Canadian Ambassador from 1984 to 1987 and I conclude this essay with the following excerpt:

I have often been asked by visiting Canadians and Chinese friends: "How do you like living in China?" For the first six months or so my usual response was "professionally fascinating, personally frustrating!" The professional fascination remains to this day and, I can add, there has been a professional sense of satisfaction that I could play a small part in the worthwhile enhancement of Sino-Canadian relations.

The personal frustrations were legion, but those that were caused only by the generally lower level of social and economic infrastructure and linguistic and cultural barriers tended to disappear as we became adjusted to the local situation.

Others, however, remained throughout. My wife and I often recalled the first look at the Official Residence en route to the hotel from the airport on the day of our arrival on which occasion we discovered a signal light on the kitchen's gas stove flashing "Help"—"Help"—"Help." We carefully backed away fearing we knew not what, wondering if this was some kind of modern "handwriting on the wall!" We later learned it was the electrical digital clock asking to be reset because a momentary power failure had offended its accuracy. When the frustrations seemed to be unbearable we would laugh and recall that our stove had tried to warn us but we had failed to heed it!

To live and operate an Embassy in a society where there is no free or open market for renting or buying office or personal accommodation, or for recruiting tradesmen, service personnel or employees, becomes a constant burden. To have only limited choice of places where Embassy personnel can live, to have the local hot water system cut off for 2-3 weeks per year while the system pipes are cleaned, to have delegations of visiting Canadians forced to climb nine floors to the Residence because the building's elevators didn't work, or to have a Ministerial Party trapped for a time in the elevator because the doors would not open, or to have the ambience of an important official dinner for guests of Ministerial rank destroyed because of inordinately long delays between the servings of meat and vegetables would tax anyone's composure and patience. Similarly, to arrive at an airport for a scheduled departure and then wait seven hours before takeoff can increase the blood pressure somewhat. As did the sometimes 3-4 hour delay to make a telephone call to Shanghai or some other major city.

On the other hand, many of these frustrations can be matched by positive experiences of successful Chinese attempts to be friendly and to help us cope with situations which they themselves find equally frustrating and annoying. In every official situation, I encountered much kindness and courtesy to help resolve problems caused by inefficiencies inherent in the systems.

Perhaps my greatest regret is that, while we have had many Chinese acquaintances who have been most friendly, helpful and good-humoured, the social contact was always restricted to official circumstances. Those Chinese would undoubtedly have liked to have become closer friends but were inhibited from doing so by the restrictions imposed on them to prevent social contact with foreign citizens, especially foreign diplomats. These restrictions were as annoying for the Chinese as they were for the foreigner, but it did put up a barrier against friendly personal contact which was the most distressing and disappointing feature of living and working in China.

To every "downside" there was an "upside" however, and the friendships forged among members of the foreign community and our own Embassy personnel were perhaps more rewarding in China than elsewhere and possibly more long-lasting.

My three years in China were very rewarding, and my wife and I would have been pleased to stay on for another year or so, but duty called us home for new challenges. At the conclusion of my assignment I sent a valedictory dispatch to Joe Clark, at that time Secretary of State for External Affairs. In doing so I mischievously used the once common, but now abandoned "dispatch form," beginning with the phrase, "Sir, I have to honour to report ..." and concluding with the closing salutation "I remain, Sir, your humble and obedient servant." I assumed that it might generate an equally mischievous reply, as would likely have been the case a few years earlier. Alas, humour seemed to have gone out of the Department by that time and my final dispatch and its attempt at light humour elicited no reaction or response whatsoever.

Richard V. Gorham joined External Affairs in 1952. After serving in Tokyo from 1954 to 1960 and in New Delhi from 1963 to 1966, he was named Commissioner to the ICSC in Pnom Penh, Cambodia in 1968. In 1971 he became Director of the Press Office at External Affairs, a position he held until his return to the Far East in 1974 as Minister in the Embassy in Tokyo. In 1979 Mr. Gorham became Assistant Undersecretary for Latin American and Caribbean Affairs. He was Ambassador to the People's Republic of China from 1984 to 1987, then Roving Ambassador to Latin America and Ambassador and Permanent Observer of Canada to the OAS until 1990. In 1990-91 Mr. Gorham was "Foreign Service Visitor" at the University of New Brunswick and is still an adjunct professor there.

10

A FOREIGN SERVICE OFFICER AND CANADA'S NUCLEAR POLICIES

J.G. HADWEN

THERE WERE THREE PERIODS in which I participated actively in the management of Canadian nuclear policies. They were: my time as Ambassador to Pakistan 1972-74, as High Commissioner to India 1979-83 and as Director General for East Asia, with particular responsibility for China and Korea, from 1983 to 1985. There were, of course, other times when the nuclear issue arose. Anyone who approaches this essay in the hope of dramatic revelations will be disappointed, but it should promote understanding of how a head of mission and a senior official in Ottawa contributes to the operations of Canada's foreign policy.

THE ROLE TODAY

What would the members of the foreign service be doing in 1996-1997, when there is worldwide concern over nuclear issues? During university studies and previous experience any foreign service officer would have had to develop a personal commitment to the value of nuclear energy and to the importance of nuclear deterrence. Under the guidelines set by the government, those with responsibilities for international trade and economic development policies would be working now on how best to pursue the Canadian interest. Generally speaking, they would support nuclear energy as one of the necessary power sources for the world and endorse Canadian technology in particular. Their approach would recall the question: "How do porcupines make love?" Answer: "With great care." A foreign service officer at any level would have to keep constantly in mind the nature of Canada's policies on the non-proliferation of nuclear weapons. The most recent example, involving many officials, was Prime Minister Chrétien's attempts in New Delhi and Islamabad (unsuccessful at least in the short term, but determined), to promote the international non-proliferation treaty and stress the strength of our commitment to International Atomic Energy Agency [IAEA] safeguards.

It is, of course, not feasible to instruct every member of a foreign service, including heads of mission, on the precise detail of Canadian government policy on all subjects. Therefore much has to be left to the good sense and experience of those involved. There is no time and no capability to provide instructions on the ramifications of policies as they affect situations abroad, often in unexpected and unpredictable contexts.

Canada's positions on nuclear deterrence and on nuclear weapons have been carefully established in documented controversy. They were clear before 1950, the year in which I joined the service. As a head of post, I was not questioned in Malaysia, Pakistan or India on Canadian nuclear weapons policy. No sensible person serving abroad would initiate a public discussion on the subject and, if questioned, would respond: "Canadian policies on this subject are on record and well understood all over the world," whether or not this was entirely true. We support and participate carefully in Allied preparations which result in nuclear deterrence, but we do not ourselves wish to produce nuclear weapons. We do what we can to prevent their widespread distribution.

There is less need for extreme caution when it comes to some of the other elements of Canadian nuclear capability. I would think that there would be few situations in which Canadian representatives abroad or in Ottawa could not support the research which Canadians have done on cancer treatments and the irradiation of food. As will be seen, there are dangers for responsible Canadians when nuclear issues of any kind arise, but there exist also opportunities to promote Canadian economic interests.

I would expect that Canadian officers serving in the nuclear weapons states, at the United Nations, at the IAEA and in NATO, would be doing their best to report, for example, on the implications of the recent Korean crisis for the countries and agencies to which they are accredited. At the same time as the confrontation was developing on the Korean Peninsula, the Chinese government conducted a nuclear test. Any Canadian representative abroad worth his salt would have done some kind of analysis, based on the best information and contacts available to him, of the implications of Chinese testing for the possible resumption of tests by the other nuclear weapons states (as France has done in 1995-96) and for the possibility of tests being conducted by the near nuclear states. When nuclear test policy becomes a matter of international concern, it has a destabilizing influence on the agencies of many governments. There will no doubt be elements in some governments who will seize on the current tensions as a justification for upgrading their own national nuclear weapons capabilities. Consideration will no doubt be given at some posts to action Canada might take which would help to reduce the effects of these latest incidents affecting the spread of nuclear weapons. It will not be easy to report on these matters, but the effort must be made and even minor pieces of information can be useful.

The intelligence agencies in all concerned countries will be producing estimates of various probable outcomes. These estimates will be exchanged with those governments with whom we regularly share intelligence information, and efforts will be made to reach some kind of consensus. This is seldom completely achievable, but it is important that no intelligence estimate be done by any one country is without input provided by other friendly and associated countries. When a crisis of the kind that has developed in Korea erupts, there is also a requirement to make sure that controls in place designed to prevent the wrongful sale or transmission of nuclear technology and materials are reviewed and, if necessary, enforced more efficiently. Vast amounts of money are available in potential nuclear weapons states to purchase equipment and information for the enhancement of their offensive capabilities. There are enough examples in the history of Canadian and other governments of the way in which, for financial gain, individuals have been willing to play the dangerous games involved in the illegal sale of nuclear weapons technology and materials. Our controls have been stringent and Canadian authorities have always been vigilant. We have successfully prosecuted those attempting to circumvent our laws. So far, in the world record books, we must be at the top of the list of countries which have worked hard to prevent the proliferation of nuclear weapons. This is such a firm and long-standing Canadian policy that it is inconceivable that any Canadian foreign service officer in the past, present or future would not be fully aware of its strength.

Assessments must be made continuously of the extent to which the potential for nuclear war exists. The experience of the world with the consequences of repeated nuclear testing has been such that there would be very few national authorities unaware that atmospheric and even under-ground tests produce nuclear fallout and thereby create widespread dangers. If China and France, or other countries, conduct nuclear tests there will be adverse consequences for many and perhaps all other peoples. If one country on the Korean Peninsula were responsible for a nuclear weapons attack on another country on the Korean Peninsula, there would be serious immediate consequences for all peoples on the

Peninsula and for the peoples in neighbouring countries. The same factors apply in the Middle East and in South Asia. We should, however, be grateful that the major East-West confrontations of great powers have been reduced, although the dangers still require analysis.

A reason why the use of nuclear weapons in 1995-96 is almost unthinkable is that in present circumstances any user of a nuclear weapon could expect the immediate destruction of his own capital city and his own major centres of population by the enemy or its allies. Few national authorities are ignorant of the consequences of the World War II bombs, and of the fact that technology has since then advanced to the point where there are enormous arsenals of nuclear weaponry around the world which might be drawn upon if the occasion required it. Thus, for reasons of national survival and because of the fear of retaliation, it is hard to imagine that any government might initiate a nuclear attack. The madness factor, however, cannot be ignored. This is one of the areas in which a Canadian foreign service officer would be expected to provide continuing analysis. There have been situations in which governments have embarked on military adventures the consequences of which for them were, either in the short term or in the longer term, clearly disadvantageous. Iraq's intransigence in 1991 demonstrated how this can happen. There may be situations in which, either now or in the future, leaders of government may lose their sanity. However, even the most unbalanced of individuals would have around him people who would reflect the truism that self-destruction is very seldom a successful feature of national policy. Still, a foreign service officer would be expected to watch for signs of the kind of irrationality that could threaten Canadian and international security. Dr. Strangelove still lives.

EARLY FOREIGN SERVICE

After the war and graduate studies, I joined the Canadian foreign service. Unexpectedly, I was rather abruptly transferred in 1951 to what was known as Defence Liaison II Division under a great figure in the intelligence and security community, G.P. de T. Glazebrook. I have no idea why I was selected for this work but, rather unusually, I remained in the division for over a year before I was posted to Pakistan in the summer of 1952.

This began a connection, which continued until just before my retirement in 1987, with the intelligence and security functions of our foreign office. I should emphasize that this was an entirely traditional

Canadian foreign service process. I suppose that, if asked to identify the subject area in which I had mainly worked from 1950 to 1987, I would answer that my responsibilities were for Canadian commercial interests and the Canadian development assistance program. My assignments in the security and intelligence field came as a matter of accident.

Those who have not worked in this field might find it hard to believe that in 1951-52 my division had very heavy responsibilities for personnel security and for a wide variety of intelligence tasks of which I was uninformed. I knew the general subjects other officers dealt with, but one of the fundamental principles in work of this kind is that of the "need to know." If you do not need to know, you are not told. My main job was the security within the Department of External Affairs in Ottawa. Another officer was responsible for security problems at our posts abroad. I also helped to process and to manage the flow of intelligence information which was received and made it available, as appropriate, to other elements of the Department.

Then followed a two-year posting to Karachi, Pakistan, from 1952-54. During this time the Canadian mission in Pakistan had only a mar-

Karachi: Fall, 1952. From left to right: Tom Monaghan (Canadian High Commission officer); Ed Ritchie; an airport guard; Protocol officer (Pakistan); J.G. Hadwen (Third Secretary); Kenneth P. Kirkwood (High Commissioner to Pakistan); Jimmy Sinclair (Minister of Fisheries, B.C.); John J. Deutsch (Department of Finance); Mrs. James Sinclair.

ginal connection with nuclear issues. It was a period of great activity under the Colombo Plan, and Canada initiated a very large program of fellowships and scholarships for the countries of South Asia, at that time India, Pakistan and Ceylon. Quite a large number of Pakistanis were processed through our office for courses of up to four and sometimes more years at Canadian universities and other educational institutions. Naturally, some of these students went to be trained in various branches of physics, including nuclear technology. It is in retrospect somewhat surprising to note that many of the students who went to Canada to study in the nuclear field came from Dacca University. I recall that, at a later period of my service in Pakistan, 1972-74, it became apparent that many of the leading figures in the Pakistan nuclear establishment were from East Pakistan and that, when that province became Bangladesh, most of them left.

Perhaps the first direct association I had with Canadian nuclear policy issues came on my return to Ottawa in 1954, when I was asked by the great Ed Ritchie to join his Economic Division. I continued to work mainly in the economic development field, but I recall taking part in exchanges on the desirability of giving "underdeveloped countries" access to Canadian nuclear expertise and technology. The basic argument was that Canada, during the war period, had developed considerable expertise in the generation of electricity by nuclear processes. We believed that Canadian technology was the most efficient of the nuclear technologies available. We thought of it as the safest of alternatives and as the one best suited to peaceful generation of electricity. A great deal of the work was done on the provision of the experimental reactor to India and, later, on the delivery of the Karachi nuclear power plant to Pakistan. Our assessment was that both Pakistan and India were capable of making use of nuclear technology for the generation of electricity.

NEAR THE SUMMIT

After assignments in Ottawa, at the UN and in Norway there was a period in which I functioned within the highest levels of the Canadian government. In early 1964 I became a special assistant to the Honourable Paul Martin, then Secretary of State for External Affairs. I was also assigned to liaison functions in respect of foreign affairs in the office of the Prime Minister, Lester B. Pearson.

I do not recall any nuclear weapons issues of major importance arising in the period from early 1964 to the summer of 1967 which required significant attention in the office of our Secretary of State for External Affairs or of the Prime Minister. I was aware of every piece of paper that came from the Department of External Affairs to its Minister, and was involved in the decision making connected with these documents. I played the same role in respect of any document that went from the Department through the Minister to the Prime Minister and back. From time to time Mr. Martin himself did, of course, take some documents directly down the hall and discussed them with the Prime Minister. It was, however, established tradition that he would not do this without informing me either in advance or afterwards, and my arrangement with Mr. Pearson's office was for any foreign affairs paper turning up there to be brought to me. I was also responsible for the organization of the papers Mr. Martin took to Cabinet and brought back.

I should note that the Cuban missile crisis had been dealt with not long before I came back to Ottawa, and that there had been other nuclear issues of importance both in Parliament and within the government in earlier years. Of course there was throughout this period a constant stream of intelligence material about nuclear threats which came to Mr. Martin and Mr. Pearson. Documents have now been released, early in 1996, revealing that British and U.S. intelligence services warned Canada in 1965 that India could be using Canadian technology to develop a nuclear weapons capability.

MALAYSIA, SINGAPORE, AND BURMA

The next four years, from the summer of 1967 to the summer of 1971, were spent as head of mission responsible for Canada's relations with Malaysia, Singapore and Burma. There was no particular nuclear program involving Canada in Malaysia and Singapore, apart from the occasional student taking physics at a Canadian university.

In respect of Burma there was one minor nuclear involvement. It concerned AECL's equipment for use in cancer treatment. Under the Colombo Plan Canada provided an outstanding nurse, Joan Goodall, and cobalt beam therapy units for the Rangoon General Hospital and for the hospital in Mandalay. Both of these units were in operation in 1967. In both cases there were Burmese nurses who had been trained in the use of these units in Canada. Everybody recalled, both in Mandalay and Rangoon, the pleasure with which they had served with Miss Goodall. I can remember making some contact with her in British Columbia in her retirement and reporting on the favourable impact of her work. The units seemed to suit Burmese capabilities very well, and I saw that they were still functional in 1994. I am currently trying to get them upgraded through non-governmental channels since we are not willing to officially support the present Myanmar government in any way.

PAKISTAN

My situation changed radically when, after a 1971 sabbatical year in Geneva, I was unexpectedly assigned to Pakistan. It had been planned, I thought securely, that I would go home in 1972.

For two years, from 1972 through '74, I was deeply involved in the nuclear issue as it affected our relations with Pakistan. The Karachi Nuclear Power Plant (KANUPP) reactor had been completed and was ready to be formally opened in 1972. This was a classic CANDU reactor, which was intended to provide badly needed electrical power for Pakistan in general and for the Karachi region in particular. It should be noted that although large quantities of gas had been discovered in Pakistan, the country had only minor deposits of fossil fuels. During the British colonial period some very modest oil resources had become available and there had been some development of marginal coal supplies. Pakistan was therefore heavily dependent on imported oil and by 1972 considerable priority was given to developing other sources of energy. In spite of great Pakistani efforts since that time, and in spite of collaboration with many foreign interests, no significant oil discoveries have been made, either on shore or off shore. I do not think that there have been any important new discoveries of coal. The gas remains, but Pakistan has been most reluctant, mainly for reasons of national security, to deplete its gas resources, which appear to be its only natural source of energy and which are obviously limited.

When I arrived in Islamabad in 1972 there were a series of administrative problems connected with the Canadian engineers who were working on the final stages of the commissioning of the KANUPP reactor.

I should note that non-proliferation issues had generally become urgent by 1972, but Pakistan accepted the safeguards we required for the reactor. The IAEA was regularly inspecting the spent fuel as it began to collect in a specially designed pool.

Eventually there came a time for a formal opening of the KANUPP reactor. It so happened that a senior CIDA official was in Pakistan at the time, on other business, and I persuaded him to accompany me to the official ceremony. However by 1972, nuclear problems had become sufficiently controversial and sensitive to make CIDA reluctant to undertake any program related to nuclear matters. Aside from the fellowships and scholarships of the past, there was no Canadian aid involved in the KANUPP reactor. The CIDA official concerned joined me, however, at the ceremonies presided over by Prime Minister Bhutto, but he did so rather uneasily and afterwards reported to me that he had been severely criticized for his participation. I had no hesitation in playing my part in the ceremony and I can recall clearing the text of the very general remarks I made with Ottawa.

We had at this point a good relationship with the Pakistanis on the non-proliferation issues and I was, to the extent possible when dealing with officials of any other government, a friend of the head of the Pakistan Atomic Energy Agency. One of my main functions was to make sure that, as the Pakistanis began to consider their long-term nuclear power requirements, Canada benefited as much as possible from the successful operation of KANUPP.

I do not believe that industry in the south of Pakistan would have developed as it did without the availability of power from KANUPP. Moreover, the fact that KANUPP was producing on a regular and steady basis significant quantities of power eased pressure on the Pakistani electrical grid and contributed to the better use of hydro-electric and thermally generated power.

In respect of the international nuclear non-proliferation treaty Pakistan had over the years refused to become a party unless India did too. Throughout the period 1972-74 there were active negotiations in Delhi between Canadian and Indian authorities in respect to bilateral Canadian safeguards and the non-proliferation treaty. We followed these closely from Pakistan because, if there was to be progress in Delhi, I was confident that we could quickly obtain corresponding action in Pakistan. At times it looked as if agreement of some kind on nuclear issues might be feasible in South Asia, but in fact there was never any substantial forward movement.

There were no particular sources of trouble in the last year of my accreditation in Islamabad until India exploded its nuclear bomb. The Indian authorities tried to describe the explosion as that of a "peaceful nuclear device," but in fact, as Canadian officials have always remarked, a nuclear explosion is an explosion and it is a bomb whatever it may be called. I believe the Indian action came as a very great shock to the authorities in Pakistan. There had, of course, been great concern in

Ottawa at the inability, in spite of very strenuous efforts at the highest levels, to upgrade our bilateral safeguard requirements with India. We received many general assurances of peaceful intent right up to 1974, but no formal commitment. We continued of course to press for Pakistani support of the non-proliferation treaty but, on balance, I think the Canadian government recognized that India and Pakistan would have to support this treaty together. Canada's nuclear relations with Pakistan and India were, and are, like almost all major issues on the sub-continent, a function of the relationships between the two countries. We have never been able to conduct our relations with these countries except in a South Asian context. The period 1972-74 on the whole demonstrated a reasonably balanced relationship between these countries and between both countries and Canada. The trauma and the hostilities occasioned by the events of 1971, when Bangladesh separated, had largely dissipated by the time I arrived. The assumption of power by Mr. Bhutto produced new conditions and, on the whole, relatively favourable conditions between Pakistan and India.

Nevertheless, when India demonstrated its ability to manufacture an explosive nuclear device, the consequences for those relations were severe. From then on, Canada had to consider the need to help control the threat of nuclear war in South Asia. It was clear that, whatever we might say, Pakistan would feel obliged to embark on a program involving nuclear explosion technology. KANUPP was not involved in these Pakistani efforts. Of course Pakistani scientists and engineers were in many cases trained in Canada and Pakistan's experience in the operation of KANUPP formed the basis of whatever program the country decided to develop outside Karachi. It became obvious, for example, that nuclear weapons research was being conducted at a heavily protected facility on the outskirts of Islamabad.

After the Indian explosion of that year, President Bhutto, and later other government representatives, made it clear that Pakistan was seeking to match India's nuclear explosion capability ("if necessary we will eat grass"). As a consequence, our relations with Pakistan in this field came to an end. One result of the Indian explosion was that in both India and Pakistan there was no possibility of selling Canadian nuclear equipment and technology. I have not heard since that time of any sales of even cancer treatment or food irradiation equipment. Certainly, no sales of reactors, heavy water or reactor parts to South Asia were possible, despite Canada's role as the first major partner, in the nuclear field, of both India and Pakistan. In general there has been no change in our position since 1974. Because of my friendship with people at senior levels of the Pakistan government, I was once asked, in later years, to approach a member of the government and determine whether there was any chance of Pakistan coming closer to the non-proliferation treaty in a way which would make for better relations with Canada. Unsurprisingly, I failed.

BACK IN OTTAWA

One assignment I was given, on my return to Ottawa in 1974, was that of Director General of the Bureau of Security and Intelligence. In that capacity I was also Chairman of the Intelligence Advisory Committee which was responsible for the coordinated intelligence work of the community in Canada. We did not have in this period any major crisis involving nuclear weapons, although we produced regular and continuing assessments of the potential for nuclear conflict anywhere in the world and on the dangers from the near nuclear or potential nuclear weapons states.

INDIA

I was made High Commissioner to India in 1979 and thrown once again back into the nuclear policy area. I had very little time for pre-posting briefing. I did participate however in discussion of my letter of instruction. At this particular time, the document was treated very seriously, even though it only took the form of a letter provided to the head of mission himself and would not be given any major distribution. It contained three or four pages intended as a summary of the objectives which the head of mission was expected to pursue during his term of office. The quality of the letters differed very much, depending on the skill and the knowledge of the drafters.

I am not sure whether a copy of this letter could be found on the present day files. If it were it would certainly be seen to contain a paragraph which noted that there appeared to be no possibility of any meeting of minds between Canada and India on nuclear matters. The lengthy and difficult discussions over the years between Canada and India on the bilateral safeguards issues and the exchanges about the non-proliferation treaty and related matters were noted. No progress on this subject was to be expected during my posting, given the firmness of the Canadian positions and the equally firm stand of the government of India. However, the letter went on, the fact that we could not cooperate in the nuclear field did not mean that we needed to hold back on cooperation in other areas which could advance Canadian and Indian interests.

Therefore the nuclear policy issue was not active formally and officially during my service in New Delhi from 1979 to 1983, but in one form or another the subject affected each day and every official contact. For example, as High Commissioner I was required to make a large number of public speeches. I believe I addressed all the Rotary Clubs in New Delhi, and there must have been twenty of them, sometimes more than once. I also spoke on many occasions throughout India, at the opening or closing of some institution, the inauguration of some Canadian project under our development cooperation program, or when I was present at the achievement of some commercial agreement.

In the question period I was always asked about Canadian nuclear policy. On each occasion I stated the nature and the firmness of the Canadian government's views and referred to the non-partisan support which these views continued to receive in Canada. I tried to frame my statements in such a way that they would not be newsworthy. I would refer to the fact that, as was illustrated by the particular occasion at which I was appearing, there were many other areas in which representatives of the Canadian and Indian governments had much work to do. It was nevertheless surprising how often and how consistently, no matter where I went in India, the issue was raised in public.

There were also many private exchanges with officials and with Indian political leaders. In some cases what would happen, even at the most senior levels, was that once we had disposed of the issue on the table between us, the comment would be made that they had never understood why Canada was unable to cooperate with India in the nuclear field. I believe this situation was created by the fact that the costs for India of continuing a major nuclear program without any form of Canadian cooperation began to be very high indeed. It was also the case that many governments took a somewhat similar, but not identical, position to our own and sharply reduced or eliminated any form of nuclear relations with India after 1974. It was known of course that India was continuing various forms of nuclear cooperation under the very wide program of relations with the USSR—as it was then—and its satellites. To my knowledge the costs of nuclear weapons activity were never questioned within the Indian government and were justified on national security grounds, in the face of what were perceived as threats from China and

Pakistan. The position of the nuclear weapon states was also resented as great power politics.

Since 1947 both India and Pakistan have spent large amounts on weaponry of all kinds and this policy had led donors to question the need for aid grants and loans. Indeed, in seeking approval for the first Canadian aid funds for the Third World, Mr. Pearson found it necessary to resist arguments in 1949 to this effect. Neither India nor Pakistan has been willing then or since to even discuss expenditures for national security with donors and, of course, the donors themselves have not been willing to discuss their defense costs in relation to their aid levels. Thus there has been a kind of tacit agreement to conduct development cooperation separately from policies involving defence expenditure.

At least once every few months from 1979-83, I also had to engage in a knock-down drag-out debate with some informed and able official during which I had to draw on every bit of knowledge I possessed about past exchanges on nuclear issues between Canada and India. I sometimes wondered if these encounters with officials represented some kind of probing, to determine whether there was an alteration in the Canadian position on the basis of which negotiations could be resumed. I believe, however, that I succeeded each time in convincing the individual concerned that there had been no change in the basic Canadian position.

Of course there was a great deal of local press attention given to nuclear issues. We kept track of it and reported any comments or information given us by friendly missions in Delhi or volunteered by Indian officials. At the same time, we kept up-to-date on Canadian thinking and were briefed by Ottawa and by Canadian missions around the world.

There were times when, as major developments were announced in India, my mission regretted that we were not able to compete for large contracts for the provision of uranium, for the supply of heavy water, or for the sale of equipment and technology for new power reactors. I was very careful not to visit any Indian nuclear installation. Had I asked to do so my action would have been taken as a signal of Canadian interest. It was hard, however, when one day, while on an official tour in Rajasthan, I had to drive by the gates leading to the two large Rajasthan atomic power projects—RAPP I and RAPP II as we called them—which had been built earlier with Canadian export financing and which were at the time the most advanced CANDU designs. I often wondered how many modifications there had been to these designs since our nuclear cooperation with India had terminated. There must have been hundreds, because our CANDU technology became safer and more economical over the years, but there was of course no question, in the period in which I was responsible for this subject in India, of Canada being able to draw commercial advantage from the very large nuclear program on which India was embarked.

We have sometimes argued with pride that Canadian safeguard requirements are stricter than those of the IAEA. The consequence has certainly been reduction in our prospects for sales of nuclear equipment and technology. Whether our somewhat isolated position has strengthened the international non-proliferation regime can be debated.

During my time in New Delhi, the international atomic energy community was becoming increasingly concerned about safety issues. Although these have come very much to the fore since 1983 and are of very great concern with respect to installations within the former USSR and its satellites, I am not aware that there have been serious safety problems at Indian nuclear sites, although there was some press speculation in the summer of 1994. There was even a reported comment at that time that the Indian authorities did not want or need Canadian help on issues concerning nuclear safety. However, if such issues do eventually arise, it is hard to imagine that Canada (the original source of the technology) would not be blamed, regardless of the historical background and the justifications for our position. Since 1990, press reports have appeared that reflect Canadian willingness to consider providing some technical assistance for the purpose of ensuring safety under international auspices at Canada installations. Such assistance would appear to have been open to both India and Pakistan. There has been no subsequent announcement of any actual program.

We were conscious in New Delhi of the geopolitical stakes involved in the nuclear policies of South Asia. It was apparent that the USSR was quite firmly committed to preventing the spread of nuclear weapons and was unlikely to be involved in measures directly assisting the development of such weapons in South Asia. It was also evident, in the 1979-83 period, that a close relationship on defence matters was developing between Pakistan and China. Depending on the state of China-USSR relations, the possibility existed of conflicts developing between Pakistan and India that would involve China and the USSR. Throughout this period, the United States remained a major influence on strategic thinking and policies in respect of South Asia. There was very little that Canada could do at any one time to try and reduce the tensions which rose and fell in

South Asia with the degree of intensity of conflicts between the great powers. The role of the Canadian High Commission in New Delhi was restricted to a modest level of watchfulness and or reporting.

INDO-PAKISTAN RELATIONS

It was very obvious during my periods as High Commissioner in New Delhi and as Ambassador in Pakistan, that Canada's involvement in South Asia was governed by the nature of Indo-Pakistani relations. Neither India nor Pakistan have been able to develop foreign policies independently of each other. From time to time each country has believed that it enjoyed alliances or associations which enabled it to function without the need to recognize that its relations with the other major country in the sub-continent were of decisive importance. Whatever influence Canada had on the region came from the fact that we had been, over the years, a source of economic assistance. We had also played our part in developments within the Commonwealth and at the United Nations and in other international bodies, particularly the IAEA, in which both India and Pakistan were deeply involved. One of the issues that arose repeatedly was whether we should use whatever influence we had in New Delhi and in Islamabad to reduce international tensions. It was a judgement call in each case as to whether a message from a Canadian political leader or an official visit to the region or a visit from the region to Canada, would be of importance, not only to Canada but also to India and Pakistan. There is a natural reluctance to use whatever international political influence you may have; it is like deciding whether to draw down a savings bank account. Generally speaking, we did not, in my time, go all out to influence either or both countries to move in what we regarded as favourable directions. Perhaps we correctly assessed our limitations. Perhaps we missed manageable opportunities.

However, during my period in New Delhi, relations between Canada and India were on the whole good. We had access to the highest levels and Indian leaders always seemed interested in Canadian views. There was of course continuing and quite widespread respect for Mr. Pearson, whose influence continues well into the 1990s. Mr. Nehru's and Mrs. Gandhi's views were always of interest to Canadian leaders. But as time went by, statements from Pakistan, and various pronouncements confirming the Indian position on its nuclear program—particularly when they occurred in times of hostility between those countries—became damaging to Canada's involvement in South Asia. Before the green revolution Canada was an important and valued source of food grains for India. We also sympathized with, and supported, India at the time of its confrontation with China in the Himalayas. But we failed completely to make progress on nuclear issues in either India or Pakistan.

Our overriding and continuing concern was with any development that suggested a revival of hostilities between the two countries. At one point the *New York Times* featured reports that India might be considering a pre-emptive strike against Pakistan's nuclear installations. Canadian officials asked me for my assessment in retirement of the likelihood of nuclear conflict between India and Pakistan. I was able to argue that the countries were so close to each other physically and had developed such a balance of deterrence between them that I did not believe either would initiate self-destructive nuclear warfare. That remains my assessment. It continues to be important for Canada to review and maintain its watching brief on Indo-Pakistan relations because of our long history of association with the two countries and a significant trade relationship built up over the years. But the most significant fact is that major nuclear installations in both countries are of Canadian origin and depend to some extent on Canadian technology. Although the importance of this factor may be diminishing over time, there are still many members of the nuclear establishment in both countries who were trained in Canada.

At the end of 1995 there were rumours, perhaps stimulated by the French tests, that both Pakistan and India might conduct nuclear tests with or without outside help, to improve their technology and to gain strategic or domestic political advantage. Again I argue that, on balance, there are grounds for hoping that neither will do so. The experience of the past thirty years shows that Canada can exercise very little influence on the nuclear weapons policy of either country. In the spring of 1996 both sides were issuing press statements reflecting "security in ambiguity" when questioned about their nuclear weapons programs. It has even been suggested that "non-weaponized deterrence" may be the best hope for South Asia. The Indian authorities went ahead with their 1974 test even though they knew it would mean the end of relations with Canada in this field. Pakistan has proceeded with its nuclear explosion program independent of Canadian views. As with most sovereign governments, what are deemed to be essential national security priorities override other domestic or international political or economic influences.

There is an enormous literature on nuclear policies in South Asia and I conclude this section of the present essay by drawing attention to an outstanding British author, H.R.F. Keating, who has created a Bombay detective. One of the volumes in the series is entitled, *Inspector Ghote Caught in Meshes*. Although Mr. Keating provides the usual disclaimer at the beginning of his novel, it is in fact the only major work of fiction I have read that is related to Indian nuclear policies. It is critical.

OTTAWA AND CHINA AND KOREA

In 1983, I was asked to return to Ottawa to be Director General of the Bureau for East Asia. This was part of a substantial reorganization of the Department of External Affairs. I wound up with responsibility for the People's Republic of China (PRC), Korea, Hong Kong, Taiwan and Indochina.

PRC representatives had made it clear before 1983 that they did not wish to be involved in a multiplicity of nuclear technologies. The Chinese had virtually decided against CANDU in favour of an American-type system. We did not have, therefore, an ongoing dialogue with the Chinese about safeguards since it seemed unlikely that there would be any Canadian-PRC nuclear facilities to safeguard. We recognized China's position as a nuclear weapons state. The Chinese, of course, were very much concerned with short- and long-term energy issues and in my bureau we came to the conclusion that our priority efforts should be directed towards collaboration with the PRC in the hydro and thermal power sectors. Of course this involved us in studies which the Chinese were undertaking—and in which we participated—on the economics of the different energy sources. We were able to assist the Chinese authorities in developing long-range energy plans which involved assessments of the comparative advantages of nuclear power versus hydro, oil, coal and other possible energy sources. When we got an opportunity, we reminded the Chinese in Beijing and out of Hong Kong, that the CANDU technology was the safest and the most economical. We maintained established Canadian positions against the conduct of nuclear tests and against the proliferation of nuclear weapons technology.

Many retired officials rejoiced when it appeared that Canada might supply CANDU reactors to the PRC, following the visit of the Canadian Prime Minister and the provincial premiers in the fall of 1994 and Chinese visits to Canada in 1995. Any contracts signed will be the result of efforts over the years to keep Canadian technology competitive and will require a lot of detailed negotiation. No one will be able to say our role in 1983-85 was "decisive" because, as in all foreign policy issues, the process before and after any particular meeting or series of meetings requires continuous effort by professional staff.

It was a completely different situation with respect to Korea. Generations of Canadian foreign service officers have worked to develop Canadian-Korean cooperation in the nuclear field. The Republic of Korea was prepared to enter into the appropriate safeguard agreements with Canada and to adopt a position on the non-proliferation treaty which we welcomed. As a result it was feasible to make nuclear sales to Korea and by 1983 Canada already had an ongoing program and a functioning nuclear reactor in Korea. In cooperation with AECL and the Canadian companies involved, we took every opportunity of making sure that the very real competitive advantages we had in the field of nuclear technology were emphasized to the Korean authorities. We were greatly helped by the fact that the Canadian reactor performed very well and that on any comparative basis Canadian CANDU technology was functioning successfully and economically around the world. Our principal competition, of course, was from the United States, and in Korea the United States had very great advantages over Canada. It was true that Canadians had made a major contribution in the Korean war and that Canada was an important market for the Korean economy as it rapidly developed. But the United States enjoyed a very much greater military, economic and political relationship with Korea than did Canada and was therefore in a strong position to ensure that its nuclear technology got as favourable consideration as possible. However, Korea is greatly dependent on imported fossil fuels since it had very limited domestic fuel sources of any kind. Nuclear energy therefore receives the highest possible priority and Canada has been and remains a natural partner in the face of the severest competition.

Hong Kong, of itself, posed no nuclear policy problems, but for any major undertaking in southern China there was always some Hong Kong connection. Therefore, when consideration was being given to the development of nuclear power plants in southern China, questions would arise in Hong Kong which might offer possibilities for Canada. We did our best to keep these in play. By the time I left the East Asia Bureau in 1985, the Chinese were beginning to think about deviating from their rigid commitment to one form of nuclear technology. This process was assisted by the fact that for some of the provinces in southern China, there was a move towards independent decision making on power projects. Although this independence was most obvious in the thermal, hydro and coal-fired energy projects, there was the beginning of some movement in the nuclear area.

Our relations with Taiwan did raise some nuclear problems. There was a gradual change over 1983-85, as direct contacts between Taiwan and the PRC began to develop, some of them through Hong Kong. This situation made more mature relationships possible between Canada and Taiwan, and it was eventually possible for the Canadian Chamber of Commerce to open an office in Taiwan for the promotion of bilateral Canadian-Taiwanese business activity. In this period there was a great deal of diplomatic activity by the Taiwanese authorities, who operated commercial offices in Canada and who attempted to formalize Canadian-Taiwanese relations in any way they could. We faced a continuing series of incidents of this kind which I believe we managed to handle without damaging our national interests in relations with the People's Republic of China.

Our possibility which appeared attractive to some elements in Canadian political life was the sale of a nuclear reactor to Taiwan. At various times the Taiwanese authorities made known their interest in the expenditure of large amounts of money for the acquisition of nuclear energy technology from Canada. There was no question of this kind of assistance to Taiwan without official Canadian government approval. There could be no approval for programs involving a country which we did not formally recognize and which might become involved in some form of hostilities with the PRC, a country which Canada did recognize and with which we had important relations on many fronts.

There was one notable occasion in Toronto when I came under very high level pressure to support a change in Canadian policy on nuclear sales to Taiwan. No doubt the event had been carefully planned in advance but it came as a complete surprise to me to be confronted at a private dinner party by experienced Canadians who claimed the very best of connections. I was pressured to indicate that some change in Canadian policy might be possible which would allow the sale of a nuclear reactor to Taiwan. It was clearly suggested that failure to cooperate could have adverse consequences for my public service career. I did not find it very difficult to describe the nature and depth of the non-partisan Canadian commitment to nuclear non-proliferation, our insistence on safeguards, and the fact that there could be no question of the Canadian government officially supporting any program to assist Taiwan in developing even a potential nuclear weapons capability. The exchange was somewhat heated, which prevented me from enjoying an otherwise pleasant social event. I never received any indication that it had any effect upon my usefulness within the Canadian foreign service.

BACK TO INTELLIGENCE, SECURITY AND TERRORISM

At the end of my time in the East Asia Bureau, I was asked to return once again to the intelligence and security area. I was responsible in 1986-87 for security issues in Canada and abroad which involved foreign policy factors. My responsibilities included running the Ops Centre, which was activated in time of any major international emergency, and our representation on the Summit Seven terrorism committee. This assignment took me to Washington, London, Bonn and Tokyo for discussion of all aspects of the response to terrorist threats. We were in close touch with Paris and Rome.

One of the elements that we considered was the possibility of some form of international terrorism involving nuclear weapons. Fortunately no such incident arose, but I can well imagine the difficulties those who are now responsible in this area may be facing as a result of the widespread distribution of fissionable materials and nuclear weapons expertise after the break up of the USSR.

The experience gained in discussing this subject with our friends and allies reaffirmed Canada's interest in strengthening the non-proliferation treaty and any existing mechanisms for inhibiting the sale of nuclear weapons equipment and technology to states supportive of terrorism. It is my belief that not only were we comparatively successful in preventing foreign governments from illegally obtaining nuclear technology from Canada, but we also contributed significantly to similar efforts at the international level.

WHAT DID WE ACHIEVE?

It is hard to separate the function of a head of mission abroad from the role of the officers in senior positions in Ottawa, I like to think that when I was Director General of various units in Ottawa I worked easily with heads of mission abroad. Indeed, one of the functions of a director general of a geographic bureau, such as that for East Asia, was to prepare the draft annual ratings of heads of mission abroad. One of my guiding principles was that, at the head of mission level, we were expected to represent the Canadian national interest in the broad sense. I always resented any suggestion that I represented, either in Ottawa or abroad, the Department of External Affairs. I argued that I felt equally responsible to the Canadian International Development Agency, the Canadian immigration authorities, the Canadian commercial authorities (however they were organized federally, provincially and even municipally), the RCMP, CSIS, and indeed any Canadian government entity functioning overseas. When you are head of mission you represent the Canadian government as a whole, as surely as Canadian federal authorities in Ottawa represent the country as a whole. The occupant of such a position is also well aware that this responsibility is to the government of the day, however its authority over him or her is exercised.

When clergy are retired on pension by a church they must ask themselves in what way their work has made a difference over the years. They may be able to point to some parish where attendance has increased and the physical building has been enhanced. They may be able to recall individuals whose lives they have been able to influence, just as a head of mission can recall individual policy problems or projects on which some personal influence could be detected. The fact is, however, that like a clergyman, a head of mission can only have the most general idea of whether his contribution was conducive to an improved presentation of the Canadian national interest.

SOME OPERATIVE FACTORS

One of the elements involved is the extent to which the government of the day in Ottawa, and the Department of Foreign Affairs in particular, considers that the position of head of mission is important and therefore how much the government and the Department relies on and seeks his or her advice. I have known situations in Ottawa when it has been decided not to tell the Canadian head of mission of some major development because that individual could be expected to make an unhelpful contribution by return telegram. There also have been periods in which the Department of Foreign Affairs has had its influence and authority reduced, so that heads of mission have not been able to play a significant role. In one period the deputy minister of Foreign Affairs was asked why missions abroad were not receiving any instructions on how to deal with national unity questions. The reply then, was that these questions were so difficult in the Canadian content that it seemed impossible to provide guidance to Canadian representatives abroad. In this situation, the head of mission has two choices: the first and most obvious is to say nothing and avoid the subject entirely; the second is to consider what positions might be taken on the basis of as careful reading as possible of Canadian government policy and then, if absolutely necessary, make some carefully structured statement. In recent years there have been periods when the political leadership and the public service have not functioned together effectively. The consequences have been harmful on all fronts and especially for heads of mission, whose relevance in such an atmosphere is greatly reduced. There must be a high degree of consultation, through every channel of communication available from Ottawa to posts abroad, to enable the head of mission to deal with crucial Canadian public issues.

One can argue that foreign policy does not exist. It could be said to consist of separate national descisions taken in an ad hoc way in an unpredictable environment. A head of mission, or any foreign service officer viewed from this standpoint, administers short-term relationships. However, as this essay illustrates, there are some continuing themes and there is a need to pursue these at home and abroad by whatever means are possible. A head of mission cannot be sure what, if anything, is achieved in support of national interests which are often very general in character, but he or she cannot fail to take whatever action is possible.

NOTES

H.R.F. Keating, *Inspector Ghote Caught in Meshes* (Chicago: Academy Chicago Publishers, 1985, reprint).

John G. Hadwen joined External Affairs in 1950. Between 1952 and 1964 he served in Ottawa and abroad in Pakistan, New York and Oslo. He was Special Assistant to the Secretary of State for External Affairs and to the Prime Minister from 1964-67. He became High Commissioner to Malaysia and Singapore in 1967, then Ambassador to Burma until 1971; from 1972-74 he was Ambassador to Pakistan and Afghanistan. Mr. Hadwen served in Ottawa between 1974-79, and was High Commissioner to India and Ambassador to Nepal until 1983. He became Director General of the East Asia Bureau in 1983, and Director General of Security Services in 1985. He is co-author of *How United Nations Decisions are Made.*

II

CRISIS MANAGEMENT IN NATO: THE POLISH CRISIS: 1980-1981

JOHN G.H. HALSTEAD

IN THE FALL OF 1980, when I left Bonn for Brussels to take up my new post as Permanent Representative and Ambassador of Canada to the North Atlantic Council, the Alliance was in a defensive and introspective mood, still licking its wounds in the aftermath of the Soviet invasion of Afghanistan. That action, the first occasion since 1945 on which Soviet forces had been deployed in combat outside the territory of the Soviet Union or the Warsaw Pact, had caught NATO by surprise.

The Alliance had no contingency plans to deal with such "out of area" situations, which did not directly engage the obligations of the allies under Article 5 or 6 of the North Atlantic Treaty. Moreover, there was no immediate consensus among the NATO members about the implications of the Soviet invasion for their security. Some regarded it as an isolated event limited to Soviet interests in a country Moscow had for some time considered to be in the Soviet sphere of influence. Others interpreted it as a potential threat—possibly a preparatory move—to attack Western oil supplies in the Persian Gulf. All condemned the Soviet invasion as a reprehensible use of force against a sovereign state, but no one was sure what could effectively be done about it.

The confusion became increasingly evident as individual NATO members took unilateral actions of varying degrees of severity, in an effort to respond to public pressure to "do something," rather than concentrating on working out a coordinated Alliance response. The resulting disarray reached a climax when the U.S. government issued a ban on participation in the Moscow Olympic Games, without ascertaining first whether its allies would follow suit or even whether its own ban was legally enforceable in the United States. Eventually the Alliance pulled itself together and agreed to apply a certain number of diplomatic and economic sanctions against the Soviet Union to punish it for its invasion of Afghanistan. These measures included an embargo on wheat shipments to the Soviet

Union, which Canada joined reluctantly at the price of a significant drop in its traditional wheat exports.

As everyone knows, those sanctions did not persuade the Soviets to withdraw from Afghanistan. Withdrawal occurred only when the guerilla war began to cost the Soviet Union more than it was worth to Soviet interests. On the other hand, NATO drew two important lessons from that experience. One was that guidelines were needed to provide a policy framework within which the members of the Alliance, and the Alliance itself, could deal with "out of area" crises. The other was that the best form of crisis management was contingency planning, and that for this purpose adequate strategic warning was essential. It was not long before NATO had occasion to put these conclusions to the test.

In July, 1980 the Polish government, beset by social unrest and strikes attributable to a prolonged deterioration of the economic situation, decided to legalize Solidarity, the increasingly popular trade union movement which hitherto had existed outside the officially sanctioned trade unions. It was the Polish government's hope that, by pursuing a dialogue with Solidarity and with the Catholic Church in Poland, which sympathised with Solidarity, it could arrest the decline in its own support and enlist the cooperation of the two most influential institutions in Poland in restoring domestic peace. The dialogue did not, however, stop Solidarity and the Church from pressing their demands for economic reform, and the Polish government was pushed into making further concessions. This in turn set alarm bells ringing in the Kremlin, from whence warnings were sent to Warsaw that the communist regime would have to crack down soon if it was to retrain control of the situation.

To back up their warnings the Soviet leaders organized Warsaw Pact manoeuvres around the periphery of Poland in the fall of 1980. With the aid of intelligence supplied from national sources the NATO military authorities monitored the situation closely and keep the North Atlantic Council briefed. In accordance with standard procedure, the Chairman of the Military Committee reported to the Council at its weekly meetings what the risk assessment of the NATO military authorities was, and the Council factored in the political and economic intelligence available from national capitals to arrive, as far as possible, at a shared assessment of the likely course of events.

The consensus in the Council at that time was that the Warsaw Pact manoeuvres were intended as a warning to the Polish leadership rather than as a preparation for immediate armed intervention. The message was clear, however: the Polish Communist Party had to pull itself together and act firmly to regain control of the situation; if it did not or could not, the Soviets would do it for them. Nevertheless the situation worsened during the winter. Strikes continued, production fell and people began to want for basic necessities. The Polish authorities tried first to buy off Solidarity and the Church, and then to scare them into submission by acts of intimidation, but neither tactic was successful. Indeed, Solidarity's demands, backed by the Church, expanded more and more from the strictly economic into the political field. Meanwhile repeated shuffles of the Polish government failed to restore its authority or to produce a solution to the country's ills, which were of course due to the central planning system, a keystone of the regime's Marxist-Leninist orthodoxy.

By the spring of 1981 the patience of the rulers in the Kremlin was wearing thin and they authorized a new round of manoeuvres on Poland's borders, more prolonged and massive than before. In Brussels we watched with mounting concern as one after another of the traditional thresholds for ideological tolerance were passed without triggering either a crackdown by the Polish authorities or a military intervention by the Soviet Union. It seemed as though Warsaw was prepared to make hitherto unprecedented concessions, even at the expense of the regime's basic claim to ideological legitimacy, and that Moscow, while exerting unrelenting pressure on Warsaw, was reluctant to undertake yet another invasion of a Warsaw Pact ally unless there was no alternative way of preventing the overthrow of that ally's communist regime.

About this time the North Atlantic Council began unobtrusively to hold restricted meetings, outside its weekly Wednesday morning sessions, for the purpose of preparing contingency plans to deal with the eventuality of a Soviet armed intervention. The meetings were chaired by the NATO Secretary General, attendance was limited for each member to the Ambassador and one note-taker, and the substance of the discussions was treated with great secrecy. The purpose was to maintain an up-to-date assessment of the situation in Poland and the risk of Soviet intervention (called the "worst case scenario") and to draw up plans, both to deter such intervention and, if it came to that, to manage the crisis. Like my colleagues, I kept my government informed of the discussions as a matter of course, and sought instructions on specific points where I felt in need of guidance, but in general I was left a good deal of discretion, because it was understood that the discussions were exploratory and without commitment at that stage.

Early on in these consultations it was agreed that the contingency plans we were considering should be drawn up within an explicit framework of Western policy. That framework assumed the peaceful and constructive evolution of East-West relations on the basis of a strict observance of the Helsinki Final Act, including respect for national sovereignty and independence and non-interference in the internal affairs of any state, regardless of its political orientation. In other words, we explicitly rejected the Brezhnev doctrine and challenged both Poland and the Soviet Union to recognize or reject the supremacy of the principles to which they had subscribed at the summit meeting of the Conference on Security and Cooperation (CSCE) in Helsinki in August 1975.

Within this policy framework we defined Western objectives in both positive and negative terms. Our positive objective was to encourage the situation in Poland to develop in an orderly way and in accord with the legitimate wishes of the Polish people for a better standard of living, and for more freedom and pluralism. The negative objective was to deter overt Soviet intervention in Poland, and thus to avert the "worst case scenario," which was likely not only to be bloody for the Poles but also to let loose uncontrollable repercussions on East-West relations.

Among the measures considered by NATO as means of pursuing the positive objective were: economic aid and credits, food aid, and support for Solidarity. Our preference was for a combination of official and private agencies (such as commercial banks) to provide economic aid and credits. The same applied to food aid, but with an even greater emphasis on private agencies in the West in contact with private agencies in Poland, in order to ensure that the food reached the people who needed it. As for help to Solidarity, we considered that this should be an entirely private and unofficial undertaking by trade unions in the West, in order to avoid any charge that Western governments were interfering in Poland's internal affairs.

The measures intended to serve the negative objective were of two kinds: those deterrent measures to be taken before a possible Soviet invasion; and those intended to exact a price if a Soviet invasion did in fact take place. The deterrent measures we considered were of both a specific and a general nature. We discussed whether to recommend that NATO should issue a warning that it would do this if the Soviet Union did that, or whether, alternatively, NATO's warning should be in general terms. It was decided that we would recommend the latter, on the grounds that we should not help the Soviet Union to calculate too precisely the costs of an invasion. The formula we adopted was that such action "would have incalculable consequences for détente." This recommendation was adopted by our governments, and in due course concerted and coordinated diplomatic *démarches* were made to the Ministry of Foreign Affairs in Moscow and to the Soviet embassies in the capitals of NATO member states.

We also discussed possible military measures by NATO. Our purpose was not, of course, to intervene directly against a Soviet invasion of Poland, which was out of the question, but rather to signal to Moscow that NATO was not unmindful of the potential threat to the NATO area posed by the massive mobilization of Warsaw Pact forces on the eastern marches. There was always the outside possibility, however remote, that the Warsaw Pact manoeuvres around Poland could be a cover for an effort to grab NATO territory as a hostage. There was also the decidedly less remote possibility that a serious continuing deterioration of the situation within Poland, or an actual invasion of Poland by the Warsaw Pact, could trigger a massive exodus of Poles across the Baltic Sea in search of safe haven in the West. If this happened, Warsaw Pact forces in hot pursuit could well enter NATO territorial waters or otherwise come up against NATO forces.

With these considerations in mind we recommended two measures which were adopted by the Alliance. The first was quietly to raise the alert status of forces under the command of the Supreme Allied Commander Europe (SACEUR) by one notch. No effort was made to conceal this measure but it was done unobtrusively and without any movement of troops that could possibly be interpreted as aggressive. In this way NATO, without being provocative, sent a clear signal to Moscow that the allies were not asleep at the switch. The second measure was to deploy the Standing Naval Force Atlantic (STANAVFORLANT), consisting of destroyers and frigates assigned to the Supreme Allied Commander Atlantic (SACLANT) by six NATO member countries, including Canada, to the Western Baltic on a "routine" training exercise. Again, the intention was to signal to the other side NATO's will to defend its territory and its interests, while avoiding any suggestion of offensive action.

As for action to be taken *after* a Soviet or Warsaw Pact invasion of Poland, if it took place, we examined only political and economic measures, having readily concluded that military measures were out of the question. NATO had never offered Poland a security guarantee, and was in no position to do so, given the balance of forces in Europe and the real danger that a military confrontation over Poland could well lead to general war and a nuclear exchange. Consequently we limited ourselves to drawing up a "shopping list" of non-military sanctions that might be applied, if NATO members so agreed, to exact a price after the fact for an armed intervention in Poland.

The political measures we examined were of both a bilateral and a multilateral nature. The former included strong statements of condemnation, limitations on Soviet (and possibly Polish) diplomatic and press representatives in allied countries, and cancellation of cultural and sports exchanges. The breaking off of diplomatic relations was considered, as an extreme measure, but was not recommended, since we judged it important to retain our respective embassies in Moscow (and Warsaw) as listening posts and vehicles of communication. Instead we recommended that ambassadors be recalled "for consultations" (as diplomatic usage has it) to mark the allies' displeasure.

Similar measures were considered as multilateral initiatives: statements and resolutions of condemnation in such forums as the UN, the CSCE Follow-up Meeting in Madrid, and the arms control talks (the Mutual and Balanced Force Reduction [MBFR] talks in Vienna and the Strategic Arms Limitation Talks [SALT] in Geneva). The question arose of whether to terminate those negotiations or only to suspend them, and our recommendation was that they should be suspended. Our reasoning was that such meetings and negotiations were as much in the interest of the West as in that of the Soviet Union, and that we would be cutting off our nose to spite our face if we deprived ourselves permanently of those means to promote Western objectives.

We also looked at a wide range of possible economic sanctions, including the boycotting of exports and/or imports, the suspension of economic and food aid to Poland and of grain shipments to the Soviet Union, and the suspension or reduction of scientific exchanges. It soon became apparent, however, that there were considerable differences of view among the allies about the feasibility and the desirability of various measures and about the possible impact on their respective economies. This led into an interesting discussion of the conditions that needed to be satisfied in order for sanctions to have a reasonable chance of success. Four such conditions were identified. First, the sanctions must hurt the enemy more than they hurt the NATO members—an obvious point, perhaps, but not one that had always been considered in the past. Second, the sanctions must be applied by all NATO members without exception, and beyond that, by all other countries that were major exporters or importers of the goods in question. Otherwise the leakage would nullify the effect of the sanctions. Third, the sanctions should be cleared, if at all possible, with the international agencies having responsibilities in the field concerned. Finally, the sanctions should be applied in such a way as to impose an equitable burden on all the allies, and by the same token to avoid imposing a disproportionate burden on one or two allies. Again, an obvious requirement but not one that had always been respected.

By far the most controversial measure discussed in the North Atlantic Council was the U.S. proposal that the Soviet gas pipeline project be cancelled. This was a project to construct pipelines into Western Europe, mainly West Germany, to supply Soviet natural gas under contracts that envisaged the construction being paid for by the natural gas exports. The Americans had been unhappy about this deal from the beginning because they saw it as bringing disproportionate benefits to the Soviet Union. They argued that such an arrangement would make the Western Europeans dependent on Soviet gas supplies, and hence vulnerable to Soviet pressure. Their main concern was probably the hard currency it would bring the Soviet Union. The Europeans argued that the proportion of their energy requirements furnished by the Soviet Union would never reach a point that would make them vulnerable to Soviet pressure; on the contrary, this arrangement would make the Soviet Union more dependent on economic links with the West. Moreover, the Europeans claimed that cancellation of this project would fail to meet the fourth requirement mentioned above, since it would impose a disproportionate burden on a few allies.

In spite of European resistance the Americans continued to press for cancellation of the pipeline project, and it was only months later that they came to recognize that the Europeans were not going to change their minds and that the continuing argument was only producing rancour and division within the Alliance. Canada was not directly affected either way by the gas pipeline project, and therefore refrained from taking sides. We did, however, let our allies know of our dismay about the disagreement and helped to persuade the United States not to insist on inclusion of their proposal in the "shopping list" of possible measures to be recommended to ministers. Later, when the Polish crisis had died down somewhat, Mark MacGuigan, who was at the time Secretary of State for External Affairs, invited the NATO foreign ministers to meet informally at a retreat in the Laurentians, where the relaxed atmosphere facilitated the search for a face-saving formula that would permit burying the hatchet.

It has been noted that the contingency planning which the North Atlantic Council engaged in, and the "shopping list" of measures it prepared, were designed to deal with the "worst case" scenario. We recognized at the time that there were a number of "grey area" scenarios that were just as plausible, but we decided not to attempt to prepare for each of them separately, because it was not feasible to deal with such a variety of permutations and combinations. In any case, it was our reasoning that in the event the *dénouement* of the crisis fell short of the "worst case" scenario, as we hoped it would, the NATO foreign ministers could pick and choose among the measures recommended in the manner they thought most appropriate to the circumstances.

In the event the Soviet Union did not intervene militarily in Poland, but General Wojciech Jaruzelski, who had taken over the reins of government, declared martial law just after Christmas 1981, probably in a calculated effort to avoid a worse disaster. With the imposition of martial law the regime broke off the dialogue with Solidarity and the Church, and embarked on a far-reaching round-up of Solidarity members and other dissidents. The reaction in the West was immediate, strong and emotional. Public opinion was deeply affected; spontaneous demonstrations broke out in many Western European and North American cities, and trade unions and other organizations called on their governments to do something. An emergency meeting of NATO foreign ministers was convened in mid-January 1982 to consider what action should be taken. They had before them the contingency plan prepared over the previous months by the NATO ambassadors, in consultation with their governments; the allies were therefore in a better position to deal with this crisis than they had been when Soviet forces had invaded Afghanistan two years before.

On the other hand, there were three factors which complicated the foreign ministers' task on this occasion. The first, and most obvious, was that the crisis was not the "worst case" scenario that the contingency plan had been prepared for, but a "grey area" scenario involving a crackdown by the Polish regime itself, without overt Soviet intervention. It was useful to have a list of practical measures ready for rapid implementation, but for the reasons I have already explained it was not specifically designed for the case at hand. In particular it did not deal with the question, which was later to give rise to so much debate, of the degree of Soviet involvement in the Polish government's crackdown.

The second complicating factor, related to the first, was that there were considerable and long-standing differences among the allies about the strategy for dealing with the Soviet Union. Some of the allies, including notably the United States, favoured a hard line designed to force the Soviet Union to back down whenever western interests were affected. Others, including France and Germany, preferred a line which today would probably be called "constructive engagement"—involving the Soviets in a dialogue designed to convince them that détente could bring more benefits to both sides than confrontation. Canada was firmly on the side of dialogue and détente, but was also in favour (as had been demonstrated repeatedly during the CSCE negotiations) of insisting on acceptable norms of conduct, and condemning behaviour that clearly contravened them. The trouble with the case at hand was that the hard-liners regarded Soviet support of repressive measures in Poland as unacceptable behaviour, whereas others including Canada wanted to keep the focus on the Polish regime's responsibility for its own actions, and to play down the Soviet role as long as the Soviet Union did not intervene militarily in Poland. If the West's reaction in the present case was to be as harsh as if the Soviet Union had invaded Poland, then there would be little leverage left for persuading the Soviet Union that détente was better than confrontation.

The third complicating factor was that some NATO members had already announced or taken unilateral measures to respond to the imposition of martial law in Poland. This was understandable, given the strong feelings that had been generated in many NATO countries and the domestic pressure to do something. As usual, pressures of this kind were particularly strong in Washington, where they were reinforced by the U.S. role of leadership of the free world and by the strongly ideological bent of the Reagan administration. Understandable it was, but helpful it was not. For it circumscribed the NATO consultative process and limited the freedom of choice of the NATO foreign ministers when they came together in emergency session. Fortunately it did not lead to any serious disarray this time, as we shall see.

As it turned out, there was also a further complication for me personally, due not to any political factors but to the weather. My foreign minister, Mark MacGuigan, was due to arrive in Brussels early on the morning of the emergency meeting. A winter storm intervened, however, and his aircraft was diverted to Amsterdam. From there he had to come on by train, which got him to Brussels just as the meeting was ending. I therefore had the unexpected honour and responsibility of representing Canada in circumstances of considerable uncertainty. I did not know when my foreign minister would arrive, and I was without detailed guidance from Headquarters, because the minister was bringing the government's instructions with him, based on last-minute consultations in Ottawa. So I found myself, as the meeting began at the familiar Council table under the chairmanship of the Secretary General, Joseph Luns, in the august company of such well-known figures as Secretary of State George Shultz, Foreign Secretary Lord Carrington and Foreign Minister Hans-Dietrich Genscher.

It soon became apparent that the principal allies had, not surprisingly, been consulting among themselves prior to the meeting, and that, whatever their differences, they were agreed on the need to act swiftly and in a united way. They knew that public opinion in the West demanded no less and they were driven by the psychological pressure of the unfortunate Afghanistan precedent. So these considerations took the lead over practical questions about the real possibilities of influencing the situation in Poland or the effectiveness of sanctions. While the foreign ministers made use of the "shopping list" prepared by the NATO ambassadors, the discussion focused mainly on two questions: the extent of Soviet involvement in the imposition of martial law in Poland; and the related question of whether sanctions should be applied to Poland only or to the Soviet Union as well.

It was generally assumed that Jaruzelski had acted with the knowledge and approval of Moscow, since it was inconceivable that he would do otherwise. That still left open the question as to whether he had acted on his own initiative or as an agent of the Soviet Union. Moreover, if sanctions were to be applied to Poland, it was not easy to see how to maximize their effect on the Polish regime and to minimize the harm done to the Polish people. If sanctions were to be applied to the Soviet Union as well, how could a sufficient deterrent be maintained against the ultimate disaster, a Soviet invasion of Poland? Although lacking precise instructions, I intervened briefly to express a preference for focusing on the Polish regime as the party that had acted in blatant disregard of the principles and norms of the Helsinki Final Act, and for pegging Western sanctions to explicit objectives. However, I indicated that I would not block consensus if a majority of the Council was prepared to condemn both Poland and the Soviet Union.

In the event, the foreign ministers were able to conclude their deliberations before the end of the afternoon and the declaration they adopted was a compromise. It satisfied the United States by including a strong condemnation of both Poland and the Soviet Union, and by recommending sanctions against both of them. At the same time it identified specific objectives—the lifting of martial law, the release of detainees and the resumption of the Polish government's dialogue with Solidarity and the Church—as conditions for lifting the sanctions against Poland. Fortunately, this compromise was also acceptable to Mr. MacGuigan when he arrived, and he confirmed Canada's support for the foreign ministers' declaration, in spite of some reservations on the part of Prime Minister Trudeau about sanctions against the Soviet Union. Mr. Trudeau felt the Russians had merely exercised their influence as a great power within their sphere of influence. Naturally, the press and the opposition in Canada tried to make what they could out of this difference between the Prime Minister and his foreign minister.

In retrospect I think this was one of the more successful efforts at crisis management by NATO. It involved proactive contingency planning rather than reactive emergency "*ad hockery.*" With more than adequate strategic warning time the Alliance was able to go systematically through the three classical steps of contingency planning: evaluating the situation; setting objectives; and fitting means to ends. While the *dénouement* of the Polish crisis could not be foreseen precisely, the planning process produced sufficient elements of a response to enable NATO governments to take the necessary decisions with dispatch and with a high degree of consensus. It gave the Alliance a new self-confidence and a new sense of solidarity (no pun intended), which helped NATO survive the Intermediate-range Nuclear Force (INF) crisis later and ultimately to win the contest of wills with the Soviet Union.

Inevitably, the decisions of 1981 were aimed as much at public opinion in East and West as they were at the Polish and Soviet governments. Inevitably, they probably had only a limited influence on the course of events in Poland and the Soviet Union in the short run. Indeed, it seemed at the time that the Russians were perfecting their technique for suppressing national revolts in their empire: in 1956, there had been bloodshed in Hungary; in 1968 Czechoslovakia had been cowed with overwhelming force; in 1980 the Poles had been manoeuvred into an act of self-suppression. Yet with the benefit of hindsight it can be argued that in the longer run the Polish crisis added a nail or two to the coffin being prepared for the already ailing communist system in Eastern Europe. That this probability was not fully recognized at the time may help explain why almost everyone in the West was taken by surprise by the speed of the final collapse of the Soviet empire.

John G.H. Halstead joined External Affairs in 1946. He served abroad in London, Tokyo and the UN offices in New York and Paris. In Ottawa he was Assistant Undersecretary and Deputy Undersecretary of State for External Affairs. Mr. Halstead served as Ambassador to the Federal Republic of Germany and then Ambassador to NATO. He is the author of numerous monographs on international affairs and has lectured extensively at universities in Canada and the U.S. He was recently awarded the Order of Canada.

12

MOSCOW, 1980-1983: THE SECOND COLD WAR

GEOFFREY A.H. PEARSON

WHEN I PRESENTED MY CREDENTIALS as Canadian Ambassador to the USSR in October, 1980, there was a political as well as a physical chill in the air. Ten months earlier Soviet troops had entered Afghanistan, leading President Carter to reflect that the détente he had worked to solidify with the signing of the second Strategic Arms Limitation Treaty was a false hope. The West had imposed sanctions, including embargoes on trade and other exchanges, and a partial boycott of the Olympic games held that summer in Moscow. The situation in Poland was beginning to look like a second obstacle to the improvement of East-West relations. The new trade union there, Solidarity, was moving towards open conflict with the Polish government, bringing charges in Moscow of Western interference in Polish affairs.

Canada had followed the American lead in imposing sanctions, and I was not in a position to offer any words of encouragement when I saw Vice-President Kuznetsov that day in the Kremlin. Yet he was cordial enough, telling me how he had worked as a young man in Detroit in the 1920s, making cars for Mr. Ford, and thus knew that the American people did not always share the views of their leaders (he must have been surprised by the election of Ronald Reagan a month later). It was to be a precursor of things to come—a courteous but unyielding defence of the Marxist-Leninist view that some day the peoples of the world would rally to the vision of a classless society, whatever the nature of current events.

An account of Canadian diplomacy in the USSR at the time must begin therefore with the advent of the second Cold War. This account ends with some personal reflections on diplomatic life in a cold climate, albeit often warmed by individual kindness and stimulated by the astonishing diversity of the "evil empire."

THE CLIMATE OF EAST-WEST RELATIONS

The election of President Reagan in November, 1980, was hardly calculated to ease the tensions of the previous year, nor did it, although the Soviets at first hoped for the best. They had had no reason to regret the defeat of President Carter, for it was he who had declared the Persian Gulf a "vital interest" of the U.S. and greatly increased defence spending. Before leaving office he was also to warn Brezhnev against military intervention in Poland, an option which I, for one, thought to be quite improbable, given the fact that the Poles would resist and that the resulting imbroglio would bring closer the nightmare of a third world war.

I was also inclined to dispute the claim made in Washington, and sometimes in Ottawa, that Soviet policy was motivated by aggressive designs on the Persian Gulf and its oil resources, a claim used to justify a massive American build-up. In this view, détente was indivisible and arms control futile.

My own views were qualified but not essentially changed after my arrival in Moscow. I wrote to my predecessor, Robert Ford, in December, 1980:

I came here with a sense of the difficulty of "communicating" anything of value to Soviet officials, given the quite different political assumptions and thus language in which to describe values and interests (except for material values such as numbers of missiles or bushels of wheat) ... the images and assumptions in the West of and about this country are so powerful and often so distorted that reason flies out the window. But still, the impression remains that it is next to impossible for any Soviet official (no doubt the ordinary person has their private thoughts) to make an objective appraisal of any social phenomenon whatsoever. This myopia, in combination with great military power, is, to say the least, alarming. Nor does this conclusion have anything to do with Western assumptions about Soviet designs for global revolution or domination, which I think are mostly wrong. Rather it follows from the apparent impossibility of challenging the doctrine that "socialism" and therefore the CPSU are beyond dispute.... Evil resides not in humanity, but in non-socialist systems. I knew all this in a way, but daily doses of *Pravda* tend to be bitter medicine.

East-West relations continued to deteriorate in 1981-82. The Polish crisis led to the imposition of martial law in December, 1981, and thus to a strengthening of Western sanctions; the conflict in Afghanistan intensified;

and arms control negotiations remained at an impasse. Misperceptions abounded on both sides. Soviet leaders blamed Western "interference" for their troubles in Afghanistan and for unrest in Poland; they defended their support for "national liberation movements" in the Third World as a kind of social Darwinism ("building a new socialist world"); and they claimed that U.S. "ruling circles" were seeking military superiority, not equality. U.S. leaders, on the other hand, perceived a Soviet attempt to expand Soviet power through terrorism and intimidation, while blocking political change in Eastern Europe. The deployment of medium-range missiles became an issue for both sides.

After a year in Moscow I concluded that a combination of Marxist-Leninist dogma about the "end of history" and traditional Russian patriotism served to satisfy members of the Party that the Soviet path to the future would prove to be correct (a view certainly not shared by most of the rest of the population). But I was also convinced that Brezhnev and his advisers wished to avoid confrontation, and were surprised by Western reactions to their threat or use of force in situations they regarded as endangering Soviet security (compare U.S. reactions to the growth of revolutionary movements in Central America and the Caribbean). They appeared not to understand, however, that the very existence of the Soviet Union, not to speak of its ideology, was bound to inspire distrust amongst its many neighbours, including those whose leaders were pledged to defend their "socialist gains."

The accession to power of Yuri Andropov in November, 1982, admitted a slight ray of hope into this gathering darkness. Since he was the former head of the KGB, it was said by some, whom I had reason to believe knew the facts, that he would bring a more sophisticated approach to Soviet politics, including foreign relations. But apart from encouraging a diplomatic solution to the Afghan War, there was no softening of Soviet foreign policy. On the contrary, the stalemate on arms control seemed to grow worse. President Reagan spoke of "an evil empire." Nevertheless, Andropov gave priority to domestic reform, long neglected under Brezhnev, and despite his failing health, hope that he would bring about real change remained. It was the destruction of the Korean Airlines plane, on August 31, 1983 by a Soviet fighter that put an end to hopes for the relaxation of tension during my time in Moscow.

This bizarre and tragic incident took place over Sakhalin Island, about as far from Moscow as it was possible to be, and cost 269 lives, including those of ten Canadians. I well recall the first Soviet press accounts of "an intruder plane stalking in the dead of night," with the implication that it was up to no good. Soviet officials repeated this thesis, speaking of a "special mission" organized by U.S. Intelligence. They said that the Soviet pilot did not know there were passengers aboard, and that he was ordered to destroy the Boeing 747 in accordance with Soviet law on violations of state borders. They expressed regret for the loss of life, but offered no apology and no response to demands for a full explanation and for compensation. They dismissed the reactions of Western governments, including the suspension of Aeroflot flights to Canada, as illegal and vindictive. President Reagan, who had described the incident as "an act of barbarism, born of a society which wantonly disregards individual rights and the value of human life," was the subject of hysterical denunciation in *Pravda*. All in all, the outlook for East-West relations looked darker than when I arrived in 1980, and I was not surprised, on return to Ottawa in October, to be asked to help plan the mission for peace on which Mr. Trudeau embarked in November.

What really happened that summer night over the Sea of Japan? There is no doubt that KAL 007 entered Soviet airspace at an especially sensitive point for Soviet air defence forces. The latter acted in accordance with rules that had been promulgated in 1982, rules that reflected the heightened tensions of the second Cold War. The Korean pilot apparently did not know he was off course, nor did the Soviet pilot know he was following an aircraft with passengers aboard. In such a fashion did human error, compounded by the atmosphere of Soviet fear and suspicion of U.S. intentions, lead to tragedy.

CANADA-SOVIET RELATIONS

Mark MacGuigan was the External Affairs Minister during my first 22 months in Moscow, and I was sometimes asked by Soviet officials whether he represented the views of Mr. Trudeau on East-West relations. This was an astute, if impertinent, question. It was known in Ottawa that Alexander Yakovlev, the longtime Soviet Ambassador to Canada, had easy access to Mr. Trudeau, and I began to wonder whether his reports were at odds with the instructions I was receiving. (Yakovlev's relations with Moscow, from where he was said to have been exiled to Canada for "political" reasons, may also have been uneasy.) Indeed, MacGuigan's public speeches on the subject struck much the same notes as those of Reagan and Haig in Washington, then at the height of their anti-communist fervour, whereas

Trudeau said little on the subject. Soviet officials made clear their regard for Trudeau, who had stimulated their interest when he visited Moscow in 1971, at a time when he was questioning the traditions of Western cold war policy. They hoped he would return (he did, in fact, return for Brezhnev's funeral in October, 1982, but this was mainly a ceremonial visit).

Aside from the Prime Minister's reputation, I had few cards to play. The high ones were hockey and wheat. Wheat exports survived all manner of sanctions, and I sometimes thought that the best-informed Canadians about the USSR might be the members of the Canadian Wheat Board, who travelled to Moscow regularly, sometimes without my knowledge. As for hockey, it helped to know the names of the Montreal Canadiens even in the Muslim Republic of Azerbaijan, where the waiters asked me for news. Wayne Gretzky was by far our most popular visitor.

Oil and gas technology, especially in Arctic conditions, was also a Canadian asset; it was no accident that Alberta was the most active province in promoting trade. Opportunities for trade were limited, given that the balance of trade was heavily in our favour. Canadians liked the price of Lada cars and the taste of Russian vodka, but the former were not well serviced and Ontario stopped importing vodka in 1982 to signal displeasure with Soviet policies. Visits, by our Ministers of Agriculture and Trade, did help to improve matters, and in the first case led to a return

Geoffrey and Landon Pearson with Wayne Gretzky and Vladislav Tretyak, Moscow 1981.

visit in 1983 by Mikhail Gorbachev, the rising star in the Politbureau, who came to Canada in a forlorn hope to learn from Canadian methods of growing wheat, but benefited mostly from the advice on East-West relations he received from Trudeau and Yakovlev in Ottawa (Yakovlev returned to Moscow in 1985 as Gorbachev's principal adviser).

In addition to encouraging the Gorbachev visit, I took advantage of the presence in Moscow of the Institute for the Study of the U.S.A. and Canada to cultivate relations with its Director, Georgi Arbatov, and his staff of talented academics, some dozen of whom specialized in Canadian affairs. Arbatov was a member of the Central Committee of the Party, a group made up of the "Who's Who" of the Soviet Union, and therefore a useful contact for a diplomat trying to penetrate the mysteries of Soviet decision making. He was regarded as a propagandist by officials in Ottawa (and even by some officials in Moscow!), but as propaganda was the daily fare of Soviet politics I found it helpful to be on friendly terms with a master of the game. At the least, he was able to give me some idea of the temperature of the Cold War in those anxious times, remarking to me once that the Soviet military were prepared to "launch on warning." Moreover, the contacts the Embassy established with the Institute were to blossom later into a program of academic exchanges that were of mutual benefit after Gorbachev rose to power, later in the decade.

But, on the whole, the politics of the Cold War took priority in Canada-Soviet relations. Western sanctions had no perceptible effect on the Soviet presence in Afghanistan, although it may be that Western warnings against military intervention in Poland made some impression. During my last year in Moscow I pushed Ottawa hard to relax the embargo we had put on government support for academic and cultural exchanges, believing that these were of greater benefit to Canada than to the USSR. Most of our allies, including the U.S., had kept up some exchanges, and I wondered whether Canadian reticence reflected lack of interest or lack of political will. Perhaps both. Certainly the few brave souls who did come were well received, both by the Russians and by the Embassy, and when such exchanges were officially renewed in 1984 they eased the way for the new Conservative government to give Mr. Gorbachev the benefit of the doubt when he rose to power. Before that, his 1983 visit to Canada had led to a return visit later that year by Jeanne Sauvé, Speaker of the House of Commons, and a group of MPs, a visit that went quite well but was quickly forgotten after the KAL disaster erased all hope of a new start in our relations.

The most sensitive issue to be raised by the MPs was that of human rights, an issue that appeared to have greater political salience in Canada than any other. It took two forms: a general concern over the treatment of political dissidents, especially those of Jewish origin, and a more particular interest in those relatives of Canadian citizens who were prevented from leaving (there were only forty-one immigrants to Canada in 1983). We had some success with the second category, although it was a slow and painful process, but none at all with the dissidents. These remained in prison until Gorbachev began to cultivate relations with the West after 1985. Soviet officials with whom I argued the case for family reunification led me to understand that "security" was involved, and they more or less admitted that the KGB had the last word. About the dissidents they were more blunt: it was an internal matter that was no business of Canada or any other country. My Western colleagues were given the same message. We all knew that the climate of the second Cold War just about ruled out any significant change in Soviet policies.

EMBASSY-SOVIET RELATIONS

A common diplomatic temptation is to interpret events through the eyes of the host government, and thus to imperil that quality of objective analysis which is the trademark of good diplomatic reporting. Western diplomats in Moscow, however, had difficulty knowing what was in the minds of Soviet officials, not to speak of the problem of deciphering the coded messages in *Pravda* editorials. There were no leaks or asides to help even the most astute observer (a long-time Swedish ambassador contented himself with sending home clips from *Pravda* on which he underlined the key passages). But it was possible to measure the quotient of emotion that lay behind the frequent outpouring of ideological or patriotic fervour, and this was usually high during my time in Moscow. There was a genuine fear of war, I thought, that was overlooked by Western opinion. And there was a growing gap between leaders and led that one could detect by audience reactions at the theatre or at the circus (the clowns knew this well), or by noting the gestures of our Russian cook when the talk turned to Soviet bureaucracy. It was possible, if not always wise, to meet with members of the dissident community (mostly Jewish). Painters and poets might reveal their frustrations, and vodka could loosen tongues.

Despite these obstacles, and our lack of fluent Russian, my wife and I were treated with courtesy and friendliness on our travels around the country, and we came to like and respect those few people—mostly with ties to Canada in one way or another—with whom we were in regular contact. The omnipresence of the police rarely prevented us from going where we wished in Moscow, although travel outside the Moscow area required advance permission. This we obtained without difficulty and soon discovered that, while the Party ruled in the capital, elsewhere it was the regional chieftains who counted in that vast country (like Boris Yeltsin, who presided over the closed city of Sverdlovsk and was thus out of the reach of diplomats). Those we met were practical people, usually engineers, who wasted little time on ideology. In some places, such as Armenia, there was a scarcely veiled hostility to Soviet orthodoxy. I had a hard time fitting this kind of experience into the Western image of a totalitarian society. It was ridiculous to think of Leonid Brezhnev in the same way as Stalin, and nobody did. Churches were few but open. Young people dressed and often acted as though they lived in Toronto or Paris, and they did not hesitate to approach foreigners in public places if they wished.

Yet these were not easy times for me or my fellow Canadians.

We had to assume we were under surveillance most of the time, and this did not make for normal relations with our Russian staff, or indeed amongst ourselves. Adding to our unease was the occasional attempt by Soviet citizens to take refuge in the Embassy building, which served both as residence and office. Either they would refuse to leave, once admitted on consular business, or, in one or two cases, they would scale the wall surrounding the back of the building at night and ask for asylum. Our task was to convince such persons that they must have a Soviet exit visa to leave the USSR, something we could not provide. The best we could do was to offer to escort them from the Embassy under our protection.

Despite these distractions, I tried to put my relations with Soviet officials on a basis of mutual respect, and where trade was concerned, on a basis of mutual interest. On the big issues of the Cold War, such as arms control and human rights, I could not expect to accomplish much, except to act as a conduit between Soviet and Canadian views, the latter generally reflecting NATO policies. My chief concerns were: a) to keep Ottawa-Soviet relations on some minimum level of civility in areas of mutual interest—prolonging sanctions served no political purpose except to exacerbate Soviet neuroses about Western hostility and to appease special interests at home; and b) to try to persuade my Soviet contacts that distrust and fear of their policies in much of the world would be less if they stopped blaming others for their own misdeeds, or pretending they did not exist. I was not optimistic about the prospects for real change: "assuming external hostility and fearing internal challenge, yet confident of the military power of their country and optimistic about its potential wealth, the Soviet leaders have many reasons to disguise both its capacities and their intentions," I reported in 1981. By 1983, I still had no reason to believe that the objectives of the revolution had been abandoned.

These assumptions were altered by the new approach to world affairs which Gorbachev displayed after 1985. Even before this change, Mr. Trudeau took the Western lead by proposing elements of common ground between East and West, an idea which Mr. Gromyko welcomed when I returned to Moscow in late 1983 as the special representative of the Prime Minister. There was little enthusiasm in Washington and London, however, and the initiative led to no immediate results. But who can say that in the course of events leading to the end of the Cold War it did not have its place, especially in the mind of Gorbachev, who had visited Canada earlier that year? In any case, it seemed to me to justify making the best of hard times for three years in Moscow.

Geoffrey A.H. Pearson joined External Affairs in 1952. He was a career diplomat from 1952 to 1984, serving in Paris, Mexico City and New Delhi, and was appointed Ambassador to Moscow in 1980. In 1984, he became the first Executive Director of the Canadian Institute for International Peace and Security. Today he is actively involved in voluntary and academic organizations connected with peace and international affairs. He is the author of *Seize the Day: Lester B. Pearson and Crisis Diplomacy*, published by Carleton University Press.

13

AFRICA AND THE CARIBBEAN: INITIATIVE AND INFLUENCE

DAVID REECE

THE TWO AREAS where I did much of my service as head of mission were Africa and the Caribbean. In the 1970s and '80s I served as High Commissioner in Trinidad and Tobago, Ghana, Jamaica and Zambia and had 16 dual accreditations to smaller countries and territories. I thought these two areas would have strong mutual ties. Since people of the Caribbean came in large measure from Africa, they naturally had an ethnic and cultural attraction to their continent of origin. This grew stronger in the 1950s and '60s as cause and effect of the mounting drive for independence. This natural magnetism worked only one way, however. I found that for the most part the Africans of influence whom I met had little interest in their long-gone cousins, who were looking homeward in the hope of cultural and political interest and assistance.

When I presumed, without instructions, to point out to one senior minister in Ghana that the Caribbean's eager, and appropriate, search for African ties and encouragement was, I thought, getting a dusty answer, he was non-committal, but he told me a few months later that I was quite right. His attendance at a conference in Jamaica had brought home to him the value of Canadian banks in the Caribbean. Could I not get one for Ghana?

A minister in another West African state looked thoughtful when I pointed out that the anti-slavery pageant we had just seen was justified, but would it not be a logical and helpful step for Africa to respond strongly to the natural and constructive urge of the descendants of the Caribbean slaves to seek out their roots and find lost racial affinities? My question was presumptuous, but it seemed to cause no resentment; instead it was given a positive reception.

Diplomatic moves are required by local circumstances or Ottawa's instructions or are, like those described above, unforced initiatives. In Jamaica I took two such initiatives with Prime Minister Seaga. I suggested, without instructions, that, since he was attending a Commonwealth

Finance Ministers' meeting in Toronto in September, 1984, Seaga might like to call on our Prime Minister at that time. (I knew there would be little competition because few of the ministers at the Toronto meeting would also be prime ministers.) Ottawa was not averse but noted that a general election at that time would annul the project. Sure enough, there was an election underway, but Seaga still managed to pay a valuable call on the new Prime Minister, Brian Mulroney. Seaga planted the idea which bore fruit the next year in a very useful conference of Commonwealth Caribbean prime ministers and Mulroney in Jamaica.

A less useful initiative was the suggestion I made after the U.S. overthrow of the communist government in Grenada. I had previously delivered to Seaga an aggrieved complaint from Ottawa about the failure of the Commonwealth Caribbean governments to consult their Canadian friends before the event. A subsequent meeting with Seaga gave me the chance to suggest, on a personal and tentative basis, that our experience in peacekeeping might make it useful for a Canadian and Commonwealth peacekeeping force to replace the Caribbean troops. The idea was bluntly squashed by Seaga. The U.S. and Caribbean states would finish the job. And they did. Just as well, since my personal suggestion might have had a frosty reception in Ottawa.

In Ghana I had two initiatives thrust upon me. The completion of a major Canadian aid project, a badly needed technical college, was stymied by the refusal of a powerful local mayor to give up the existing use of a piece of land needed for the essential services plant of the college. Fortunately I had been in the country for some time and knew relevant local leaders. One was a very influential figure, the head of the paramount chiefs in Ghana. With the help of the chief, the regional governor and two cabinet ministers, one of them my favourite partner on the tennis court attached to our residence, I was able to overcome the understandable parochial concerns of the mayor. He had wanted to retain the land for dumping the night soil of his citizens. Other space was found.

In such a case instructions were not needed. The need and the action were clear. Another case in Ghana precluded seeking Ottawa instructions because there was no time. I was summoned one evening by a visiting Canadian business executive who was potentially in deep trouble. He had refused to accept a low offer for the Canadian company's plant and facilities in Ghana. The local bidder was a businessman of eminence and influence. He immediately threatened to have the Canadian visitor arrested. After hearing this tale of threats and a failed deal, I decided that the local man was out of court. I told him any police action against the Canadian would be immediately followed by an approach on my part to the Head of State and Government, protesting the action taken in the strongest terms and demanding on behalf of the Canadian government the release of the Canadian executive. In the event no action was taken against him but I was delighted to see him off on a plane departing next day, especially as it was six hours behind schedule—suspense sustained!

Another event in Ghana turned out well because of interaction between Ottawa, the Ghana government and myself. Ghana was anxious to have us provide half the military instructors needed for the first phase of a senior staff college. We were pleased to cooperate in a project intended to stimulate human rights concerns as well as military training among senior Ghanaian officers, but financial difficulties stood in the way. We did not have enough money available in our military assistance budget to do the trick. The locals could not pay the heavy costs. At the last moment, when this useful cooperation project, which had a significant human rights factor, seemed about to abort, I had a simple and overdue idea. I persuaded the Ghanaians to pay the local costs of the Canadian officers and this slice off the total cost enabled us to pay the larger part—the salaries, travel and other dollar expenses.

In Trinidad and Tobago I encountered a situation where I had an initiative forced upon me which amounted to direct disobedience to Ottawa's instructions. I was told to make high level noises to the Trinidad government—soothing noises. They were becoming heated over an erroneous belief that we were intent on collaborating with a third party, another Caribbean government, to the detriment of Trinidad. This was untrue. I sought out my favourite cabinet minister, who luckily was the relevant one, and put the Ottawa case. He was swiftly convinced. But a snag arose. His crusty Prime Minister would not be convinced unless he could see our position stated in writing. My instructions were clear and firm: do not give them our explanation in writing; the matter is too sensitive. After exploring and querying my minister friend's rigid assertion that the matter was such that it was imperative to present his boss with our explanation in writing I agreed, and gave him the relevant text of my instructions. Should I confess to the Ottawa chiefs that I had precisely disobeyed them? I almost did not. I had done the right thing. Why should I be caned for it? In the end I confessed and the response was stony silence.

Situations like those described above are exceptions from the normal embassy routine. Its head and its staff are mainly concerned with diurnal tasks, bread and butter if you like, in pursuit of various programs including aid, trade, consular and immigration services. These activities, and reports on them, as well as general economic and political reports on the local and regional scene, have a continuing influence at the working level and higher up. But there are times when a post needs to pipe up on high if a decision is at issue and contrary to what those in the field see as Canadian interests.

In one post the issue was clear-cut. I was instructed to seek support for a Canadian candidate for a major international job. He was superbly qualified but I was still reluctant to make representations on his behalf. Why? Because there was a respectable local candidate for the same office. To make noises about our man would undoubtedly cause intense local annoyance and have no effect, except perhaps to spur on their efforts to line up regional support for their man and deny it for ours. When my first attempts to persuade Ottawa to change its mind on this issue failed to annul the instructions, I aimed at the top of the Department and won. They were annulled, and my compromise suggestion that, in working for the candidate, we should make *démarches* only to the other countries in the region, was implemented with my own participation.

On another occasion, and in another embassy, we should have requested the omission of one part of Ottawa's instructions on a trade matter. We did obtain an amendment and some improvement to the text, but not in the offending section. Instead of rebelling, I reluctantly called on the foreign affairs minister. When I implied that failure by the local government to stop giving unfair preference to a rival trade country might cause us to complain internationally, the minister erupted with fury. This *démarche* did us little good.

In Zambia I made an approach on behalf of Bata Shoe aimed at impending government measures which would be to the detriment of this international company based in Canada. I was cordially received, since our instructions contained no threats. The proposed measures were aborted and Bata continued to give the country useful footwear, including sturdy miners' boots popular in the copper mines of Zambia.

This varied and handsome country was deep in debt, like many others in Africa. In 1987 Zambia dropped its International Monetary Fund commitment and targets. Soon after Canadian officials decided that Zambia would be an exception to the new Canadian decision to wipe out the debts of African developing countries to Canada. Luckily this decision had not been finalized or published before our mission heard of it. I

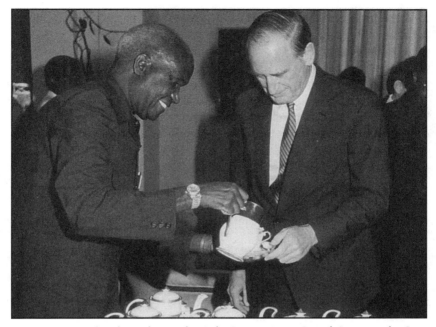

President Kaunda of Zambia with High Commissioner David Reece at the State House in Lusaka, 1988.

sent a brisk telegram at a high level, pointing out that this discriminatory decision had been taken on insufficient grounds and was also very ill-timed. The Vancouver Commonwealth Summit was imminent. The Zambians, as leaders of the Front Line States around South Africa and veterans of the long struggle against apartheid, would inevitably play a key role. At Vancouver strong, realistic Zambian leadership, in conjunction with our own firm but moderate stance, would be a major factor, promoting a beneficial outcome from which Canada would obviously gain. My reiteration of the obvious worked. The Ottawa officials concerned were overruled. Zambia's past aid debts to us were wiped out and the country was not adversely singled out by us from among its confrères. President Kaunda played a major role in the constructive decisions at Vancouver, including the creation of a new committee to ride herd on South Africa and encourage the imposition of sanctions against it.

My last two examples of embassy attempts and obligation to influence policy are taken from the aid field. When I was in Trinidad in 1973 CIDA proposed to establish a regional aid office in the eastern Caribbean. Based in Barbados, this office would take all aid decisions relating to the area. Heads of mission would have no say. Their aid staffs would report to the area office and not to them. Their authority would be eroded and their influence with the governments to which they were accredited would be of no use in aid matters, which were a major reason for our maintenance of embassies in the region. I pointed this out with polite vigour. Other posts doubtless did the same. The idea was dropped, perhaps not simply because of the sound reasons referred to but also due to the unlikelihood of the regional office being given sufficient fiscal authority to do its job adequately. Ottawa grasped that authority firmly in its own hands.

Eventually, after area aid authority became larger and looser, a regional aid bureau was set up in Harare, capital of Zimbabwe. It was operated as a substitute for Ottawa in decision making on aid programs and projects. So there I was in the last half of my last posting confronting a regional rival. However, this time the arrangements were more sensible than those originally proposed for the Caribbean in the early '70s. Politely I was asked for my views about the new scheme. I suggested amendments to preserve the role of the High Commissioner in the aid field. These were largely accepted. More of the aid work in Zambia would be done by visiting officials from Harare, but the envoy would still be in charge of the aid work in his own bailiwick. His standing, contacts and influence in Zambia would still be used to the benefit of the aid program. How this has worked out in practice I know not, but it began well, with flexible and able officers involved in and from Harare.

The examples given in this essay are high points. They should not hide the fact that the envoy and his staff are involved in myriad daily tasks which, in sum, much outweigh in influence, effectiveness, and results those moments when an ambassador steps in locally or deals with Ottawa to seek substantial decisions. In this context I would mention the role of a posting outside the Caribbean and Africa. During my four years as ambassador and head of delegation to the arms control talks in Vienna from 1978 to 1982, I and my staff spent much of our time working out the texts with our Western colleagues, for minor and sometimes major moves in negotiation with Eastern bloc ambassadors. There was usually no time and too much detail for decisions to be sought from Ottawa. So would-be subtle and crafty Canadian compromise drafting suggestions would live or die in the Western envoys' group and then in the East/West forum, which rumbled on for years.

AFRICA AND THE CARIBBEAN

REPORTING

Reporting is an important and ongoing segment of an embassy's duties. Its target may be high or wide. Some reports seek to augment the knowledge and interest of senior echelons in Ottawa and in other Canadian embassies regarding major features of the post's work and significant events in the country concerned which are relevant to Canadian interests.

These reports often play a substantive role in decisions on programs, e.g. aid and trade. Some reports are technical and vocational and are aimed at desk officers. The ambassador often employs his experience and contacts to draft his own reports rather than delegating this function to a colleague.

The following are excerpts from reports I wrote as a head of mission in a scatter of countries. The first was prepared in India in 1969 when I was Acting High Commissioner.

There is some danger that the Congress government will seek to improve its election prospects in 1972 by having a "peaceful" nuclear explosion shortly before then. My personal view is that we should avoid taking on any further nuclear aid commitments in India as a government and we should discourage Canadian private firms seeking our advice from entering this field. We are more vulnerable than anybody else to criticism if India explodes a nuclear device before unsafeguarded resources of plutonium become available in the mid-'70s or later.

India did in fact explode such a device a few years after my prediction, and Canada reacted by cutting our aid, except for food and agriculture, for about three years. We suspected that this "peaceful" device might have been made with plutonium produced from a research reactor in India which we had aided with research, not bombs, in mind.

In 1972 I wrote an appraisal of the situation in Trinidad and Tobago, where I was High Commissioner.

On credit side economic development in real terms is taking place with solid per capita income gains, substantial industrialization, some agricultural diversification and recent gas and oil strikes of strong potential. Government economic policy, although erratic, seems to have struck fairly good balance between economic nationalism and foreign capital needs, between overall economic control, welfare financing and economic growth incentives. Racial tension between main communities, black and Indian, is evident but seems well below danger point, although friction could increase rapidly if a charismatic leader ever appears from the Afro-Caribbean community.

In Ghana in 1976 I took advantage of a farewell lunch given for me by the Foreign Minister to express complimentary thoughts about this very interesting country where I had had a busy time.

Since Ghana first suggested the Commonwealth Secretariat, a seed which has taken such useful root—and flower—I should point out the membership of our two countries in this unique institution has also been an important focus of our bilateral relations. The Commonwealth is of unique value. Its membership provides an overlapping of many different rings of regional membership interest and concern. This provides enrichment to the regional groupings involved as well as the Commonwealth itself, which is made up of a network of multilateral and bilateral ties. The strong links between Ghana and Canada have in turn strengthened the Commonwealth as a whole.

Back in the Caribbean I was accredited to other countries from my home base in Jamaica. One affectionate memory was Belize, which I visited for the first time in 1982. According to my report, the "general impression I received of Belize was, physically, slightly reminiscent of Canadian prairies of my early youth with Belize City not unlike an abandoned film set from quote 'High Noon' scripted by Graham Greene. Racially and linguistically, [the] mixture seemed more harmonious—and Spanish flavoured—than expected." This description was perhaps a shade fancy, even churlish, but was balanced by the useful exchanges I had with Prime Minister Price and the good impression I increasingly gained of him and reported to Ottawa.

My last sum-up report was from Lusaka in 1990, where I was High Commissioner to Zambia. I noted that:

In 1989-1990 Zambia returned to an acceptable Structural Adjustment program blessed by the donors and IFIS (international financial institutions). Canada had thus begun new aid commitments here although regrettably confined in volume by our own severe constraint necessities. Since independence in 1964 President Kaunda's relations with successive heads of Canadian government have been warm and sustained including Kaunda's visit to Montreal in 1989 for international AIDS conference and official visit to Ottawa.... Our relations have remained strong and constant not only due to personal affinities but from common approach to the problems of southern Africa rooted in Republic of South Africa apartheid.

In a report on Malawi, to which I was also accredited, I pointed out that "our evaluation of Malawi human rights must take into account an important plus, namely Malawi's open-handed reception of about 800,000 Mozambique refugees and its humane policy of not forcing repatriation. Consequent strain on Malawian infrastructure is another reason why Canada should maintain its aid volume for the time being, as is the other cost to the Malawian economy from the Mozambique civil war which has much reduced Malawian trade routes through Mozambique."

14

FROM PAKISTAN TO BANGLADESH 1969-1972: PERSPECTIVE OF A CANADIAN ENVOY

JOHN SMALL

MUCH HAS BEEN WRITTEN about the breakup of Pakistan in 1971. Much more will follow but it could be years before a definitive account appears. This essay does not attempt to provide one. Nor does it offer a detailed running account of events as they occurred. It simply provides sufficient facts to place in context the operations of the Canadian High Commission during the crisis years of 1969-1972. The perspective is that of the author, who was then Canadian High Commissioner, later Ambassador, to Pakistan and, concurrently, non-resident Ambassador to Afghanistan. The narrative is a personalized account of the interplay between the Canadian High Commission's views and actions and those of officials in Ottawa charged with taking policy decisions, together with the effects of those decisions on Canada-Pakistan relations.

BACKGROUND TO BREAKUP

When I arrived in Islamabad in August 1969 the martial law regime of General Yahya Khan was firmly ensconced, having succeeded the disintegrating administration of Field Marshal Ayub Khan on March 25 that year. The agitation which led to Ayub's downfall was championed by Zulfikar Ali Bhutto, leader of the Pakistan People's Party based in West Pakistan. It was widely supported in East Pakistan, where Sheikh Mujibur Rahman (Mujib) and the Awami League were dominant, because the Bengali inhabitants of that province hoped it would serve their nationalist political aims.

Bengali nationalism and West Pakistani insensitivity to it were at the root of the events which led to the birth of Bangladesh. In addition, the limited Bengali representation within the national civil and military administration left Bengalis frustrated and angry. Equally aggravating to Bengalis was the fact that the proceeds of East-wing industry, exports and foreign exchange earnings, a major portion of the total, were employed largely in development of the West-wing, as was the bulk of foreign aid. For these reasons East Pakistanis considered themselves to be colonized and exploited, with virtually no control over their own destiny.

My arrival in Pakistan coincided roughly with Yahya Khan's efforts to accommodate East Pakistani nationalism. On assuming power he had promised early elections. In November, 1969 he went further by conceding maximum autonomy to each wing and representation by population, thereby abandoning East-West parity and ensuring a majority in the National Assembly for the East-wing Bengalis. This was not welcomed among West Pakistanis who feared Bengali domination. It was to become a prime contributing element in the chemistry of East-West ferment which continued to grow and ended in disaster.

West Pakistani fears were realized in the general election of December 7, 1970 when Mujib's Awami League won 167 out of 169 seats contested in the East wing, giving it an absolute majority nationwide, but no seats in West Pakistan. Bhutto's Pakistan People's Party captured 81 of 138 West-wing seats but none in East Pakistan. These results led to confrontation between the two parties which meetings between Bhutto and Mujib, in January 1971, failed to resolve.

The impasse between the political leaders of East and West Pakistan led Yahya to reinstate full martial law rule and postpone *sine die* the constitutional session of the National Assembly scheduled for March 3, 1971. This provoked defiance by the Awami League, which proceeded to assume *de facto* control of East Pakistan. The Yahya regime's response came in the form of a military crackdown on the night of March 25-26 which resulted in Mujib's arrest, civil war in the East wing and, ultimately, war with India.

Eight months of guerilla warfare and, finally, Indian military intervention on December 3, ended in the surrender of Pakistani forces in Dacca (now Dhaka) on December 16, 1971 and the birth of independent Bangladesh. Yahya Khan resigned and was replaced as President and Chief Martial Law Administrator by Zulfikar Ali Bhutto.

PAKISTAN-CANADA RELATIONS

Historically, Canada's relations with Pakistan have reflected the Canadian government's desire to pursue, *mutatis mutandis*, parallel policies toward India and Pakistan. This stemmed logically from the evolution in 1947 of these two former British colonies into independent states and full members of the Commonwealth. The South Asian events of 1970-72, which resulted in the partition of Pakistan and the emergence of Bangladesh, attenuated the old official doctrine of parallelism, though there linger to this day elements which come into play to ensure that policies adopted toward the one do not have undesired effects in the other.

Broadly speaking, Canadian relations with Pakistan, apart from the obvious Commonwealth link, were weighted toward economic development. Trade was marginal in total terms and, where significant, related to development assistance through the provision of equipment and commodities. At the time under consideration, Canada was Pakistan's second largest provider of aid and Pakistan was Canada's second largest recipient.

Beyond aid and trade, Pakistan was a growing source of new Canadians —at the time about 1000 annually—requiring a strong immigration presence in the High Commission. Consular affairs, a bread and butter activity in foreign missions generally, were enlivened in Islamabad by virtue of its situation athwart the hippie route between Afghanistan on the one hand and India and Nepal on the other. This situation obliged us, besides engaging in routine passport duties, to make repeated efforts to get and keep Canadians out of jail, both in Pakistan and Afghanistan.

Political and economic reporting commanded substantial efforts and resources, given the endemically disturbed internal economic and political situation and, on the external side, the consistently bad relations with India. Regional peace and stability were constant concerns of the mission, since Pakistan-India relations had a built-in potential to affect international security through involvement of the great powers and, ultimately, the United Nations. This environment, together with a military training and officer exchange program, amply justified the presence of a military attaché in Islamabad.

In general, relations between Canada and Pakistan were harmonious and suffered only from two notable irritants, both relating to India. The first was Kashmir, concerning which Canada studiously avoided taking sides. While Pakistan would have preferred Canadian support, it grudgingly accepted Canada's impartial stance. The second and more serious irritant was Canada's nuclear power assistance to India, which Pakistan saw as contributing to India's nuclear weapons capability and, therefore, to its overall military potential. These two points of friction have never been resolved to either Canada's or Pakistan's satisfaction.[1]

THE VIEW FROM ISLAMABAD

The Canadian High Commission in Islamabad was located on the top floor of the Shaharazad Hotel, the only hostelry in the new and unfinished capital of Pakistan. It offered basic accommodation with no frills beyond a magnificent view of the nearby Margalla Hills. These quarters were scheduled to be replaced by a new chancery, together with residences for the High Commissioner and other Canadian personnel. The building program, undertaken during a time of national crisis, added considerably to the mission's workload. Moreover, the change of regime, late in 1971, brought constant pressure from the Pakistan government to move our mission out of the Shaharazad to make way for the Ministry of Foreign Affairs. During my final months in Pakistan I waged a rearguard action to ensure that we could stay put until completion of our new facilities. This was largely successful, though the new chancery was not fully operational when the move was made early in 1973.

When I took up my posting in August, 1969 the High Commission had a substantial presence, with a dozen officers providing services in the areas of political, economic and consular affairs, trade, development assistance, immigration, military affairs and administration. Together with the necessary Canadian and Pakistani support staff, the total work force comprised some thirty-five members.

As I pursued the initial and customary activities of presenting credentials in Rawalpindi[2] and Kabul, being briefed by High Commission staff and establishing official contacts, it became apparent that, while East-West irritants persisted, together with the myriad of socio-economic problems endemic in each wing, there was restrained optimism concerning the future of a united Pakistan. While Yahya's military credentials were impeccable, he was an unknown quantity politically. Nevertheless, he appeared at first to be moving in the right directions. The key to the survival of a united Pakistan appeared to depend upon an early general election, expected in 1970, and the establishment of representative government. When I presented my credentials to Yahya as President, he impressed me as a straightforward soldier whose duty it was to achieve the desired ends and withdraw as quickly as possible from the seat of power which he had not sought. While no intellectual giant, he was aware of East-West disparities and frictions and seemed determined to move toward democratic solutions.

Understanding Pakistan demanded travel and this was especially important in a diverse and divided country where the barriers to nation building and survival were particularly daunting. My previous two-year posting in Karachi had given me a basic understanding of Pakistan but now my knowledge needed updating. I started my travels with a visit to

Karachi in December, 1969. This former fishing village was now Pakistan's only major port in the West wing and was rapidly becoming the financial and industrial hub of the country. Since my departure from Karachi, four years earlier, its population had doubled to 3.5 million.

A source of Canadian pride and concern was the Karachi Nuclear Power Project (KANUPP), a joint effort of the governments of Canada and Pakistan. This CANDU reactor was then nearing completion with the help of some 65 Canadian technical personnel. It had been the cause of considerable concern during my 1963-65 posting in Pakistan and now seemed to be coming back to haunt me. Nuclear safeguards, an initial problem were, in the end, agreed upon with Pakistan and the International Atomic Energy Agency [IAEA] and the completed project was officially inaugurated with the participation of Prime Minister Trudeau during his visit in January 1971.

As Canada, unlike Britain, the United States, Australia and others, had no official representation in East Pakistan, it was High Commission policy to visit the East wing regularly. During 1970 and 1971 there was rarely a month that I or other officers did not travel to Dacca and outlying areas, to apprise ourselves of the situation there, to keep a finger on the political pulse and to maintain touch with Canadians who were dispersed throughout the province. Without such visits we would not have been able to keep Ottawa informed or to advise on the type, scale and feasibility of aid in an increasingly unstable situation.

In keeping with our travel policy, I embarked on a tour of East Pakistan during the first fortnight of 1970, accompanied by my wife, whose presence was much appreciated by both Bengalis and, especially, those Canadians who were situated in remote stations. Besides acquiring basic knowledge and a feel for that part of the country, we were able, during our journey, to fulfil our consular responsibilities by keeping in touch with and ensuring the well-being of the 150 or so Canadians working there, mostly in development or educational programs. The former group were sponsored by either CIDA or the World Bank. The latter were largely members of the Holy Cross religious order from the province of Quebec, which had been involved in the area for close to a century.

On January 3 we joined President Yahya Khan near Chittagong, where he laid the cornerstone of the satellite earth station being built by RCA of Canada and funded by a Canadian soft loan. Later in the year, I joined the President in Karachi where he officiated again at the launching of a twin satellite earth station funded by Canada.

Back in Dacca, I called on a series of central, provincial and institutional authorities. The most interesting of these were the Governor, Vice-Admiral Ahsan; the Martial Law Administrator, Lieutenant-General Yakub; and the Awami League leader, Sheikh Mujibur Rahman (Mujib). Ahsan, just five months in office, had won the grudging respect of Bengalis through his sympathetic approach to the problems of the East wing. Yakub, a linguist, had likewise earned high marks from Bengalis for taking the trouble to learn their language. Both were particularly interested in Canadian constitutional arrangements and both thought South Africa's semi-annual shuttle of parliament between Pretoria and Capetown offered a possible precedent for Pakistan. Ahsan came through as intelligent, humane, pragmatic and motivated by a will to get the job done which, he said with feeling, was not one for a sailor. Yakub was clearly an able soldier who impressed with his insights and views on how to deal with a difficult situation in a manner calculated to keep Bengalis on side.

It was a tragedy of the time that the advice of these two most senior East Pakistan authorities, Ahsan and Yakub, was largely ignored by Yahya and his advisers in Rawalpindi. The direct consequence of their attempts to translate their own understanding of the situation in East Pakistan into practical action was their disappearance from the scene at a crucial moment in Pakistan history. Ahsan was unceremoniously removed on March 1, 1971 for being too soft. Yakub resigned on March 5 when the President rejected his plea to proceed at once to Dacca to repair the damage done by postponement of the National Assembly session without setting a new date. For Yakub, this was only the final straw on top of a heap of actions by his superiors of which he disapproved.

My call on Sheikh Mujibur Rahman was both interesting and enlightening. He received me graciously but shouted imperiously at the hangers-on who were noisily chatting nearby. He was clearly many things to many people. He was vain, inclined to demagoguery, a brilliant orator and crowd mover, charming, politically astute up to a point but insufficiently so to control events once they were in motion. He recognized this weakness but in the end believed his power stemmed from the people whose servant—and leader—he was. He said he was for a united Pakistan and was prepared to work for it, but only in the short term. He was unequivocal in stating his readiness to part company with West Pakistan if his demands (the Six Points[3]) were not met. He added with an engaging smile that an independent Bangladesh would, however, remain a member of the Commonwealth.

Mujib ran through the litany of Bengali grievances against the West and was convinced that East Pakistan's ills could be cured by the acquisition of political and economic autonomy. He expressed admiration for the Canadian federal model and the British parliamentary system. He rejected the American presidential system of government as too restrictive of the President's powers. He expressed his belief in Yahya's promises to withdraw after elections but clearly distrusted Yahya's advisers. He set a high price for unity: a weak central government, provincial autonomy, a fair share for Bengalis of central jobs and army recruitment, more attention to the East wing by central ministers and alternate sessions of the National Assembly in East and West Pakistan.

After talking to those mentioned above and to a host of others in East Pakistan, I returned to Islamabad with qualified optimism, partly because the senior personalities involved, the President, the Governor, the Martial Law Administrator and many others in authority seemed to be struggling to meet the demands of Bengali nationalism. At the same time, they were deeply conscious of the social and economic problems caused by poverty and overpopulation, too few resources of all kinds and too much corruption and incompetence. The other part of my optimism stemmed from the Bengalis themselves, who reflected promise and a touching confidence that all would be well once the levers of power were in their hands.

CIVIL WAR

Yahya Khan's first year in office, March 1969-March 1970, could be characterized as relatively successful. He had reduced the violence which preceded his assumption of power. He had produced a time table for general and provincial elections. He had relaxed martial law to the extent of employing a cabinet of civilian ministers, had demonstrated flexibility in dealing with tensions in both wings of the country and had removed the ban on political activities on January 1, 1970.

As 1970 wore on, the political parties succumbed to the old Pakistani disease of inter-party strife and fragmentation of the parties themselves. Disputes and hostility arose between East and West over allocations in the Fourth Economic Plan; food shortages in East Pakistan added to the existing East-West economic disparity and the Bengali sense of grievance. This problem was aggravated by disastrous floods in July and August in the East and again in November, when some three million people were affected by a cyclone and tidal wave and hundreds of thousands perished.

John Small, Canadian High Commissioner in Pakistan, presents a cheque for $1000 to Pakistan Foreign Secretary Mr. Sultan M. Khan, February 4, 1971—a donation towards the President's East Pakistan Relief Fund in Islamabad.

In the light of these developments, the High Commission was kept busy observing and interpreting events to Ottawa, and with advising on development assistance needs and practicalities. The advice was in general "steady as she goes," along with emphasizing the desirability of increasing Canadian food aid, especially for East Pakistan. On this score, the High Commission and Ottawa saw eye to eye.

With the elections over and the political parties jockeying for position, it seemed the right time for another foray into East Pakistan. For this purpose my wife and I timed our visit to coincide with the arrival of a relief shipment and with the opening of the National Assembly on March 3, 1971. While preparing to fly from Islamabad we learned, on March 1, that the Assembly opening had been postponed *sine die*, guaranteeing further trouble in East Pakistan. Given this dimension, I decided to proceed to Dacca as planned to try to put together a picture of the likely course of events which, inevitably, would affect our substantial aid program in the East and the safety of Canadians working there.

Our flight involved two hours of travel to Karachi and another six hours to Dacca via Ceylon (Sri Lanka), instead of the customary direct flight of about two hours. This was because India had banned Pakistan International Airlines [PIA] overflights following the hijacking of an Indian Fokker aircraft by two Kashmiris to Lahore on January 30. A subsequent Pakistani judicial inquiry concluded the incident resulted from an Indian conspiracy aimed at providing a pretext for the overflight ban. Whatever the reason, it subjected travellers to a tedious journey which left them in a less than positive frame of mind on arrival in Dacca around 9:00 p.m. This was not improved by learning that a curfew had been imposed on Dacca and we were destined to spend a night in the unusually crowded airport.

After a few hours of waiting and being rebuffed in attempts to arrange some sort of transport to our hotel in town, I chanced on an old friend from Karachi days, a retired major-general who was now a National Assemblyman, and sought his assistance. He promised to help and then disappeared for an hour or so. He finally returned with the good news that he had arranged transport under escort to the hotel. He then boarded his flight to Karachi and we waited. Around 1:00 a.m. our vehicle, a small open personnel carrier, materialized with escort. As there were other diplomats in the airport, all from East European countries, we thought we should share our good fortune and invited them to join us. When the truck rolled up to the entrance our communist colleagues elbowed us aside, threw their bags in and climbed aboard, leaving no room for us. Rather than create an international incident we let them go with our mental imprecations. An hour or so later our transport returned and we clambered aboard with what dignity we could muster and reached our destination at 3:00 a.m. The approach to the Intercontinental Hotel entrance was impressive, with a gaping hole in the plate glass from a bomb placed in a nearby toilet earlier that day.

The reaction in Dacca to the March 1 announcement of the Assembly's postponement was immediate. Rawalpindi had given Mujib advance notice through the Governor on February 28, and the Awami League wasted no time in organizing their hostile response. Within half an hour of the March 1 announcement, mobs surged through the streets of Dacca armed with *lathis* (long bamboo sticks), looting (mainly non-Bengali shops), overturning vehicles and shouting abusive slogans. A complete *hartal* (protest general strike) was called for March 3 throughout the province and general chaos ensued. All economic, industrial, central and provincial government activity was hamstrung and ground to a halt.

This meant I was confined to Dacca but there was plenty to do there. Because Canada had no representative office in East Pakistan we relied on the British should evacuation become necessary. Through their system of wardens (some of them Canadians) I contacted as many Canadians as possible to confirm their well-being and to warn them to think about evacuation if it should become necessary, although I did not consider the moment had come for that. At the time we had 126 Canadians registered in East Pakistan and the number fluctuated eventually around 150. Nearly half of these were Holy Cross missionaries and they, as expected, said they would not leave whatever happened. Most of the other Canadians were with Acres International on a World Bank contract for the East Pakistan Water and Power Development Authority. Others worked for W.P. London Associates on an EPWAPDA training program, for RCA (Canada), building the satellite ground receiving station, for Pelletier Inc., involved with the Sidhirganj transmission line, and for the East Pakistan Institute of Graphic Arts. All these were CIDA projects. My considered opinion was that evacuation was not then necessary, though the situation was unstable and would have to be kept under constant review.

This opinion was not shared by all the foreign agencies or diplomats in Dacca. The Germans evacuated their personnel immediately, their decision being influenced by an unhappy experience in Africa when they waited until tragedy struck. They were soon followed by the Japanese, Russians, East Europeans, United Nations personnel and, finally, British women and children and some non-essential personnel. At about this time Ottawa questioned my judgement and administered a mild slap on the wrist for arguing against evacuation when even the people on whom we depended for transport, the British, were starting to move out their citizens. My views were influenced by a variety of factors. First, the Canadians with Acres International were reluctant to leave because they had a widely distributed network of people throughout the countryside who saw no occasion for alarm. Moreover, if they pulled out on their own their contract would be violated and they would not receive compensation. Secondly, the Bengalis with whom I was in contact, from Mujibur Rahman down, urged me and other foreigners to stay. The turbulence in East Bengal was not xenophobic but aimed, rather, at the perceived enemy: the Martial Law regime and West Pakistanis generally. In addition, I was not alone in my view, as both the American and French Consuls General and the Australian Deputy High Commissioner, a longtime resident of East Bengal and a former missionary, shared my perception of the lack of danger at that time.

Being confined to Dacca, I occupied my time, besides contacting Canadians, with keeping in touch with diplomatic colleagues and those authorities still willing or able to see me, but the number was shrinking because of the Awami League-sponsored *hartal*. Being without an office or facilities for communication with Ottawa or, for much of the time, with Islamabad, I cast about for a way to surmount this difficulty. I was pleased when I discovered the British Deputy High Commissioner (resident in Dacca) was an old friend from an earlier mutual posting. I knew the British and Americans each had their own radio link, respectively, with London and Washington and was sure my friend would allow me to send messages to Ottawa via London. When I approached him he was in a highly nervous state, on the verge of breakdown, and permitted me to send a single short paragraph but no more. This being unsatisfactory, I sought help from the American Consul General, with whom I shared views on evacuation which were not entirely acceptable in either Ottawa or Washington. He graciously allowed me to address Ottawa via Washington every day or two, on condition my communications did not exceed one page. As we had not yet arrived at the era of the personal computer and I had not brought my portable typewriter, I bought locally the longest pad of foolscap paper available and proceeded to draft my near-daily telegram in the smallest script I thought the Consulate secretary could decipher. To her and the Consul General's credit they accepted my efforts and, indeed, Washington later admitted it was as interested in my reports as Ottawa was.

On March 8 I was able to meet Mujibur Rahman for a full hour. What I heard from him and reported to Ottawa was not encouraging. When I asked if he was in direct touch with the central authorities in Rawalpindi I was appalled to find communications between them were virtually non-existent. He said he had had no contact with the new Governor-elect, Lieutenant-General Tikka Khan; nor had he been in touch with the Martial Law Administrator, Lieutenant-General Yakub. His only word had been an oral message conveyed by an emissary from Rawalpindi that President Yahya Khan would travel to Dacca within the next week. He did not ask me directly but left the clear impression he wished me to pass a message that he was prepared for peace and was ready to sit down and talk modalities. He said there was some flexibility in his position but that it was fast disappearing, by virtue of the fact that he had a gun pointed at each side of his head: one by the communists, the other by the military. He had lost confidence in Yahya and considered he was no longer either impartial or in control of the situation. With the Canadian educators involved in a number of East Pakistan institutions in mind, I sought Mujib's assurances concerning the reopening of schools (closed by Awami League fiat) but received none. He feared for the lives of students should there be a military clampdown. However, he did not want foreign advisors to depart and said he could provide voluntary guards for them if desired. He added that these would be of no use in the event of a military confrontation, for which he was clearly prepared.

With respect to the rapidly deteriorating economic situation in East Pakistan, Mujib said he was prepared for a continuing downward spiral if the military sought to maintain control. They should hand over power to civilians and the elected National Assembly could take it from there. He still spoke in terms of drafting a new constitution within 120 days under his guidance as majority leader. At the same time, he said that although he had not yet called for independence, it was what Bengalis wanted and he was being forced in that direction. He thought that if independence came there could still be close links with Pakistan, for example through a mutual defence agreement. All this was said without rancour but with confidence.

In my message to Ottawa reporting on this meeting I held out a shred of hope based on the President's impending visit to Dacca; but I warned of an end to the Canadian aid programs if a military crackdown ensued, which I did not rule out because of the ongoing build-up of army reinforcements. I continued to counsel against the withdrawal of experts. In addition to the arguments recorded above, I added the appeals to me by Mujib and by Asghar Khan, former Air Force Commander-in-Chief, Chairman of P.I.A. and now leader of the Pakistan Democratic Party, to keep our advisers in East Pakistan. I pointed out that their departure would both aggravate the existing economic malaise and have an adverse psychological effect on the already gloomy situation. Further, I argued that teams of advisers, once gone, would be difficult and costly to stitch together again. Finally, their absence would magnify the extent of an international rescue operation which might be needed before long.

A few days later I responded to a message from Ottawa, courtesy of the Americans, which had criticized my reluctance to recommend evacuation of Canadians from East Pakistan. By this time a few Canadian families had decided to leave and were taking opportunities to catch BOAC flights to London and other international services to Bangkok and Singapore, about forty persons in all. However, for a variety of reasons, the majority remained reluctant to leave.

My report went on to outline the stringent measures, designed to immobilize the economy, that had been taken by the Awami League as the effective government of East Pakistan, the only exceptions being the military cantonments. All governmental and quasi-governmental operations, including schools and courts remained closed. Money supplies were beginning to run short. Prices were rising and vital cooking kerosene was scarce. Despite the consequent dislocation and discomfort, the Awami League's support from Bengalis was disciplined and virtually unanimous. Observing the departure of some foreigners, the local populace concluded they had knowledge of impending danger and began to head for the villages outside Dacca. There was an air of suspended animation as everyone waited for the promised arrival of Yahya Khan. His foot-dragging was both misunderstood and a source of distrust among Bengalis, who noted the continuing arrival of army reinforcements. My own view was that his hesitation reflected his wish to be sure of his welcome and a continuing distaste for, and bafflement over, what seemed to him an intractable problem. I ended my report by reiterating my view that evacuation at that time was unnecessary, but added that this would change if the impending Yahya-Mujib discussions ended in deadlock, as then the struggle would assume a new and serious dimension.

My next report to Ottawa, dated March 16, 1971 described Yahya's arrival on March 15, and his travel to the President's residence, the route lined by troops with machine guns and automatic rifles and his vehicle escorted by a fleet of similarly armed troop carriers. Mujib had earlier pronounced that the President would be welcome as a guest of Bangladesh. At the last moment, to avoid further embarrassment to the President, he agreed to the removal of a check point put in place by the Awami League. I witnessed Yahya's convoy passing by the Intercontinental Hotel and his cheery wave to a crowd of spectators was met with sullen silence, in contrast to earlier visits when he had received a friendly welcome.

As a prelude to the President's arrival, Mujib released his action program for the week commencing March 14. This superseded, and considerably expanded on, the program proclaimed a week earlier. If ever there was any doubt about who was running East Pakistan, it was dispelled by this latest list of "directives," 35 in all, which covered the entire range of commercial, financial, economic, service, fiscal and institutional activities.

I went on to report that the situation was basically calm, notwithstanding some increase in violence and lawlessness, and that foreigners were still not the butt of Bengali animosity. I concluded my report saying that if all went well in the Yahya-Mujib talks, my wife and I would return to Islamabad by March 20; if the talks failed, we would all be running for cover. The taxi driver I used that day put it succinctly: "President is in big fix; if he give us our freedom, West Pakistanis kill him; if he does not, Bengalis kill him."

From March 16 onward I was caught up in the game of talks watching. The President's House, the seat of negotiations, was a short walk from the Intercontinental Hotel, which was the refuge of foreign correspondents, diplomats, foreign advisors and other interested parties. It became apparent from the mood of Mujib and his followers, as they entered and left the President's House, how the daily talks were faring. On March 16 the President and Mujib met alone. There was no public announcement but the grim faces of those involved told their story—no progress. This situation prevailed until March 18, when I witnessed a jubilant Mujib and his team emerge from the gate of the President's House. To my questions, grinning Awami League members said that everything had been fixed and all was well. They seemed relieved that a military solution had been averted. I returned to the hotel and consulted with my wife, who was anxious to be in Islamabad for meetings with the All Pakistan Women's Association. As it seemed the immediate crisis was over, we decided she would return at once and I would follow a few days later if it appeared a settlement would ensue.

After seeing my wife off at a distant part of the airport, which was in a state of chaos, I went back to talks watching and liaising with Canadians. Up to and including March 20 there was an air of optimism, bolstered by the arrival that day of A.K. Brohi, the noted constitutional expert, and it appeared that Yahya and Mujib had reached a tentative accommodation. This was based on the withdrawal of martial law and the transfer of power to representatives of the people. However, from Yahya's standpoint it required approval of Bhutto and his Pakistan People's Party.

Feeling optimistic, I flew back to Islamabad on March 20, naively thinking that a political solution had been found and a crisis averted. This was not to be. Bhutto arrived in Dacca on March 21 and would not agree to the Yahya-Mujib formula on the grounds that "it contained the seeds of two Pakistans" and, in any case, would need "to be put to and approved by the full knowledge of the people."

Pakistan Day, March 23, was deemed by the Awami League to be "Resistance Day." Mohammed Ali Jinnah's portrait and effigy were burned, as was the Pakistan flag, in the place of which the new flag of

Bangladesh was hoisted. On March 24 the Awami League raised the ante again with a proposal to hold two Constitutional conventions to draft two constitutions, one each for East and West Pakistan. Subsequently, the National Assembly was to meet to meld the two constitutions into a Confederation of Pakistan. These proposals were unacceptable to Bhutto and the President. Bhutto and his aides flew back to Karachi on March 24, followed by Yahya on March 25. The army moved on the night of March 25-26. Sheikh Mujibur Rahman was taken into custody and the die was cast. Eight months of guerilla warfare ensued. Pakistan and India went to war officially on December 3 and the war in the East ended on December 16 with the surrender of the Pakistan forces to the Indian army in Dacca. In the West, it concluded with the unilateral offer of a ceasefire by India on the same day.

Meanwhile, back in Islamabad, our task became more focused. We watched and reported assiduously on the political situation, with particular reference to developments in East Pakistan and with special concern for our aid program and for the Canadians still in that Province. We advised two Canadian experts with the East Pakistan Institute of Graphic Arts to leave, which they did. Acres International, W.P. London Associates and RCA (Canada) personnel soldiered on with mounting difficulties. At the end of March, the assessment I sent to Ottawa was that the Pakistan army would be able to control the cities of East Pakistan temporarily, but that the Bengali opposition would grow and ultimately triumph.

I returned to East Pakistan again at the end of April, specifically to assess the value of keeping high-powered teams of Canadians on jobs where there was now little or nothing they could do. During my visit in March and again now I met daily with General Allen Clark of Acres International and his Canadian experts to share information, theirs being derived from their perspective on outlying areas where they had personnel and mine on political developments, from my sources in town. These exchanges proved to be invaluable to both of us when it came to making decisions on whether to remain or leave.

On this visit I was anxious to make the rounds of Canadians, in order to advise them again of the situation and the need to consider departure while it remained possible. PIA was still flying in and out of Dacca and Burmese and Thai airlines were doing so intermittently. I was able to fly to Chittagong, where once more I met with the Brothers and Sisters of the Holy Cross order and received the expected response that they were committed to their work in Bengal and would not leave, whatever might happen. I travelled to the satellite earth receiving station, accompanied by the RCA (Canada) site manager, Paul Wajtowicz, who, in the face of nearly insuperable difficulties, had completed about two thirds of the foundation. Back in Chittagong I sought another Canadian, Mr. R.L. Hande of James Findlay & Co., who was an adviser on electrical power. By chance, I discovered him dealing with a small transformer station which was smouldering after sabotage by the Mukti Bahini (guerillas). His heroic efforts were largely responsible for keeping power flowing in Chittagong at that time. Neither he nor Wajtowicz was ready to leave at that point, but they did so later when their work became impossible.

Another group of Holy Cross Canadians lived and worked in Barisol, a substantial town on the Jamuna River. At the time it was inaccessible by land, boat or air. So I arranged to call on the Governor, Lieutenant-General Tikka Khan, who had replaced the summarily dismissed Vice-Admiral Ahsan on March 1. In the course of our discussion I appealed for help in finding a way to visit the Canadians in Barisol. He promised to think about it and the following day I was roused at 6:00 a.m. to find the Governor on the line. He offered to take me to Barisol if I could be at his residence by 7:00 a.m. As it was my only hope of contacting the Canadians there, I accepted with alacrity. We flew in an army helicopter to Barisol where two Holy Cross Brothers, forewarned by the Governor, greeted me. We drove to their nearby mission and had an hour's meeting, then returned to the airport. Like their confrères in Chittagong, they cheerfully declined to consider leaving but asked me to arrange for some insulin for one of their members, which I did on my return to Dacca. Before we left Barisol one of the local commanders drew me aside to say he was fully aware that the Canadian Brothers were at times harbouring Mukti Bahini who were on the run. He suggested I warn the Canadians that if caught doing so they would be in deep trouble. I responded with thanks and what I hoped was an enigmatic smile.

The Governor, of course, had not arranged this trip for my benefit. He was traveling to Barisol, Khulna and Jessore to receive first hand reports from his army commanders in those areas. As there were no Canadians in Khulna or Jessore at the time, I attempted when we landed to move off and leave Tikka with his army cohorts, but he insisted I stay. The result was that I was privy to the reports given by each officer who had been pulled in from outlying areas. It was fascinating but embarrassing. The sum of the reports was that everything was under control. In fact, that was the situation at that time, though there was still isolated violence around the province, as I had witnessed in Chittagong.

I made two more visits to East Pakistan in 1971, one at the end of August, by which time the Martial Law regime and army were becoming embattled and the Mukti Bahini more numerous and better trained and armed by their Indian patrons. The final journey was on November 1, in the company of CIDA President Mr. Gerin-Lajoie and a planeload of relief goods. It was later alleged by critics that these items were misused, some blankets having turned up in local markets. The criticism was largely misplaced, since many families that received gift blankets did in fact sell them to obtain money for items of greater need. The effect was as desired: practical help to the needy.

CANADA-PAKISTAN DIALOGUE

Throughout 1971, besides monitoring the political situation, we were engaged in a dialogue with Ottawa over the aid program. In addition, we were consulted a number of times on the appropriate content for letters from Prime Minister Trudeau to President Yahya Khan. On one occasion I was instructed to deliver a message in person to the President, which diplomatically suggested Bengali bashing was hardly the way to win hearts and solve problems. From my own viewpoint I doubted the value of such an exercise, as the President was not amenable to persuasion by criticism. My doubts were soon confirmed. The President could hardly wait for the end of my presentation before he exploded in a burst of self-righteous indignation, absolving himself as the cause of the civil war in East Pakistan. The message itself would have been less irritating had the timing been more felicitous. At the time Yahya was the butt of both domestic and foreign criticism and did not take kindly to it.

What pressure Canada exerted on Pakistan throughout this trying period was consistently constructive and aimed at promoting East-West dialogue and political solutions. To our colleagues in New Delhi our advice and Ottawa's responses were often considered to be much too gentle. But it was obvious to those who lived in Pakistan that Yahya was not a man who responded positively to attack. He was straightforward and prepared to listen and be persuaded. Indeed, if he was to be criticized it was for being too easily swayed by his Principal Staff Officer, Lieutenant-General Peerzada, the Army Chief of Staff, General Hamid, and other hawks at army headquarters. Another less than positive influence on the President was Bhutto, who frightened him into postponing the March 3 session of the National Assembly and, in the third week of March, ended all hope of any form of reconciliation by rejecting the tentative Mujib-Yahya agreement.

Early in May, in a reply to a letter from the President dated March 31, 1971, Prime Minister Trudeau expressed the concerns of Canadians over the casualties in East Pakistan. Acknowledging that the search for solutions was the responsibility of the government and people of Pakistan, he first stated his hope that it would soon be possible to resume that search and second, observed that it would be tragic to be diverted from the accepted objectives of political and economic progress. In a reference to the disastrous typhoon and tidal wave suffered by East Pakistan late in 1970, the Prime Minister said Canada was prepared to join with the international community to provide emergency relief. He closed with wishes for a speedy resolution of Pakistan's current difficulties.

In another letter near the end of July 1971, the Prime Minister noted the lack of progress toward political solutions or the resumption of political dialogue and urged on the President the need for early forward movement on constitutional development. He underlined the importance of normalization for encouraging the return of refugees (then pouring into India from East Pakistan) and said a more active search for political compromise was a precondition for the return of these people. He placed his frank comments in the context of views offered by a Commonwealth colleague.

Again in August, I was instructed by Ottawa to deliver a letter from the Prime Minister to President Yahya Khan at the highest level possible. I consulted the Foreign Secretary, Sultan Khan, about the feasibility of personally delivering the letter to the President. He was candid in stating it would be best for all concerned if I were to give him the letter, which he promised to deliver immediately to the President. His argument for this procedure was that Yahya was then receiving other letters from foreign governments and was exceedingly "touchy." This being so, he thought personal delivery might be counter-productive.

The message in this case was a plea concerning the treatment of Sheikh Mujibur Rahman, who was in custody in West Pakistan and whose trial had been announced by the President on August 9. In his usual diplomatic way, the Prime Minister said many outside Pakistan would regard Mujib's trial as a political rather than a judicial act. He asked the President to consider the significance for Pakistan of a humane and magnanimous decision with respect to Mujib. When I met the President at a reception a few days after this letter had been delivered, a director in the Ministry of Foreign Affairs started to introduce me but the President waved him off saying "Oh, I know him well. He's been pressurizing me." He went on to say everyone was trying to "pressurize" him concerning Mujib and added that he would not reply to either Prime Minister Trudeau or to any of the others.

Our exchanges with Pakistan were not always at such an exalted level. For example, under instructions from Ottawa, I called on the Foreign Ministry on March 27, 1971 (two days after the army crackdown in East Pakistan) to register concern for the safety of Canadians in the East wing. Our military attaché did the same with the Ministry of Defence. We were assured that foreigners in East Pakistan were in no danger and this proved to be the case. At the same time, some thirty foreign correspondents, including Canadians, were unceremoniously loaded on a plane in Dacca and dumped in Karachi after being stripped of their films. Thus ended the slow but steady progress toward press freedom and a more open society which had been achieved over the previous year.

As 1971 wore on, we in the High Commission and Ottawa carried out a dialogue on the possibilities of salvaging and executing the Canadian aid program. We were of one mind in this respect for the situation gave us little choice. The March 25 military onslaught in East Pakistan effectively terminated our program there. One of the main objectives of my several trips to East Pakistan and of the travels of our development assistance officers through the summer of 1971 was to assess the feasibility of carrying on or of modifying the program to accommodate the new situation. We found the various authorities involved, without exception, were most anxious for us to carry on. But as time passed it became clear that this would be impossible. Outlying areas became infested with Mukti Bahini and even cities like Chittagong were subjected to their attacks. Moreover, the Awami League's *hartal* stopped all institutional activity.

In mid-November our development and immigration officers, Emil Baran and Gibby Gibson, travelled to East Pakistan in attempts to salvage what was possible from the tatters of our aid and immigration programs. It became clear that development assistance to East Pakistan would be impossible for the time being. By agreement with Ottawa the emphasis in our original program shifted away from development toward social justice and humanitarian relief. It was decided in Ottawa there would be no new aid commitments but that those undertaken for 1971-72 would be maintained. It had already been decided, in May, 1971 that future commitments would stem from a re-examination of past undertakings, with a view to developing broader policies which would encourage peace, rehabilitation and, eventually, continuing development. Canada made it clear to the Pakistan government that it stood ready to work with other members of the Pakistan Consortium to provide humanitarian relief to Pakistan and, at the same time, to help India to deal with the extraordinary influx of refugees from East Pakistan. Despite some disposition in Canada and in certain diplomatic quarters to cut aid to Pakistan, we in the High Commission opposed such a move, and Ottawa agreed, on the ground that it would simply compound the tragedy for the people of Pakistan, both East and West.

Throughout 1971 the Canadian government consistently favoured restoration of democratic government under civilian rule, on the basis of the elections to the National Assembly in December 1970. In July 1971, to add teeth to its declarations, Canada prohibited the export of aircraft spares and other military equipment to Pakistan and to the subcontinent generally, a move which substantially lowered Canada's popularity in Pakistan in both official and other circles.

WAR WITH INDIA

The situation in East Pakistan continued to deteriorate in 1971, especially after November 21, when India increased its pressure with stepped-up attacks on border posts and towns in the East wing. On November 22 Yahya declared a State of Emergency throughout Pakistan and on December 3 all-out war between India and Pakistan commenced. Late that evening I, the British High Commissioner and the Ambassadors of Belgium, France, Germany, Italy and Sweden were summoned to the Foreign Ministry for a briefing by Mohamad Sultan, Director-General for the Americas and West Europe. Characterizing Indian army attacks on East Pakistan on November 21 as the start of war with Pakistan, he alleged now that the Indian army, with air support, had attacked West Pakistan at Sialkot, Chumb (near Lahore) and Rajasthan in the Rahimyar Khan area, commencing at 3:30 in the afternoon. He said the Pakistan Air Force had responded at 6:00 p.m. with attacks on Indian targets at Amritsar, Avantipur, Pathankot and Srinagar in Kashmir.

During the two weeks following the outbreak of all-out war, in Islamabad we watched Pakistan's Canberra bombers flying east to Indian targets and corresponding westward Indian flights aimed mainly at the Rawalpindi airport and the nearby Attock Oil refinery. Both sustained considerable damage but insufficient to stop their operation. The only

Indian success at the airport was the destruction of an UNMOGIP Caribou aircraft, built in and supplied by Canada, the American Embassy air attaché's small aircraft and a non-flying wooden mock-up plane. The runways sustained inconsequential damage. One or two bombs fell harmlessly in Islamabad which lacked industry or anything of strategic importance (the decision makers were situated in Rawalpindi).

Karachi was a different matter, as the Indians made a more determined effort to knock out the Pakistan Airforce airfield and station, which were adjacent to the civil airport and, more seriously from a Canadian standpoint, to hit KANUPP where some 65 Canadians lived and worked. RCA (Canada) personnel were also in the area, as well as a miscellany of other Canadians. As the bombing intensified, the question of evacuation became urgent and my recommendation to Ottawa was the removal of Canadians from Karachi by Canadian Armed Forces [CAF] aircraft. At no time did I suggest Canadians in northern West Pakistan should be withdrawn. However, when Ottawa decided to make a CAF Boeing 707 available for the Canadians in the Karachi area, it decreed that those in the north should go too.

This required an enormous amount of hard work in a very short time. Most of the burden fell on our Counsellor, Bill Brett, acting as chief coordinator, our administrative officer, Doug McCue, who had to contact Canadians spread over a wide area, and our military attaché, Colonel Trower, who had the difficult task of arranging at short notice flight clearances in Karachi and Rawalpindi. It also required the help of our High Commission in Delhi which had the equally, if not more, difficult mission of persuading the Indians to guarantee a gap in their bombing to enable the Canadian flight to pick up its passengers unscathed. A convoy of Canadians and other nationalities drove via Baluchistan to Kabul, but this route had a variety of drawbacks, including danger of attack by local tribesmen and the lack of accommodation en route and in Kabul. So, on December 12, the CAF Boeing 707, after picking up the remaining Karachi Canadians, touched down in Rawalpindi, along with British and Soviet planes on the same mission for their nationals. We were proud to be able to accommodate a variety of other nationals on our plane. This was both helpful and useful because the plane's first stop was Teheran, and the fact that it carried a number of Iranian officials and families undoubtedly eased the process of obtaining flight clearance and the visas which were required.

As our convoy of Canadians in minibuses was disgorged at the airport, we were surrounded by a shouting, heaving mob which initially took us for Russians. As backer and signatory of a treaty with India, the Soviet Union was highly unpopular in West Pakistan. But, as I led our departees across the tarmac to the waiting Boeing 707, the atmosphere changed. The word spread that we were Canadians and we were cheered and beseeched not to leave and to return soon. The Russians were roughed up and their planes sustained some damage from showers of stones. Our own pride at being able to assist other nationalities, together with our own citizens, was enhanced as we left them in the competent hands of the CAF. Some of the passengers disembarked in Tehran but most proceeded to Canada via Lahr, where empty seats were filled with Canadian forces personnel, disgruntled at the delay occasioned by the flight's diversion to Pakistan. Our evacuees were less than impressed with their attitude and still less with their rush to occupy the best seats and spread themselves, to the disadvantage of those who had already travelled so far under cramped conditions.

Back in Islamabad our scaled down High Commission crew of eight (myself, the military attaché and his sergeant, the administrative officer, one immigration officer and one aid officer, one communicator and a guard) rattled around our now largely unoccupied chancery and residences. We busied ourselves with gathering information and reporting daily to Ottawa on the war situation. It had not been easy to select from among our top notch High Commission team those who would go and those who would stay. With one exception, all had volunteered to be part of our skeleton crew.

We were to celebrate Christmas on our own, so we did our best to make it an occasion. We joined forces and our combined culinary staff provided handsomely. Our toasts rose warmly to absent ones so far away. Following our sumptuous Christmas fare, and to assuage our sense of loss, we repaired to the golf course, where our scores ballooned in consonance with the expansion of our postprandial waistlines.

AFTERMATH OF WAR

With the war over, the High Commission exodus was reversed in January 1972, but the number of returnees was substantially reduced. Those whose tour of duty was nearly over did not return and when the dust had settled our complement was slimmer by four officers and several support staff.

Priorities elsewhere, the loss of East Pakistan and the war-induced slowdown in trade, aid and immigration justified the reduction in numbers. Perhaps more serious was the loss of a first-rate team and the high morale and efficiency which had marked its performance. It was to be many months before full recovery would take place.

I like to think that, throughout the crucial year of 1971, our efforts in the Canadian High Commission were integral to the policies developed in Ottawa toward Pakistan and the historic events then unfolding. Those policies in the early stages deplored the shattering of Pakistan's geographical and national integrity and, particularly, the way in which this took place: first, through internal conflict and, finally, through foreign intervention. Canada urged on Pakistan quick action to introduce civilian, representative government in East Pakistan and counselled patience to India. Canadian views had little effect. The rulers of Pakistan offered a limited number of gestures to Bengalis of the East wing and these were too little, too late. India refused to discuss refugees with the government of Pakistan and would not countenance international involvement with them, other than the provision of funds to India to support them.

Throughout the historic events of 1971 the international community, by and large, stood by helplessly and watched as Pakistan moved inexorably toward civil war and, finally, dismemberment by outside forces. Despite some eloquent pleading by Bhutto in New York, the UN proved to be little more than a powerless bystander in the face of the shattering events which it could neither influence nor control. Amongst the great powers, the U.S. purportedly "tilted" toward Pakistan but could find nothing better to demonstrate this than a futile deployment of an American fleet in the Indian ocean. The Chinese, ostensibly backers of Pakistan, were equally ineffectual, merely backing their muted words of support with a $200 million line of credit for arms. The British, as the former colonial master, sought gingerly to avoid exacerbating relations with either India or Pakistan though, after the war ended, it was the early decision by Britain to recognize Bangladesh that triggered Bhutto's withdrawal of Pakistan from the Commonwealth. The only international action that significantly influenced the war over Bangladesh was taken by the Soviet Union. Through the conclusion of its Treaty of Friendship with India the latter gained both the material and the psychological support required for a move from covert aid to the Bangladeshi guerilals to all-out war in the form of an invading army.

Canada regarded both India and Pakistan as belligerents once the shooting between them started. Shipments of offensive military *matériel* to both was banned. Beyond this, Canadian energies were directed toward: a) Terminating the war as soon as possible; b) limiting the spread of the war (India's alliance with the Soviet Union and Pakistan's with China held the potential to embroil the great powers, with undesirable consequences); c) providing humanitarian aid (aid to refugees was to be channelled through international agencies while the war lasted); d) limiting development assistance projects to existing commitments to India and Pakistan while the war lasted; e) avoiding the provision of assistance that might support the war-making capacity of either India or Pakistan.

In sum, Canada's priorities were first, cessation of fighting and second, provision of humanitarian assistance. We in the High Commission were at one with Ottawa with respect to both its concerns and its priorities. The only substantial difference between us occurred with respect to the evacuation of Canadians. In East Pakistan this was no more than a shading with respect to timing. In West Pakistan, we did not favour the evacuation of Canadians from the north but were in complete agreement with respect to the south. These were minor differences considering the stakes involved.

The differences with our colleagues in New Delhi were more acute but not more so than one would expect when looking at situations from the widely different perspectives of India and Pakistan. Indeed, in an effort to minimize differences and to understand each other's points of view, I travelled to New Delhi at the end of May, 1971 to discuss the situation with my colleague Jim George. With some effort we were able to collaborate on a joint telegram to Ottawa in which we urged priority consideration to the welfare of Bengali refugees, reasoned that there was no longer a need to pursue a rigid policy of parallelism toward India and Pakistan, and suggested it might be appropriate at the June meeting of the Pakistan Consortium to put pressure on Pakistan to observe restraint in the East wing.

Pakistan's defeat by India and the surrender of its forces in East Pakistan to the commander of the Indian invasion forces on December 16, 1971 effectively terminated the war and brought the swift replacement of Yahya Khan as President and Chief Martial Law Administrator by Zulfikar Ali Bhutto, on the basis of the latter's electoral victory in West Pakistan in December 1970. Having achieved his long-held ambition to reach the pinnacle of power, Bhutto set about restoring the fortunes of West Pakistan.

In this he was largely successful, though his initial hope for some form of confederation or link with newly independent Bangladesh failed. His achievement was to lift a defeated and demoralized country and give it confidence once more. He introduced a workable government and channelled national energies into solving the country's many problems. He instituted land reform and cleaned house in the military establishment. In April, 1972 he convened the National Assembly, where he gained a vote of confidence and approval for an interim constitution. An assembly committee was established to draft a new constitution before August 14, 1973. He released Mujib unconditionally. He realigned Pakistan's foreign policy, emphasizing bilateralism but tilting toward the Muslim world. He consolidated relations with China. He negotiated peace with India on respectable terms and secured the return of Pakistan's prisoners-of-war. He terminated martial law and, in 1973, introduced a new democratic constitution under which he became Prime Minister.

In January, 1972 I was instructed to deliver a letter from Prime Minister Trudeau to the President which offered good wishes on his assumption of the presidency and expressed confidence that under his leadership progress toward peaceful solutions would continue. It closed with an invitation to Bhutto to get in touch if there was anything the Prime Minister could do to contribute to the development and progress of Pakistan or if he wished to exchange views. I was instructed in my oral presentation to indicate the likelihood that Canada would move on recognition of Bangladesh with our Consortium partners, as this would provide for a useful influence in Dacca.

Presentation of the letter became a problem as, early in January, Bhutto had embarked on a travel program which took him to the Muslim countries of the Middle East. On his return, he proceeded to his ancestral home at Larkhana in Sind, to which he had invited all heads of mission and their wives. In consequence, I delivered the Prime Minister's message in an exotic environment reminiscent of the days of the British Raj. In response, Bhutto pleaded for a short delay to provide him with the time to reach agreements with Mujib. Moreover, he considered recognition would be inappropriate while Indian troops were still occupying Bangladesh. Recognition would complicate matters for him domestically. Britain's intention to recognize Bangladesh in the near future had been made known in London and Bhutto now said that, if Britain took this action prematurely, the result would be Pakistan's withdrawal from the Commonwealth.

With respect to Bangladesh, Bhutto initiated his own version of the Hallstein Doctrine, threatening to break relations with countries prematurely recognizing Bangladesh. It was on this issue that we in Islamabad parted company with our colleagues in the Canadian High Commission in New Delhi. The latter argued for immediate recognition, as did Arnold Smith, the Commonwealth Secretary General. I argued that what was at issue was not recognition per se: not whether but when to recognize. This being so, I suggested there would be no advantage to be gained from seeking the favour of Bangladesh at the cost of losing good relations with Pakistan by granting immediate recognition. Nothing would be gained by premature recognition but it could result in Pakistan's withdrawal from the Commonwealth and, possibly, a break in diplomatic relations such as occurred with Bulgaria, Mongolia and Poland or the withdrawal of ambassadors in the cases of Burma and Nepal. Further, the pro-recognition promoters argued that such a move would facilitate the provision of aid to Bangladesh. My answer was that immediate help could be offered through international institutions and voluntary agencies whose channels to Bangladesh already existed.

In my view, by the time Canadian supervision of our contribution to reconstruction was required, the question of recognition would be but a memory. I saw no reason to delay resumption of aid to either Pakistan or Bangladesh until that question had been settled. Further, there was a suggestion that Soviet and East European recognition, already accorded, if combined with quick aid, would give the communists a monopoly on influence in Bangladesh. I suggested any assistance these countries might offer should be welcomed. Their record on development assistance to the Third World had never been commensurate with either their obligations or capacity. Whatever they provided would be far short of Bangladesh's needs and, as elsewhere in the developing world, it would in the end be Western help which counted. In sum, my advice was that a modest degree of patience on the question of recognition would achieve all our aims in both Pakistan and Bangladesh.

In the event, the debate ended quickly on January 30, 1972 when the British informed Bhutto of their intention to recognize Bangladesh on February 4. At the invitation of President Bhutto, Arnold Smith, Commonwealth Secretary General, had arrived in Rawalpindi early in the afternoon of January 30. I was among those who greeted him at the airport, along with the Pakistan Chief of Protocol. My recollection varies slightly from Smith's, in that I understood Bhutto had already decided to withdraw from the Commonwealth, whereas Smith's memoirs record that the Chief of Protocol said Bhutto was then in session with his Cabinet considering how to react to the British decision. These memory nuances are of no consequence, since Pakistan's decision to withdraw from the Commonwealth was announced later that afternoon by Radio Pakistan. Smith was understandably upset as he had dashed to Pakistan in the hope of persuading Bhutto against such action. His immediate impulse was to return to London without seeing the President. Bhutto, however, dissuaded him and they met privately before a working dinner with the provincial governors and members of the cabinet. Smith records that by the end of the evening Bhutto and his ministers "seemed somewhat shaken and showing regret at their precipitate action."

The debate on recognition of Bangladesh having opened up old tensions and conflicts of view between India and Pakistan and between Canada's diplomatic missions in New Delhi and Islamabad, as well as their protagonists in Ottawa, Jim George and I were summoned home toward the end of February, 1972 for the proverbial "consultations." We both saw the Prime Minister and the relevant authorities in the Department of External Affairs. While exchanges of views at home base are always useful—and these were—it seemed to me that our temporary recall had more to do with public relations in Canada, India and Pakistan than with substantive issues. The pace in the subcontinent had its own momentum and timetable and Canadian views at this point, while sensible, seemed irrelevant to the subcontinental powers. Pakistan was tilting toward bilateralism and the Muslim world and had little time for other countries beyond the U.S., Soviet Union, India and China.

Pakistan's departure from the Commonwealth had a number of practical consequences. I had by virtue of that act become an Ambassador and the High Commission an Embassy. The question posed for all Commonwealth envoys was whether we would be obliged to present our credentials afresh and whether formal recognition would be required. What would our countries' policies be regarding visas, Commonwealth trade preferences, Colombo Plan assistance and other preferred treatment customarily accorded Commonwealth members? I met with Commonwealth colleagues and with the Foreign Ministry to discuss these matters. Happily Ottawa agreed to our proposals for maintenance of the status quo with respect to preferred treatment for Pakistan, as had been done with respect to the Republic of Ireland, a former Commonwealth member. All agreed that continuing official business with the Pakistan government would make recognition a non-issue and there would be no need to present credentials once more. The only immediate change in our status was the replacement of our High Commission nameplate by a new one with the Embassy designation.

As the summer of 1972 proceeded our Embassy was adjusting, not without pain, to the loss of four officers (political, aid, trade and immigration). Our team had changed substantially following the evacuation of December 1971-January 1972 and all were adapting to the new political and economic situations, a new aid program and the beginnings of growing instability in the country. Local costs were rising, currency devaluation intruded and our post index was adjusted abruptly without consultation and, in our view, without sufficient analysis of the situation. Morale was slow in returning.

By midsummer, 1972 my posting to Beijing had been decided on and it was time to make my farewell calls in Pakistan and Afghanistan. My call on President Bhutto, on August 8, 1972 revealed him at his best. Banishing formality and protocol he invited me into the garden of his residence where we sat in easy chairs as the dusk gathered, scotch in hand. He was completely relaxed and looked fit despite his wearing schedule and the fact that he had skipped the PPP's Central Committee meeting that afternoon by reason of "indisposition." He talked freely of Pakistan's internal political and economic situation, of Bangladesh, Bengalis in Pakistan, POWs and India.

On the home front, the President laid the burden of Pakistan's economic difficulties at the door of the successive dictatorships of Ayub Khan and Yahya Khan. He said the establishment of his government signalled a fundamental change and both labour and management would have to come to terms with the new situation.

With respect to Bangladesh, he was forthright in saying he accepted Bangladesh's independence as irreversible. He had sent a message to Mujib promising instant recognition of Bangladesh the moment the two leaders met but Mujib had not responded. His rigidity and immobility were playing into the hands of right-wing extremists in Pakistan. He acknowledged the existence of what he termed "pockets of resistance" in the country, especially in Lahore. His own hesitation was motivated by his wish to bring the entire nation with him.

As for the Bengalis remaining in Pakistan, they could "go home tomorrow" provided the question of Pakistan POWs and civilian internees was settled. When I said the increasingly harsh treatment of the Bengalis in Pakistan was incomprehensible, he looked thoughtful, said he would think about it and concluded by promising "I'll do my best for them."

Referring to China's assurance it would veto Bangladesh's application for UN membership, Bhutto said this was not just an indication of support for Pakistan but was a matter of principle: Bangladesh had not complied with UN resolutions on the return of POWs and the withdrawal of foreign forces.

He explained the failure of the Simla Agreement with India to include restoration of diplomatic relations as an attempt by India to pressure Pakistan into recognizing Bangladesh. He contrasted this with his voluntary good-will gesture that day in releasing unconditionally 6,000 Indian civilians. At the same time, he said, the 600 Indian military POWs held by Pakistan would have to await further developments on the question of Pakistani POWs in Indian hands.

I left Pakistan at the end of August carrying with me the impression of a President who was fully aware of the enormity of the problems he faced but confident and perfectly at ease with his task.

NOTES

1. See John Hadwen (Chapter 10), pages 162-65.
2. The new capital, Islamabad, housed most of the government's offices and ministries but the President and Chief Martial Law Administrator and the military command remained in the twin city, Rawalpindi. Physically, the two were about 10 miles apart.
3. The Six Points envisaged a federation of the two distinct parts of the country and allocated only defence and foreign affairs to the central government. All residual powers, including taxation, were to be vested in the two federating states. Bengalis looked upon these proposals as a demand for autonomy. West Pakistanis believed them to be a step on the road to secession.

John Small, born in China and educated in Canada, served with the Royal Navy in World War II in the North Atlantic, the Mediterranean, Australia and Normandy. After the war he worked for five years as an Agricultural Trade Commissioner in Holland, Belgium, Luxembourg and Denmark. After transferring to External Affairs as a China specialist, he was posted to Hong Kong and Karachi. Between 1955 and 1984, Mr. Small served as Permanent Representative to the OECD in Paris, High Commissioner to Pakistan, Malaysia and Brunei, as Ambassador to Afghanistan, China and Vietnam, as well as Deputy Secretary General (Economic) of the Commonwealth in London.

15

NATIONALIZATION IN GUYANA

J.A. STILES

THE MOST DIFFICULT and important problem during my years as Canadian High Commissioner in Guyana (1970-1973) arose in 1970 from the threat by the Guyanese government to nationalize the Demerara Bauxite Company Ltd. (Demba), a wholly owned subsidiary of the Aluminum Company of Canada (Alcan). This raised the question of what action the Canadian government should take in such circumstances. Should diplomatic pressure be brought to bear on behalf of the Canadian company? Should Canadian government representatives be involved in a mediatory role? Should development aid be discontinued?

Following full consideration, the Canadian government decided: a) to urge the Guyanese government to consider very carefully before making such a move, but to acknowledge the right of Guyana as a sovereign nation to take whatever action in the development of its national resources it deemed appropriate; and b) should the nationalization route be chosen, to indicate to the Guyanese government that Canada expected that there would be no discrimination against a Canadian company in favour of another non-Guyanese company; and c) should a decision be taken to nationalize, to encourage a strong effort to reach agreement among the parties concerned regarding compensation.

In the event, the Guyanese authorities did nationalize Demba on July 15, 1971. This essay reviews the Demba case from my viewpoint, describes the international implications involved and recounts the considerable drama that unfolded before a mutually acceptable agreement on compensation was achieved.

BACKGROUND

In the late 1960s and early 1970s a number of developing countries, particularly in Africa and South America, decided that the time had come to take control of their natural resources which were then being developed by foreign companies. Guyana, formerly British Guiana, which had obtained its political independence in 1966, felt strongly that it had not been receiving a sufficient return from the production and export of its bauxite. Demba was Guyana's principal bauxite producer and by 1970 bauxite was the country's main export and leading source of foreign exchange. The only other bauxite producer in Guyana was the U.S.-owned Reynolds Metal Company, a much smaller operation than that of Demba.

Observing the apparent success of the Zambian government's takeover of its copper industry from the Belgians, the Guyanese authorities in 1970 decided to see if they could do the same with the mining of their bauxite. In this they were egged on, not only by strong nationalist elements in Guyana, but also by a leading Jamaican economist, Dr. Norman Girvan, who had specialized in the study of the Caribbean bauxite industry and was a strong proponent of nationalization. Dr. Girvan was hired by the Guyanese government as special adviser in the period leading up to the takeover of Demba.

Indications of the Guyanese government's plans soon became known to Demba and Alcan headquarters in Montreal. Alcan President Nathanael Davis, D.D. Mackay, President of Alcan Ore Ltd. and E. Hugh Roach, Alcan Public Affairs Adviser, visited External Affairs in Ottawa in May, 1970 and stressed to Minister of External Affairs Mitchell Sharp and senior departmental officials the growing trend towards economic nationalism in the area. They hoped the Canadian government would help to ensure Demba was treated fairly in the negotiations with the Guyanese government, which they anticipated would take place within a few months.

From the outset the Canadian officials in the departments concerned (External Affairs; Industry, Trade and Commerce; Energy, Mines and Resources; Finance; and the Prime Minister's Office) fully realized the significance of the threat to nationalize Demba. From a domestic viewpoint Guyanese bauxite was at that time important to Canada's aluminum production. Not only did the industry bring substantial employment to Canadians in Arvida, Quebec and Kitimat, British Columbia but its aluminum output constituted Canada's sixth leading export.

In the past, Canada's approach to nationalization issues affecting Canadian firms abroad had been to treat each case on its merits. The 1970 nationalization by the Spanish government of the Barcelona Traction Company (a subsidiary of Barcelona Light and Power Company Ltd. which was incorporated in Canada) concerned a company largely owned by Belgian interests and only 0.2 percent by Canadian nationals. The case of the International Petroleum Company, nationalized by the Peruvian government, concerned a wholly owned subsidiary of Standard Oil of New Jersey which had registered its head office in Toronto. Thus, neither of these involved the substantial Canadian interests that were associated with Demba.

Externally, Canada in recent years had been active in building up relations with Third World countries, largely through increased development assistance. The Commonwealth Caribbean countries, Canada's closest Third World neighbours, comprised an area of Canadian aid concentration where our development assistance programs were increasing steadily.

Canadian officials were also aware of the extensive U.S. involvement in the region and shared the U.S. government's concern about the potential "demonstration effect" of a Demba nationalization on U.S. and Canadian interests in other countries in that part of the world, particularly Jamaica, Trinidad and Surinam.

CHRONOLOGY OF EVENTS (APRIL, 1970-JULY, 1971)

The Pre-negotiation Period (April, 1970-December 7, 1970)
In April, 1970 the ruling political party in Guyana, the People's National Congress [PNC], at its annual meeting called on the government to secure a minimum controlling interest of 51 percent in Guyana's forest and mining resources. Many members of the party had been questioning why their country, which had acquired political independence in 1966, had not yet been able to bring an end to "foreign, white economic domination." At the time of the designation of Guyana as a Cooperative Republic in February, 1970 the Prime Minister had also pledged to work "for the complete emancipation of the economy."

The Guyanese government then began to make thorough technical preparations for taking control of the bauxite industry. Various strategies were considered which were greatly influenced by the Zambian copper case. In the Zambian negotiations the foreign company had in the end managed to secure a management contract, which in practice gave them continuing control of the industry. The Guyanese wished to avoid this if at all possible. The Guyanese team also realized that it must prepare for full nationalization if necessary. It must also consider Guyana's capacity to market the bauxite after a takeover and it must be satisfied that it could attract personnel to run the company. The team felt that all this was feasible, although there might at first be some serious dislocation.

During this time a concerted, government-inspired campaign developed in the press to discredit Demba. Demba was depicted as a "cold, capitalistic enterprise which is misusing Guyana's natural resources and providing foreign owners with huge profits."

The President of Demba in Georgetown, Mr. J.G. Campbell, in response to many local queries as to "why don't you say something," broadcast over Georgetown radio stations on August 26, 1970 and presented the facts from the official accounts of the company. These indicated that over Demba's 50-year operation 23 cents of every dollar earned went to Demba employees, 36 cents were spent on supplies and services and 19 cents on plant investment, 13 cents went to the Guyana government for income taxes, royalties and customs duties, leaving only 9 cents of each dollar received as the owner's share.[1]

The Guyanese press leaped on this disclosure, strongly maintaining that far too much had gone to overseas suppliers for materials, parts and services. Why hadn't Demba obtained more local supplies?, they asked.

Demba officials maintained that they *had* in fact developed numerous local sources of goods and services for their operations. They pointed to their machine shops, the largest in the Caribbean, which gave employment to some eight hundred Guyanese; to the Alcan-financed diversification of Sprostons which employed over a thousand Guyanese. Sprostons, besides managing navigation on the Demerara River, had built a dry dock (which made possible the building of barges and tugs sold to Trinidad oil producers and others) as well as a foundry, machine shops and a Caterpillar engine-rebuilding facility. All of these helped to reduce the country's, and Demba's, reliance on imports.

Demba officers might also have referred to the Mackenzie Hospital, built in 1923, which looked after not only Demba employees but also the emergency needs of much of the interior of the country. The company had also built an excellent trade school which facilitated the technical training of many Guyanese. Sadly, all of these and other Demba accomplishments, such as the important work on the control of malaria carried out by the eminent specialist, Dr. Giglioli, who had been recruited by Demba, were either ignored or overlooked by the Guyanese.

Throughout September and October, 1970 the media war in Guyana continued, with an accompanying deterioration of relations between Demba and the Guyanese government. Demba was expecting the date of the start of negotiations to be set at any time and had been preparing as best it could without knowing in detail what the Guyanese authorities had in mind.

On October 14, Senator Paul Martin arrived in Guyana to discuss with the Guyanese Canada's decision to end the customs rebates it had been granting on imported Guyanese sugar and its proposal to replace this concession with an agricultural development fund. I arranged for him to meet Prime Minister Burnham and Foreign Minister Ramphal for a discussion of this fund and also for a review of the Demba situation, and I accompanied him to this meeting.

Senator Martin indicated to Prime Minister Burnham that, while the Canadian government accepted that it was Guyana's right to nationalize its resources, should this appear to be in the nation's long-term interests, Canada was also interested in seeing that the Canadian company was not discriminated against and was treated fairly. Mr. Burnham replied that no discrimination was planned and that Demba would be receiving fair treatment. He added that he was under great pressure from the "young turks" in his party to achieve quick results in regard to control of the Guyanese economy.

Prime Minister Burnham appeared to deliberately misinterpret Senator Martin's comments at a personal meeting he had with Demba President Campbell in Georgetown on November 24, when he told Campbell "the Canadian government does not really care what happens," in reference to the forthcoming negotiations with Demba. Campbell promptly relayed this to Alcan in Montreal and that company arranged for a high-level visit with External Affairs in Ottawa. The result was a "flash" message (highest priority) on December 1 to the Canadian High Commission in Georgetown, requesting that Prime Minister Burnham be assured that the Canadian government did in fact care very much and that it expected Demba to receive fair and non-discriminatory treatment. In my meeting that day with Prime Minister Burnham, at which I relayed this message, he said "there must have been a misunderstanding." He again reassured me that Demba and Alcan would be treated fairly and that any action his government might take would in due course be applied in a similar manner to other foreign interests. He added that, should Canada decide to discontinue its development aid to Guyana (then approximately $3.5 million annually), such action would not deter Guyana from its plan to assume control of the local bauxite industry.

On November 28, 1970 the Guyanese government wrote a "confidential" letter to Demba setting the date of December 7 for negotiations to

begin. In their letter they included what they called their "non-negotiable" terms. These were that:
- the Guyanese government would have a majority participation in Demba;
- government participation would be effected by means of the purchase of a share of Demba's assets;
- valuation of the assets would be made on the basis of their written-down book value for income tax purposes, as at December 31, 1969;
- payment of the government's share would be made out of future, after-tax, profits;
- the government's majority was to carry with it effective control; and
- the effective date of the government taking control would be January 1, 1971.

Demba and Alcan were shocked by these "non-negotiables" as they had expected terms to be worked out after detailed negotiations. On November 30, in order to meet Securities and Exchange Commission obligations, Alcan issued a statement saying that it was preparing to meet with the Guyanese government representatives on December 7 and at that time it planned to seek clarification of the government's "non-negotiables." The statement included an assurance to its employees, shareholders and customers that their interests would be safeguarded. It concluded with the comment "if supplies (of bauxite) are affected, Alcan believes alternative supplies can be arranged."

Demba and Alcan were immediately accused by the Guyanese of having disclosed publicly the contents of the government's "confidential" letter and of issuing unwarranted threats. The atmosphere for the forthcoming discussions deteriorated still further as the Guyanese press renewed its campaign to discredit the Canadian company.

The Negotiations (December 7, 1970-February 20, 1971)

The first meeting of the negotiating teams took place on December 7, with Guyana's delegation being headed by Mines Minister Hubert Jack and the Canadian delegation being led by Fraser Macorquodale from Alcan, who had returned to Alcan headquarters in Montreal in 1967 following ten years as legal officer and secretary of Demba. He was accompanied by Robert E. Rosane, Demba's Coordinator of Administration and Gerald Clark, Chief Financial Officer of the Raw Materials division of Alcan in Montreal. No progress was made in connection with the "non-negotiables." Prime Minister Burnham told me later that day that the Guyanese government had no real wish to get involved in running Demba. It just wanted effective control of the management of the company.

On December 15 Burnham, in a conversation with U.S. Ambassador Spencer King, commented: "the Guyanese Government is doing a favour to the Canadians by negotiating," hinting that outright confiscation was a possibility; apparently he abandoned this concept, on reflection, probably because he realized the adverse affects such an action would have on Guyana's future need for foreign investment and development assistance.

Further meetings between the teams then took place without agreement being reached on the essential point of controlling interest. The talks were eventually broken off on December 21 with agreement to meet again on January 5. The Guyanese wanted to have a quick decision to enable Prime Minister Burnham to make an announcement on February 23, the first anniversary of Guyana becoming a Cooperative Republic. The Alcan-Demba team, on the other hand, was prepared to continue negotiations for six months, or longer if necessary, to achieve an acceptable outcome.

On January 14 Burnham (who had clearly been making all the major decisions) left Guyana for Singapore to attend the Commonwealth Heads of Government meeting. At this conference, as had been recommended by Canadian officials in Ottawa and Georgetown, Canada's Prime Minister Trudeau spoke with Burnham privately. He indicated to him that fair and non-discriminatory treatment of Demba was expected.

In Georgetown negotiations had bogged down in the absence of Burnham, who was not due back until February 5. The Alcan-Demba team had submitted a proposal whereby Guyana was to borrow (possibly from the World Bank) 25 million dollars to help pay for its share of a new company that would concentrate on an increased output of the profitable calcined bauxite, in the production of which Demba was already a world leader. This product is used in the manufacture of abrasives and high temperature linings of industrial furnaces.

Alcan and Demba felt that by this method both sides could come out winners through increased profits and employment, plus additional taxes for the Guyanese government. However, the proposal did not sit well with the Guyanese, who felt that they would be seen as paying in advance for their own resources.

A recess in negotiations until February 8 was proposed and agreed to; by this time Prime Minister Burnham would have returned. The local press seized on the delay, claiming that the Alcan-Demba team was "dragging its feet."

By early February the U.S. authorities and U.S. aluminum industry representatives were becoming increasingly concerned about the effect a Guyanese takeover of Demba would have on other bauxite producing countries in the region. A senior U.S. Embassy officer in Ottawa called on External and referred to the substantial U.S. ownership in Alcan (in 1971, 39 percent of Alcan's common shares were U.S.-owned, 49 percent Canadian-owned and 12 percent owned elsewhere). Would the Canadian government consider a combined Canada-U.S. approach to Prime Minister Burnham? The answer was no. If they wished to approach Burnham directly that was up to them.

On February 9 U.S. Ambassador Spencer King in Georgetown, following instructions, called on Burnham and referred to the U.S. Hickenlooper Amendment which authorized withholding a U.S. sugar import quota if the supplying country had not made a prompt and adequate settlement in convertible foreign exchange following the nationalization of a company in which the U.S. had a substantial financial interest. He urged that Burnham not be hasty in his Demba nationalization efforts.

Negotiations resumed on February 12, but the Guyanese found it politically unacceptable to agree to Demba's suggestion that they raise 25 million dollars to buy into the proposed new company. Minister Jack then said Demba would be receiving a letter by February 20 which would indicate Guyana's final decision.

On February 17 Prime Minister Trudeau telexed a letter to the Canadian High Commission in Georgetown for Prime Minister Burnham and I delivered it that day. In his letter Prime Minister Trudeau referred to their recent meeting in Singapore and reiterated that he expected Demba would be accorded treatment no less favourable than that given to any other foreign investor in Guyana. After reading the letter Burnham again confirmed that this was certainly his intention. He complained to me that he felt the Alcan-Demba team was "not negotiating in good faith."

On that same date a senior officer in Alcan's headquarters in Montreal telephoned External to say there was a strong possibility of an imposed solution and that Alcan was concerned about the security of its expatriate personnel in Guyana. Another "flash" External telegram was sent to the Canadian High Commission in Georgetown asking that the Guyanese government be requested to give assurances regarding the safety of Demba and Alcan personnel. These were promptly given to me by Prime Minister Burnham. At the Canadian High Commission emergency evacuation plans for Canadian personnel were brought up to date and all Canadians in Guyana were advised of steps to be taken in the event of trouble.

On February 18 Canada's representative (and also Guyana's) at the World Bank, Dr. Claude Isbister, arrived in Georgetown and tried to see Prime Minister Burnham, without success. It was becoming clear that the Guyanese government was not really interested in trying to raise 25 million dollars to meet the Alcan proposal for a restructured Demba. On February 19 and 20 the negotiating team met but failed to reach agreement.

Negotiations were finally discontinued on February 20 and the stage was set for an announcement on February 23 of the decision to nationalize. On that day Prime Minister Burnham, at a mass rally in Georgetown celebrating the first anniversary of Guyana becoming a Cooperative Republic, announced the government's decision to take complete control of Demba. In an emotionally charged speech he accused Demba of "contempt and arrogance for the Guyanese Government and people." He added: "We have seen in Guyana and in other underdeveloped countries foreign-owned extractive industries prosper while the native population remained poor and destitute. We must now get the large share of the cake, otherwise what is the difference between Guyana and a colony? What shall we tell our children when they ask us to explain the gaping holes in the earth whence rich minerals have been won? You tell me." [2]

In the same speech Burnham said: "We have no quarrel with the friendly Canadian government; no quarrel with the friendly Canadian nation or with the Canadian people; only with the system which Alcan epitomizes and Demba illustrates."

Back in Ottawa, in response to a question asked on February 23 by the Hon. Heath Macquarrie (Hillsborough) in the House of Commons, Mr. Pepin, the Industry, Trade and Commerce Minister said: "I would not like to leave the impression that the Canadian government had not made proper representations to the government of Guyana. Conversations were held to that effect. The point I made a moment ago to the effect that we expect the Canadian companies to be properly treated was made in these bilateral conversations." [3]

In Montreal Alcan issued a statement saying that every effort would be made to ensure that the transition would be effected in an orderly way. It added, "Alcan does not expect these developments to affect its aluminum smelting operations in Canada."

In Kingston, Jamaica, Prime Minister Shearer was reported in the press as saying: "Jamaica does not wish to go the road Guyana is taking." In Port of Spain, the *Trinidad Guardian* editorialized: "Burnham will either go down as a rash, intemperate leader, or as a man who pressed ahead faster than anyone else with the new nationalism in the region today."

On March 4 the Guyanese parliament passed the Bauxite Nationalization Bill. This legislation abrogated, for the bauxite industry alone, the provision of the Guyana Constitution guaranteeing adequate and prompt compensation in the event of nationalization. The new law stated that in the event of nationalization payment of "reasonable compensation" was to be made. What was "reasonable compensation" now became the prime issue before the negotiation teams. The Guyanese were encouraged by the recent passing of a UN resolution on Permanent Sovereignty over Natural Resources, which they had co-sponsored and which said: "*appropriate compensation should be paid in accordance with the rules in force of the state concerned.*"

Negotiating Compensation

On March 25, Prime Minister Burnham replied to Prime Minister Trudeau's letter of February 17. He again promised that Demba would be receiving fair and equitable treatment. No discrimination against a Canadian firm was intended and in due course Reynolds would be offered the same set of "non-negotiables."

Alcan continued to hope that some solution other than nationalization could still be found. They stressed again to Canadian officials in Ottawa the very difficult situation that would prevail in the aluminum industry in North America as a whole if other Caribbean countries followed Guyana's lead. Alcoa in the U.S. was urging the U.S. government to condemn Guyana's actions and impose reasonable economic sanctions if necessary.

On April 12, Trinidad's Ambassador in Washington called on Canadian Ambassador Cadieux to say that Trinidad was maintaining a neutral position regarding Guyana's actions. If Alcan, which owned an essential bauxite transshipment terminal in Trinidad, at Chaguaramas, denied the use of this terminal to Guyana he believed the Trinidad government would be in an awkward spot. Black Power demonstrations were possible and he hoped a negotiated settlement would be achieved as soon as possible. He added that Trinidad had no wish to be a party to pushing the Guyanese government to the wall. At the same time it had no quarrel with Alcan.

On April 14 Prime Minister Burnham, through the Canadian High Commission in Georgetown, enquired if the Canadian government could assist in reaching a settlement in the matter of compensation. The reply was that it would be preferable for the parties directly concerned to try to work out an agreed solution.

A general work stoppage then took place at the Demba mine at Mackenzie, because of the workers concern about their pension funds, which were held in Montreal by Royal Trust. Eventually, they were reassured sufficiently on this question and a prolonged strike was averted.

Several meetings between Alcan and External officials were held in April and May but the gap between Alcan's view of adequate compensation and that of Guyana remained. For their part Alcan wanted well over 100 million U.S. dollars, as this was what it would cost at current prices to replace the existing assets.

On the other hand Guyana was insisting that the written-down book value for income tax purposes—approximately 46 million dollars—was an appropriate settlement figure. Alcan felt this was unfair, as they had some years previously received permission for an accelerated depreciation on an expansion of their calcined bauxite facilities. This was in accordance with the provisions of the Guyana Income Tax Act, which entitled any taxpayer to claim accelerated depreciation on any outlay for new production facilities. Alcan considered that the Guyanese proposal was in fact taking back tax incentives given earlier to encourage new investment.

On June 11 Prime Minister Burnham invited Mr. Justice Goldberg, a former U.S. Secretary of Labour and a friend of Burnham's, to come to Guyana to see if he could assist in reaching a settlement. Goldberg, coincidentally, was acting legal counsel for the Reynolds Metal Company. No progress was made regarding the compensation question. Burnham was reminded that not making a "fair" settlement would make future foreign investments in Guyana very difficult.

U.S. Assistant Secretary of State Meyer arrived in Georgetown on June 22. In conversation with the U.S. Ambassador he said that the solution to the Demba problem lay in the hands of industry, not government. He added that it was becoming increasingly difficult to use the "big stick" in Latin America. "It is even difficult," he added, "to reduce sugar import quotas without being accused of economic aggression under the Organization of American States Agreement."

On June 30 the Canadian High Commission in London advised that Gerald Metals of London had been appointed sales representative for six months for Guyana's bauxite and alumina. They were reported to have made substantial sales of Guyana's bauxite to Eastern Europe and the USSR. On the same date the Russian Ambassador to Brazil telephoned

Prime Minister Burnham asking "if he could be of assistance."

The Demba-Alcan negotiating team continued to hope that a compensation agreement could be reached before vesting day. They rejected the Guyanese offer of Demba's written-down book value as the basis for determining compensation.

Prime Minister Burnham then announced, on July 4, that Alcan President Nathanael Davis and Mr. Justice Goldberg would be coming to Georgetown for discussions on the compensation question on July 12. He confirmed July 15, 1971 as Vesting Day for taking over formal control of Demba.

At a dinner party on July 12, at the home of Demba President Campbell in Georgetown, Alcan President Davis commented to me, "If we reach agreement with the Guyanese in the present discussions the Canadian government's policy in this case will have proven to be the correct one. But I fear there is only a 100-to-1 chance of this happening."

Guyana's Prime Minister Forbes Burnham in conversation with Canadian High Commissioner John Stiles and U.S. Ambassador Spencer King (background). Georgetown, Guyana: July 4, 1971.

However, on July 13, following a strenuous late night session, settlement was in fact reached between Prime Minister Burnham, Foreign Minister Ramphal and Alcan President Davis and his colleagues. The Guyana government agreed to pay Alcan 53.5 million U.S. dollars for Demba, with payments to be made over a 20-year period, at an interest rate of six percent, subject to the Guyana withholding tax. Davis said that he was satisfied with the outcome.[4]

For their part the Guyanese were jubilant. Guyana's Foreign Minister Ramphal called me to say they were extremely pleased with the result. He paid high tribute to the "understanding attitude of the Canadian government throughout this difficult negotiating period."

On July 28 Alcan President Davis wrote to Undersecretary of State for External Affairs Ed Ritchie in Ottawa: "Settlement is within the Alcan guidelines as expressed in my remarks at the Alcan shareholders' meeting on April 1, 1971. While we regret the act of nationalization of Demba, the quantum of compensation to be paid by Guyana is in all the circumstances acceptable to Alcan. Please let me express to you and your associates our deep appreciation of the interest you have taken in the Guyana developments."

LOOKING BACK

From a perspective of 25 years after the event some observations can be made. First, the Guyana government, despite having to renegotiate the debt agreement with Alcan on two occasions, eventually met its obligations to Alcan by paying in cash or bauxite. Canadian development assistance to Guyana continued and Alcan for a while bought bauxite from Guybau (Guyana Bauxite Company, successor to Demba) for its Arvida alumina plants.

Alcan also increased its reliance on other sources of bauxite, including Brazil, where shipping facilities were more convenient and economical than those in Guyana.

Alcan's policy concerning local equity participation in its bauxite interests in Brazil changed. Alcan found it expedient and helpful in gaining access to local capital markets to agree to 51 percent of the new company's shares being held by Brazilians.

The possibility of discrimination against Demba has been referred to above; in actual fact the Guyanese government, some four years later, did take over the U.S.-owned Reynolds Metal Company. It offered them the same terms that had been extended to Demba, which were accepted.

The Demba takeover was just the first step in Guyana's nationalization plans. Subsequently, the government elected to assume control over other local companies. Eventually more than 80 percent of Guyana's industrial output was nationalized.

Guybau, after some initial success, experienced mining and administrative problems which appeared to be beyond the capabilities of the staff available. The alumina plant, in dire need of rebuilding, had to be closed in 1981. The once profitable Guyanese calcined bauxite business has all but disappeared.

A very different and better result might have been achieved if the discussions could have been maintained for two or three months longer. It was a difficult experience for both sides and was in fact a clash of two very different ideologies and cultures. In hindsight, it is clear that the Guyanese never completely understood how they would have been better off in accepting a reconstructed Demba, concentrating on calcined bauxite production, over which they could have had the majority control.

It is impossible to overstress, too, the importance of the strong nationalistic feelings and the emotionalism in Guyana at the time, which were kept stirred up by the local press and worked against rational discussions of the problems involved.

Canadian official policy in regard to the Demba case remained the same from beginning to end, i.e. respect for Guyana's sovereign right to nationalize its resources, should this be considered in Guyana's long-term interests, combined with insistance that there be no discrimination against a Canadian firm and, in the event of nationalization, that agreed compensation should be achieved.

Spurred on by Alcan's requests for assistance, strong Canadian diplomatic efforts were made to carry out this policy, including two personal interventions by Prime Minister Trudeau with Guyana's Prime Minister Burnham.

The deal which Alcan-Demba negotiated with the Guyanese may be compared with the results of the nationalizations of U.S. copper mining interests in Chile and Peru in 1969. Following the nationalization of the U.S. Anaconda Mining Company in Chile on June 26, 1969, Anaconda agreed to the establishment of a new company in which the Chilean government would hold a 51 percent interest. Compensation was to be made in the form of government-guaranteed 6 percent dollar bonds over a 12-year period from January 1, 1970, based on *book* value of the stock at 197 million U.S. dollars. An option for the Chilean government to purchase the remaining 49 percent might be taken up after 61 percent of the purchase price for the 51 percent interest had been paid, but not before December 31, 1972.[5]

On June 24, 1969, President Velasco of Peru announced his government's intention to expropriate several foreign-owned operations including the U.S. Cerro de Pasco copper mining company. Following heavy pressure from the U.S. Government and nearly five years of negotiations, Cerro de Pasco received 58 million U.S. dollars, although it had originally sought close to $200 million. Cerro de Pasco called the settlement "reasonable under the political realities in Peru today."[6]

My conclusion is that it was certainly a very questionable action on Guyana's part to overturn a 50-year relationship, which had brought extensive benefits to the country, after less than 50 days of discussion. Subsequent events—the severe decline of the Guyanese economy and its standard of living, resulting in "a tragic story of years of unnecessary human deprivation"[7]—would seem to bear this out. Had the Guyanese chosen to forego the nationalization route, there is little doubt that their country would be much better off than it is today. The financial resources they committed to acquire existing production facilities could well have been used to help finance the many new industrial opportunities which existed at that time.

NOTES

1. "The Demba Record in Guyana 1919-1969," Demerara Bauxite Company Ltd., Guyana: September 1970.
2. *Guyana Graphic*, February 25, 1971, 5.
3. Canadian House of Commons, *Debates*, Hansard: February 23, 1971, 3658.
4. Demba had a gross value of about 114 million U.S. dollars (undepreciated) on Alcan's books; it had a net value (depreciated) of slightly more than 50 million U.S. dollars, and a net book value, for Guyana tax purposes, of 46 million U.S. dollars. Alcan considered the 53.5 million U.S. dollars settlement was probably equal to, or not far below, what would have been awarded by an independent arbitrator. See Duncan Campbell, *Global Mission: The Story of Alcan*, vol. II (Montreal: Alcan Aluminum Ltd., 1989), p. 693-94.
5. *Keesing's Contemporary Archives*, London, England, August 1969, pp. 23533-35A; *The American Metal Market*, New York: November 18, 1969.
6. *Facts on File*, New York: February 23, 1974, 134.
7. Letter to J.A. Stiles from former senior Demba officer R.P. Guselle, dated December 30, 1993.

BIBLIOGRAPHY

1. Litvak, Isaiah and Christopher Maule, "Nationalization in the Caribbean Bauxite Industry," *International Affairs* 51(1), January 1975, 43-59.
2. ———, "Canadian Investment Abroad: In Search of a Policy," *International Journal* 31(1), Winter 1975-1976, 159-79.
3. ———, "Forced Divestment in the Caribbean," *International Journal* 31(3), Summer 1977, 501-32.
4. Chodos, Robert, *The Caribbean Connection*, (Toronto: James Lorimer, 1977), Chapter 8.
5. Campbell, Duncan, *Global Mission: The Story of Alcan*, vol. II (Montreal: Alcan Aluminum Ltd., 1989), Chapter 14.
6. Canada. The Senate. Standing Committee on Foreign Affairs, no. 3, November 25, 1969, Appendix C, "Alcan in the Caribbean" (Ottawa: Queen's Printer, 1969), pp. 3:27-3:35.
7. Canada. House of Commons. Standing Committee on External Affairs and National Defence, Sub-Committee on Canada's Relations with Latin America and the Caribbean, no. 16, February 11, 1982, Appendix, Alcan Statement "Alcan in Latin America and the Caribbean" (Ottawa: Supply and Services Canada, 1982), pp. 16A:1-16A:48, especially the section on Guyana, pp. 16A:39-16A:43.

John A. Stiles served in the Canadian army from 1941-45, earning the rank of captain. He joined the Trade Commissioner Service in 1945 and was posted to New York, Caracas, Bonn, Sydney and Tokyo (including accreditation to Korea). From 1954 to 1957 he was Assistant Director of the Trade Commissioner Service. In 1970 he joined External Affairs and was appointed High Commissioner to Guyana, then Ambassador to the Republic of Korea in 1974. In 1977 he was named "Foreign Service Visitor" at Mount Allison University. Mr. Stiles went on to serve as Special Advisor on international relations with the Public Service Commission in 1978, then as Chief Inspector, Foreign Operations, Canadian Government in 1981-83. He is the author of *Developing Canada's Relations Abroad*.

16

A NEW BASE FOR PROMOTING CANADA'S INTERESTS IN JAPAN

J.H. TAYLOR

THIS ESSAY DEALS WITH THE EXPANSION of the Canadian government's network of establishments in Japan in the period 1990-92. The principal developments were the opening of a new chancery in Tokyo in May 1991; the appointment of honorary commercial representatives in Sapporo, Sendai and Hiroshima, also in May 1991; and the opening of consulates, principally for trade purposes, in Fukuoka in the summer of 1991 and in Nagoya in November 1992. This program represented the largest expansion of Canadian facilities in Japan since Canada originally established diplomatic relations and opened a legation in Tokyo in 1929. While it unfolded rapidly, it was the product of years of planning and preparation. The new network of trade offices, together with the Consulate-General in Osaka, opened in 1986, created a basis of support for Canada's trade and other interests in all the principal regions of Japan. In the capital the new chancery, Canada's largest and most modern foreign outpost, provided a focus for Canadian activities that was both beautiful and efficient. From the moment of its opening the building began to prove its usefulness, not only to the federal government, but also to the provinces, the private sector and individual Canadians. It is arguably the best building of its kind ever commissioned by the Canadian government. It may simply be the best embassy owned by any government anywhere in the world—and it was completed virtually without cost to the taxpayer!

The extraordinarily rapid expansion was all the more remarkable for having been carried out in a period of shrinking resources. Throughout the 1980s and into the 1990s, as the program was being pursued to completion, pressure on government budgets was increasing. The conflict between needs and resources grew sharper. Priorities had to be more clearly defined and more vigorously defended. It took a clear sense of purpose and sustained determination to see the program through, as the pool of people and money for which it competed shrank progressively. In effect, the resources for Canada's program in Japan had to be found by double compressions elsewhere among the government's other overseas programs. That they were found is the best evidence of the government's commitment to strengthening relations with Japan.

This recognition of Japan's importance to Canada had deep roots, going back to the beginnings of our history as a sovereign state. When Canada acquired control of its external relations as a result of the constitutional developments of the 1920s, one of the decisions faced by the government of the day was whether to open missions abroad and where. The legation in Washington was the first such mission established; the legation in Tokyo was the second. How the Canadian government came to acquire the splendid property it owns today in central Tokyo is a fascinating piece of history that sprang from the decision to open relations in 1929. The story has often been recounted: how Herbert Marler, Canada's first minister to Japan, after unsuccessfully arguing with both the King and the Bennett governments that land should be acquired in Tokyo and a residence and chancery built at public expense, finally persuaded the Bennett government to give him permission to proceed on his own initiative, by offering them a buy-back proposition too good to refuse.

Arranging his own financing, Herbert Marler purchased a site of about three acres in 1932, opposite the Akasaka Palace grounds in downtown Tokyo, where the homes of the Imperial family are located. The previous owners, the Aoyamas, were one of Japan's great feudal families. Their name is commemorated in the name of the avenue on which the property stands, Aoyama-dori. On this land Marler built a large residence and a smaller office building, surrounded by handsome Japanese gardens. The property, in the hands of a custodian during the War years, survived unscathed the virtual destruction of central Tokyo by bombing in 1945. It was extended in the 1950s by a key acquisition that carried its boundary out to Aoyama-dori and enlarged it to 4.3 acres. It is in fact this later land acquisition that underlies most of the new chancery, which could not have been built on the site without it.

The splendid house Herbert Marler built, which rightly bears his name, celebrated its 60th anniversary in 1994. Marler House is an elegant reminder of another age, when guests arrived by three-funnelled white Empress steamers at Yokohama, fully equipped with steamer trunks to stay at the residence for months. Its high-ceilinged reception rooms and gardens, now grown to maturity, are much admired by the thousands of Canadians, Japanese and other guests who are received in the house

The Canadian ambassador's residence in Tokyo. The salon of Marler House (inset).

every year. As a physical symbol of Canada's presence in Japan, it has enormous intangible value, quite apart from its worth as a piece of real estate. Many would claim it is Canada's finest embassy residence. In 1982 the Architectural Institute of Japan declared it to be one 2000 buildings of particular architectural value erected in Japan since the Meiji restoration. There is no doubt that Canada would damage its own reputation in Japan were Marler House ever to be destroyed or thoughtlessly altered.

History and beauty are hard to value. Judged by more prosaic standards, however, Marler House has not seemed rational to some. Treasury Board experts, retrospectively applying standards of their own devising, have pointed out that it is more than twice as large as the largest residence now allowed under their guidelines to an ambassador. Property managers claim that it is in the wrong place for today's needs—that if it were knocked down or moved, the land could be developed more sensibly (the house is essentially a box of reinforced concrete, which, for all its size, could apparently be moved). Yet Marler House stood in the centre of the property because it was the most important structure on it; and when the question arose how best to develop the property in postwar years, everything turned on a prior decision as to whether the residence was to be kept, destroyed, moved or modified. Only when that had been settled was it possible to proceed.

The debate went on for years. It took until 1983 to reach a decision. By then a dozen possibilities had been considered, covering the full range of options from selling everything to keeping everything. The final decision was to keep all the land and to keep the old residence and to build a new chancery and staff apartments on a part of the remaining property.

At one time it seemed as if the discussion about the fate of the property might turn in circles forever. The residence was splendidly equipped to fulfil its functions. Some maintained it was, if anything, over-equipped. Everyone agreed, however, that something had to be done about the old chancery. Even when extended, it had never managed to find room for all Canada's postwar services in Japan. There was a great deal to be said for entertaining in a fine old residence that breathed the gracious atmosphere of another age; there was much less to be said for trying to work from an office that barely met the standards of the 1940s.

Meanwhile, as managers wrangled over what to do with the property, Tokyo and Japan recovered, grew and prospered all around it. With its miracle of postwar reconstruction and export-led growth, Japan became more important to the world and to Canada with every year that passed. By the 1980s it was the world's second largest economy. It was home to the world's largest financial institutions. It had risen from eighth to third place as a supplier of foreign capital to Canada. It was Canada's second largest trading partner: trade with Japan exceeded trade with Britain, France, Germany and Italy combined. Close to half a million Japanese visited Canada every year. While investing massively in their own economy, the Japanese were the principal suppliers of capital to Asia as well. As Asia's only fully industrialized economy Japan contributed to the extraordinary growth rates in which Asia led the world. Canadians excited by the glowing prospects of the Pacific Rim were advised that Japan was the key: "If you don't have a Japan Strategy" they were told, "you don't have an Asia Strategy." This was the message to both public and private interests.

So far as the government was concerned, the messenger was pushing against an open door. Documents from the early 1980s reflect a recognition not only of Japan's growing importance but of the need to have facilities in Japan worthy of Canada. A memorandum of March 1982 states, for example, "Japan is second only to the United States as a country of significance to Canada ...[and] is now emerging as a regional and global power of the first order.... Our embassy in Tokyo must be able to reflect, represent and support in every possible way Canada's interests vis-à-vis Japan.... The location of our property in Tokyo could scarcely be better and from both the point of view of practical convenience and political symbolism, this location has served us well in the sense that it creates a positive impact on the Japanese. It remains only to maximise the advantage by constructing the kind of office facilities and official presence that the property requires."

Unfortunately, this kind of presence was slow in coming. In 1983, the Department of External Affairs had to respond to criticism in the Public Accounts Committee that it had allowed development plans to become years out of date through failure to act. In those years, witnesses in other committees were pressed to show what all the fine words about the importance of Canada's relations across the Pacific boiled down to in practice. It became indispensable for the government to demonstrate that, even if budgets shrank, resources would be found from programs judged of lower priority and transferred to high priority projects such as strengthening relations with Japan.

If everyone recognized Japan was important, why was progress in developing a plan for Tokyo so slow? One reason was simply the value of the assets. The Tokyo property was enormously valuable—probably the most valuable single piece of real estate abroad that was owned by the Canadian government. As Tokyo land prices boomed in the 1980s, estimates of its value rose rapidly. In 1983, the whole property had been appraised at about $150 million. By the mid-1980s, the appraised value of just that portion of land which it had been decided to develop had risen from $200 to $400 million. In 1986, the value of the whole property was said to be about $750 million. At the height of the Japanese boom in 1988-89, the property may have been worth somewhere in the neighbourhood of $1 billion. This was at the time when the most expensive land in the world was said to lie a mile or so away on the Ginza, and fanciful calculations maintained that the grounds of the Imperial Palace were worth more than all the assets of California or Great Britain.

Although asset inflation was a great stimulus to fantasizing, the grounds of the Imperial Palace were not on the market. Neither was the Canadian property on Aoyama-dori. Speculating about how much it might be worth if it were sold was an intriguing exercise, but of limited use. Whatever its value, the land was plainly an enormous asset. No wonder that those in charge of deciding what to do with it went about their business carefully.

As the value of the land rose, so did the cost of building on it. When testifying before the Public Accounts Committee in 1983, officials said that building a new chancery was a $30 million project. What was finally built less than ten years later cost $200 million. But there was one enormous difference: whereas the $30 million would have been a direct charge on the Department's estimates, and therefore on the Canadian taxpayer, the $200 million project was financed by Japanese investors, essentially at no cost to the Canadian taxpayer. Even $30 million would have been too much for the Department's overstretched capital budget. Ironically, the circumstances of 60 years earlier were repeating themselves. What the government wanted and needed in Tokyo was far beyond its means. It was probably far beyond what Parliament would have found tolerable. In 1932, an imaginative and novel solution had been found to a similar dilemma; now, nearly 60 years on, another had to be found.

It was the government's willingness to enter into partnership with the private sector in Japan that broke the impasse. A consortium was formed with the Mitsubishi Trust and Bank Corporation and the Shimizu Construction Company. No land was sold. A new chancery and staff apartments were to be built on land that remained entirely Canadian with money supplied by the Japanese partners. To permit the partners to recoup their investment, the chancery building was built to a size roughly double the Canadian government's space requirements. About half the space in the building was designed as a chancery, for Canadian purposes, with the special status accorded to diplomatic properties by international law; the other half was configured as normal commercial office space, with the rents repaying the investment of the Japanese partners. These arrangements, approved by the Japanese government, were governed by a trust agreement with a maximum life of 30 years, which provided for reversion of the commercial portion of the building to Canada. In practice, the reversion period was expected to be substantially shorter than 30 years.

Once the key decisions had been taken, namely, to retain Marler House and to develop the rest of the property under the consortium arrangements described above, the project went ahead rapidly. The first sod was turned on July 1, 1988. A temporary chancery was built where, for the first time since the War, all Canadian government services in Tokyo were united under the one roof. The old chancery was demolished—it was a tough nut to crack—and the site was cleared. By the end of 1989, the new chancery was at ground level. By the following April, the topping-out ceremony was held. A year later, the building was

The new Chancery of the Canadian Embassy in Tokyo, designed by Moriyama and Teshima. Photograph courtesy of Shimizu Corporation.

finished and handed over to the Canadian government. It was officially opened in May, 1991. Immediately thereafter, the temporary chancery now lying vacant behind it was quickly pulled down. An apartment block capable of housing about half the Canadian staff of the Embassy was then erected on the site. This allowed the government to surrender a number of private leases in Tokyo, at savings of several million dollars annually. With the completion of these apartments in the autumn of 1992, construction work came to an end. It had lasted almost four years.

The organization of the project by the Japanese partners was superb. Order, discipline and cleanliness reigned. Noise and confusion were kept to a minimum. Deadlines were unfailingly met. Each important stage of construction was marked in the Japanese way, by appropriate Shinto ceremonies with prayers, ritual music and dance, and ceremonial cups of sake. The residence nearby continued to serve as the focus of the Embassy's representational work and the temporary chancery functioned without interruption from its offices only yards away as the new chancery moved swiftly and methodically to completion. Visiting Canadian experts were unanimous in praising the high standard of organization and the quality of work displayed by Shimizu Construction.

In May 1991, the new chancery was opened officially by Prime Minister Mulroney before a distinguished Japanese and Canadian audience that included Prince and Princess Takamado, Prime Minister Toshiki Kaifu and four former prime ministers of Japan. Approval of the project was overwhelming. The leading Japanese architectural journals published long and favourable articles. Japanese friends noted that Canada had chosen not to sell any of its land, thereby preserving the integrity of an important site in the capital while enhancing its beauty. The building itself, although impressively large, had been designed so as not to overwhelm the avenue on which it fronted. The architect, Raymond Moriyama of Toronto, had angled back on two sides the huge cantilevered glass tent that roofed the upper floors of the building. In that way minimum shadows were cast by the building in adjoining Takahashi Park and the privacy of the Akasaka Palace grounds opposite was respected. While some older cherry trees had been unavoidably cut down to permit construction, the builders had undertaken to leave the site as green as they had found it. New trees—maturing cherries and Japanese maple—were transplanted to the Embassy garden to compensate for the trees that had been lost. Some wondered how considerations of security and openness could be reconciled in the design. Raymond Moriyama and his associates had squared that circle as well. The embassy portion of the shared building was designed to meet high standards of security, yet large public areas were easily accessible to casual visitors. The wide balconies of the fourth floor, at treetop height, provided one of the best views of Tokyo. They were as open and welcoming as Canadians would wish a Canadian embassy to be.

Visitors promptly began to come to the building by the thousands. Some had been invited; some had business with one or another of the Embassy's services; some had simply heard that the building was one of the sights of the city and was worth a visit. Mounting a long outside escalator to the lobby, they entered an immense space lifted above Tokyo's crowded streets that recalled the vast quietness of Canada's own spaces. Around three sides of the building at this level ran a great symbolic map of the geography of Canada's relationship to Japan: on the east, a pool representing the Atlantic; then Canada from sea to sea with the Shield, the North and the Rockies represented by stone shapes; then another pool representing the Pacific, leading by stepping stones to Japan, on the west, represented by a Japanese garden of stones, raked gravel and flowering shrubs.

At the core of the building, surrounded by this garden-map in stone and water, was a large, glass-walled space capable of holding 1000 people. Like a bare stage when not in use, it could be quickly set for a variety of shows, fairs or exhibitions. This was the principal commercial display area. Elsewhere in the building visitors could admire the cultural facilities, grouped around a two-storey lobby as around a town square; a library capable of holding 20,000 volumes and intended to become the best collection of Canadian material in Asia; a gallery for exhibitions of painting and sculpture; and an auditorium of 233 seats, equipped both for concerts, film shows and lectures. Its design was inspired by the Japanese Noh theatre.

At selected locations in the building were specially commissioned works of Canadian art and sculpture. These included two important bronzes, one by Ted Bieler and the other by Maryon Kantaroff of Toronto, representing the waves of the Atlantic and the Pacific; a Cape Dorset *inukshuk* [a stone sculpture shaped like a man] by the Inuit artist Kananginak Pootoogook, symbolizing the Arctic (but reinforced by hidden cement and rods to permit the work to withstand earthquake); and a large stained glass window-wall by Warren Carther of Winnipeg. Private sponsors enhanced this collection with additional generous gifts. The offices contained other examples of Canadian art, crafts and design. Efficient work stations were located in the unconventionally shaped spaces created by the intersection of the interior partitions with the sloping glass roof-walls of the upper floors of the building. The interior equipment and furnishing of the new chancery was the only part of the cost directly charged to the Canadian taxpayer. It amounted to about $16 million in a project totalling over $200 million.

While the flagship chancery was being commissioned and passing its trials, the pace of the Embassy's activity continued to be intense. There was an unbroken stream of visitors: the Governor General; the Prime Minister; most of the senior federal ministers; many of the provincial premiers and many more of their ministers; business executives and university presidents; writers and editors; artists and musicians. The largest Canadian cultural festival ever held in Japan took place successfully. The Montreal, Toronto and Vancouver Symphonies all toured. So did Tafelmusik and the Orford Quartet. Robert Fulford, John Polanyi and David Suzuki lectured; Jon Kimura Parker played; Robert Bateman's paintings were exhibited; the National Ballet visited Japan for the first time in over twenty years; "Anne of Green Gables" played to packed houses.

This activity extended far beyond the Embassy to theatres and concert halls all over Japan. But in Tokyo the old residence and the new chancery were often at the centre of events. Two of the provinces, Alberta and British Columbia, had opted for space in the new building. All the provinces found they benefited from access to its resources. So did thousands of businesspeople and private visitors. Many requests to use the facilities on a commercial basis, especially the theatre, were received. This was impossible under international law and practice. Rules had to be worked out to permit Canadians, and Japanese with Canadian interests, to use the building in ways compatible with its status and acceptable to the Japanese authorities. Meanwhile there was never a lack of demand. The staff assigned to manage the new facilities worked to near exhaustion. Even a year after it had been put into service, the building's novelty had not worn off. Bookings for its public spaces had to be made months in advance.

The running-in period went remarkably well. Raymond Moriyama paid frequent visits to Tokyo as the new building neared completion. He was patient and engaging in explaining to the staff of the embassy the sources of his inspiration and the logic of his design. Sensibly, he warned not to expect perfection. Some details had been deliberately left by the architect to the users to decide on, in the light of experience. He advised against making snap judgements: it was better, he suggested, to work with the building for six months or so, noting things that might be changed and only deciding on alterations after mulling them over. Given the scale of the project, there were in the end remarkably few changes. These were accommodated without difficulty and at no increased cost.

Even as the new chancery was brought into service the government had turned its attention to improving Canadian representation outside the capital. Better promotion of our interests in trade, investment and tourism was the objective. Canada had a long history of being represented in Japanese cities other than Tokyo. There had been trade offices in Yokohama and Kobe long before the Canadian legation in Tokyo was opened in 1929. But following the restoration of relations after the War, a hiatus of more than a generation occurred before a Canadian trade office was to be opened outside the capital.

There was some argument in favour of this delay, although it was not overwhelming. Japan was the most highly centralized of the major industrial countries. There was a strong postwar tendency to concentrate even more national functions in Tokyo. The capital became, in a sense, New

York, Washington, and Los Angeles combined—to make a comparison with the United States. Furthermore, the country had the best railway system in the world and an internal air service that used jumbo jets like taxis. Yet it was evident Japan was too large and complex a market to be served effectively from one office in Tokyo. The facts of geography alone would discourage any attempt to do so. Since the Japanese islands lie in the same latitude and extend the same north-south distance as the eastern United States, trying to cover all Japan from Tokyo was, so to speak, the equivalent of trying to handle everything from Maine to Texas from one office in Washington.

Furthermore, the regional markets of Japan were simply too big. The country had the second largest economy in the world; its regional economies were therefore as large as those of many nation states. For example, the Kansai, centered on Japan's second city, Osaka, constituted an economic region as large as Canada. Kyushu, the southernmost of the major islands, had an economy equalling that of the Netherlands. Each of the major economic regions was as big, in economic terms, as a South Korea, a Taiwan, a Malaysia or a Thailand. With over half of Japan's GDP and 60 percent of its population, the regional economies taken together surpassed in size those of Britain, France and Italy combined.

By the 1980s, Canada's thinking about Japan had come to include a recognition that ways must be found to operate more effectively in the regions. This was acknowledged, for example, in the National Trade Strategy. Within that framework, a Consulate-General, largely devoted to serving trade interests, was opened in Osaka in 1986. By 1991, the Osaka office was able to identify more than 80 Canadian firms that had registered significant successes in exporting to the Kansai thanks to its assistance. The exports were valued at over $50 million. The office had been instrumental in arranging Japanese investments in Canada worth $70 million. Typically, Osaka had helped small or medium-sized Canadian firms and stimulated sales of value-added products; its success was not based on a few large commodity deals.

This experience suggested that a well-established office in a major Japanese city might hope to stimulate $40 to $50 million worth of annual exports. Furthermore, these would tend to be exports with value added at the higher end of the spectrum, to which Canada had to look increasingly for its future as a trading nation. And while for many Canadian firms, depending on their corporate objectives, the best point of entry to Japan might still be Tokyo, and a partnership with a major Japanese trading company, there were many other Canadian firms who might find compatible partners among smaller Japanese firms in the regions. The government could help this process with a modest investment of its own resources. While the parallel was not exact, mini-offices had worked in the United States. But in the United States these offices had functioned in English; in Japan they would have to work in Japanese. This meant guaranteeing a permanent supply of Japanese-speaking trade specialists to staff the offices before it would make sense to open them. Training took time—a minimum of two years of full-time instruction. But by 1989, the Pacific 2000 dimension of the government's "Going Global" program had provided resources for two new small trade offices in Japan, one to be opened in 1991 and a second in the following year.

Where would it be best to locate these offices? In 1990-91 the Embassy in Tokyo organized a careful survey of five cities: Sapporo, Sendai, Nagoya, Hiroshima and Fukuoka. These were centres of major regional economies down the length of the Japanese islands. Each presented attractive prospects for furthering Canadian interests. Some already had important connections with Canada. Sapporo, for example, was the capital of the northernmost island, Hokkaido, which was twinned with Alberta. The Tohoku region, centred on Sendai in northern Honshu, and the Chugoku region, centred on Hiroshima in southern Honshu, had for years been important markets for Canadian coal and uranium through their regional power companies. It soon became clear that no sensible analysis was going to result in a recommendation to pick two of the cities surveyed and ignore the three others. Resource constraints notwithstanding, something had to be done in all five.

It was therefore decided to name career trade specialists as consuls in two cities, Fukuoka in 1991 and Nagoya in 1992, and to designate prominent local businessmen as Honorary Commercial Representatives in Sapporo, Sendai and Hiroshima. Three leading executives agreed in 1991 to serve in this capacity: a Canadian, Daniel A. Guyot, General Manager of the Ramada Renaissance Hotel in Sapporo; and two Japanese, Toshio Tamakawa, President of the Tohoku Electric Power Co. in Sendai, and Koki Tada, President of the Chugoku Electric Power Co. in Hiroshima. The announcement of this program of expanded regional representation formed a prominent part of Prime Minister Mulroney's visit to Japan in May 1991. The new representatives were introduced to the Prime Minister at a reception deliberately held in Osaka, to symbolize Canada's determination to be as active in the regions of Japan as in the capital. As if to confirm this new perspective, this was the first time that an official visit to Japan by a Canadian prime minister had included a program of substance outside Tokyo.

With the opening of the consulate in Nagoya in November 1992, the program of expansion was complete. There had been nothing like it in the two generations since Canada had first established relations with Japan. There will probably be nothing else like it for another generation. If Japan's weight in the international system, and its relative importance to Canada, continue to grow in future, the time will come when the government will be glad to have at its disposal all the additional space which will revert to it in the new chancery in Tokyo. By that time also, it may well be that the network of trade specialists working for Canada in Japan's major regional centres will have been enlarged as well. Meanwhile, the government has available what is perhaps the best-conceived and best-equipped embassy building in the world, and a network of trade offices running the length of Japan. If it is a government's obligation to lead in setting national priorities and creating a framework within which public and private interests can work together to pursue their common interests, then that obligation has been well discharged by the Canadian government in Japan.

The famous phrase says: "To govern is to choose." In this case, the Canadian government chose to give priority to Japan. It set goals, assembled resources and persisted until it had brought the program of expansion to a successful conclusion. Those responsible for implementation had shown ingenuity and imagination in finding novel solutions to old problems and a respect for the taxpayer's interests of which bureaucracies are often said to be incapable. This, then, is a success story, for all that Canadians are supposed to be bad at recognizing and accepting their own successes.

What part does the head of mission play in the story? This was a large program, carried out over a period of years at a large embassy. Hundreds of officials, both in Ottawa and in Tokyo, had a share in the final result. The advice of the Ambassador was influential on key issues. For example, it made an important difference that both Bruce Rankin and Barry Steers, who between them led the Embassy for close to 15 years, were ardent defenders of the preservation of Marler House. As their successor, I served in Tokyo as the plans of the previous years were coming to maturity, and was responsible for seeing that the normal work of the Embassy continued while the new chancery was being brought into service and the new offices in the regions of Japan were being established. This chapter is intended to give some impression of the importance, scope and intensity of the work involved.

James H. Taylor joined the foreign service in 1953. His postings abroad include Vietnam, India, France, Russia, Belgium, and Japan. In 1982 he was Ambassador to NATO, a position he held until 1985, when he returned to Ottawa to serve as Undersecretary of State for External Affairs. Mr. Taylor was Canada's Ambassador to Japan from 1989-93.

17

CULTIVATING RELATIONS WITH SADDAM: 1986-1988

ERIK B. WANG

IT IS SAID THAT DIPLOMACY is more like gardening than engineering. If so, Baghdad was arid desert terrain. This was an unyielding environment in which to practice the traditional tasks of diplomacy. When the host country is preoccupied with a struggle for survival there is little room on the agenda for issues unconnected to that struggle, and little room for meaningful dialogue.

A WAR AND ITS LEGACY

When I arrived in Baghdad in 1986 the Iran-Iraq war was in its sixth year. The Iranians were pressing at the gates. While suffering terrible losses themselves in the course of successive "human-wave" assaults, the Iranians had managed to gain a substantial foothold on the Fao peninsula, on the west bank of the Shatt-al-Arab. They had briefly held part of the Baghdad-Basra highway before being pushed back. There was fighting in the outskirts of Basra, Iraq's second largest city. Baghdad was under intermittent missile attack. The civilian economy was showing signs of severe strain. Iraq was spending a billion dollars a month on the war. Iraq's international payments and credit standing was in a shambles. Morale amongst the civilian population, and amongst the almost one million men under arms at the front, was dangerously low. Iraqi casualties numbered over a thousand a day during the major Iranian offensives.

It was a close-run thing. The fall of the Shah and the return of the Ayatollah in 1979 had unleashed internal convulsions and strong revolutionary pressures on Iraq. Full-scale hostilities were initiated in 1980 by Iraq in response to these Iranian provocations. By 1986 the war had become for the Iraqis a brutal struggle for survival against a more powerful and populous neighbour.

I departed Baghdad in August 1988, shortly after the UN-brokered cease-fire which brought an end to eight years of war. Saddam Hussein declared the cease-fire stalemate a victory. It was greeted by the Iraqi people with an explosion of rejoicing, relief and expectations of what surely must be better days ahead.

It is part of a diplomat's function to alert his government to emerging international issues likely to impact upon national interests. I wish I could say that when I left Baghdad in 1988 I foresaw a risk that Canada, along with other members of a UN coalition, might soon be engaged in hostilities with Iraq over Iraqi aggression against Kuwait. Well, not quite.

To foreign observers in Baghdad in that summer of 1988 the war seemed to have transformed Iraq, for better *and* worse. Whether Iraq would emerge as a more peaceful, moderate and responsible member of the international community was a topic of lively debate. Had the leopard changed its spots? The new signals emerging from the leadership were not easy to decode. Information was strictly controlled and usually distorted by wartime propaganda. A mistake or an indiscretion could cost officials and even ministers not just their jobs but their lives, and the lives of relatives and friends. All decisions of any consequence were referred upward to Higher Authority, the President's office. For diplomats, the President himself was usually beyond reach, except at ceremonial occasions with hundreds, if not thousands, of others present. Very few of my diplomatic colleagues were prepared to make confident predictions. My valedictory reports reflected a view that, on the whole, and with important qualifications, the future trend-lines seemed favourable.

On the one hand (would a diplomatic analysis be complete without the symmetry of balanced arguments?), it seemed safe to assume that Saddam Hussein would emerge from the war chastened by the terrible price his people had paid for his blunder in invading Iran in 1980. He would have little appetite for renewed conflict, least of all with his immediate Arab neighbours and allies.

Saddam Hussein had forged strong ties with Arab moderates, especially Saudi Arabia, Kuwait, Egypt and Jordan, which had provided funds essential for the war effort, or crucial use of ports, highways and pipelines for Iraqi imports and oil exports. Most Arab regimes saw Iraq as a bulwark against a particularly virulent, expansionist strain of Islamic fundamentalism, as the "eastern flank of the Arab world." The ideology of the ruling Baath party had been transformed beyond recognition. The once potent Baath slogan "unity, freedom and socialism" had been gutted or turned on its head. The slogan, as applied by the Baath, had for many years led Iraq perversely in the direction of three dead-end policies: pursuit of the myth of pan-Arab unity, freedom from foreign influences, and socialism on the Soviet model.

The strident call for Arab unity and confrontation with Israel had given way to a more realistic recognition of the differing national interests of other Arab nations. Saddam had stated publicly that Iraq was not a front-line state vis-à-vis Israel and that it was for the PLO and Israel's immediate neighbours to make peace with Israel as they saw fit. Iraq would support them in whatever course they chose. Iraq, he implied, would no longer be the "bad boy" of the Arab world.

During the war Saddam Hussein had resumed relations with the United States, broken off during the 1967 Arab-Israeli war. Trade relations had improved with the West generally. Socialist dogma had given way to a pragmatic respect for the vitality of the private sector. All signs seemed to point to a period of post-war reconstruction with a more open market-oriented economy. Senior Iraqi officials acknowledged that the enormous pent-up domestic pressures for economic development could only be met by Western technology and trade.

Iraq had the second largest oil reserves in the Middle East (100 billion barrels confirmed, as compared, for example, with confirmed Canadian oil reserves of 8 billion), a significant population base (16 million), water from the Tigris and Euphrates river systems and rich expanses of arable land. Iraqis had grounds for confidence in bright long-term economic prospects for their country.

On the other hand, there were clouds on the horizon. Between Iraq and Iran there was no peace, merely a cease-fire of uncertain durability, and a legacy of suspicion and animosity which would probably cause Saddam to maintain sizeable armed forces, as a hedge against future Iranian pressures and to maintain domestic order, particularly against continuing Kurdish insurgency. Iraq came out of the war with its forces largely intact: fifty battle-hardened divisions, and more than 4000 tanks and 600 aircraft. The existence of forces on this scale could create options and therefore temptations for Iraq to engage in confrontation in other directions. Israel in particular feared a renewed threat to its security.

The war had left Iraq with an enormous debt burden. For several years Iraq had been the largest importer of military goods in the world, at the cost of depleting Iraq's healthy prewar foreign exchange reserves and accumulating debts in the order of $80 billion, including an estimated $45 billion non-Arab foreign debt. The pace of postwar reconstruction would be governed by Iraq's ability to service this debt, and maximize oil revenues. In spite of the recuperative powers of rich oil reserves, Iraq would be highly vulnerable to oil price fluctuations.

Saddam Hussein's personal hold on power was greatly strengthened during the war. Under a ruthless dictatorship it may be futile and irrelevant to try to assess undercurrents of public opinion. But Iraqis could point with genuine pride to the impressive benefits—roads, schools, hospitals, housing—with which Saddam had earlier endowed the nation. The enormous oil revenues that flowed into the country after the 1973 oil price rise had on the whole been invested wisely for the benefit of his people. Corruption, endemic elsewhere in the Middle East, had been virtually eliminated in Iraq. Many Iraqis seemed to feel, in spite of their fears, that a firm hand was required at the helm if their country was to survive under the threat of deep social, ethnic and sectarian divisions and predatory neighbours. In a time of national emergency, in a war against the historic Persian foe, many had felt there was no one else who could rally the country.

The widely broadcast Iranian war objectives—to liberate the Shia holy shrines at Najaf and Karbala, and install an Islamic regime in Baghdad as a stage towards liberating Jerusalem—were repugnant to most Iraqis, accustomed to a secular government. The Shia of Iraq—a majority of the population—had rejected appeals from Khomeini to rise up against the Sunni oppressor and had stood firm in defence of the country. In the dark days of military defeat morale did not crack. Foreigners found the cult of the personality carried to absurd lengths but many Iraqis, united behind the leader as never before in the country's history, saw nothing absurd about Saddam comparing himself to the great historic figures, Saladin, Nebuchadnezzar and Hammurabi, the lawmaker.

The party and the military were totally subservient. The national legislature had never been more than a stage prop. Dissent had been rooted out by an elaborate state security system of agents and informers controlled by Saddam and his kin. The Iraqi Mukhaberat—secret service—was closely modelled on the East German Stasi, which had numerous advisors in Baghdad in a grotesque technical assistance role. For Iraqis cooperating with the regime there were a range of rewards, including access to scarce consumer goods, foreign travel, military service deferment, career advancement and privileged education for children. The uncooperative could expect harassment, intimidation and, ultimately, torture and execution.

Accordingly, at the end of the Iran-Iraq war, in August 1988, Saddam Hussein stood at the pinnacle of his power domestically, and at the height of his prestige in the Arab world. With Iraq's oil wealth redirected to civilian reconstruction, many Iraqis felt that anything and everything was possible. At the same time, however, as subsequent events would underscore, there were no moderating or countervailing influences within the regime to restrain the leader from overreaching himself. Saddam's judgement of the outside world was fundamentally distorted by the cult of personality in which he had become enveloped.

In the brilliant light of hindsight, the folly of the invasion of Kuwait two years later can be understood as a convergence of these three potent legacies from the first Gulf War: the existence of a huge army, the frustration of a faltering economic recovery under a mountain of debt and depressed oil prices, and the unchallenged ambitions of a capricious, ruthless leader. The second Gulf War can now be seen as flowing from the first. In the hopeful summer of 1988 none of this seemed preordained to observers of the Baghdad scene. If I failed to predict Saddam's invasion of Kuwait, I take some comfort from the fact that neither did anybody else, including Iraq's closest Arab friends and neighbours.

For diplomatic representatives the physical environment during the war years was uncomfortable, and the political environment no less so.

Baghdad was only 110 kms from the Iranian border and the front lines, well within the 300 km range of Iranian missiles. There was no confidence in the accuracy of the "Scud B" missiles that Iranians were deploying against Baghdad. It was a missile of Soviet origin, developed in the fifties to carry a nuclear warhead in circumstances where pinpoint accuracy was not important. With a payload of 400 kg of high explosives, it fell on Baghdad indiscriminately. But unless one happened to be within 50 metres of impact one could carry on. The wry quip circulated widely: "It's not the missile with my name on it which worries me, it's the one addressed To Whom It May Concern." On several occasions, during the most active periods of the "war of the cities," we evacuated Canadian Embassy personnel temporarily into the desert to the west of Baghdad, beyond Scud range.

There was little warmth in Canada-Iraq relations. Canadian public opinion focused on Iraq fitfully, and the image was often that of Iraq as an implacable enemy of Israel, a supporter of international terrorist organizations, an unsavoury dictatorship and a user of chemical weapons, with aspirations to develop a nuclear bomb. At the same time there was little sympathy for Iran under the Islamic revolutionaries. Canada had closed its Embassy in Tehran in 1980 after assisting American Embassy personnel to escape. It was clear that an Iranian victory would have profoundly destabilizing consequences for the Gulf region and the Middle East generally. Most Canadians felt that neither side should win. This sentiment was transcribed into appropriate diplomatic language, endorsed by Canada in the declaration of the G-7 Economic Summit at Venice in 1987: "We favour the earliest possible negotiated end to the war with the territorial integrity and independence of both Iraq and Iran intact."

This was in fact a positive element in our bilateral relationship with Iraq: our mutual desire to bring the war to an early end. When the Security Council adopted Resolution 598 in July 1987, calling for a cease-fire on carefully balanced terms, Iraq immediately accepted it. Iran did not. At that point Canadian and Iraqi diplomatic goals at the UN converged behind the resolution and the efforts of Secretary General Pérez de Cuellar to mediate a cease-fire. Indeed, a slight Canadian tilt set in. Canada indicated it would support a UN-sponsored arms embargo against Iran, if that country continued to refuse to accept the terms of Resolution 598. It followed that, when Ayatollah Khomeini finally accepted the "poison" of the cease-fire, Canada was invited by Iraq to contribute troops to the UN peacekeeping force—the UN Iran-Iraq Military Observer Group (UNIIMOG)—which was established along the Iran-Iraq border to monitor the cease-fire. Canada was not acceptable to Iran as a force contributor. Canadian personnel were accordingly stationed only on the Iraqi side of the border. With their professionalism and experience in UN peacekeeping operations the Canadian contingent, numbering approximately 370, played a prominent role in deploying UNIIMOG quickly and effectively, to shore up what was initially a very shaky cease-fire.

In one other important area Canada and Iraq found common ground: trade. Support for Canadian business interests was a major priority for the Embassy. Every effort was made to maintain Canada's position in the much reduced civilian market, so that Canadian exporters would be able to take full advantage of its sizable longer-term potential once the war ended and Iraq turned to reconstruction. The underlying assumption was that Iraq could be expected to favour those countries which maintained an active presence through the lean war years.

ENCOURAGING TRADE

Canadian goods and services were clearly competitive in quality and price, specially in the foodgrains, telecommunications and automotive sectors. The 13,000 Canadian-built Chevrolet "Malibu" cars, bought by Iraq six years earlier, were seen frequently on the road in 1986 and following years, and were much valued by Iraqis for their solid durability under harsh conditions (the earlier contract dispute with G.M. Canada over optional extras had long been forgotten). The role of the Embassy as a door opener and facilitator was important for Canadian businesspeople seeking access to unwieldy, state-controlled agencies, where real power centres were not easy for outsiders to identify. Canadian exports to Iraq had peaked at $300 million in 1981, when the war began to bite into the economy.

By 1986, wartime economic priorities, reduced oil revenues, scarce foreign exchange and mounting international indebtedness had made financing and credit arrangements essential to doing business in Iraq, at least on the non-military side. We kept a close eye on Iraq's economic relations with third country trading partners and on financing terms offered by the competition. Canadian exporters sought our advice on the most effective use of available credit facilities in order to take advantage of new market opportunities. Iraqi officials (and Canadian businessmen) periodically complained that Canada was not as forthcoming in the matter of export credits as other western governments. I was able to point out that at least on Canadian wheat exports, which made up a large bulk of our trade, Iraq had a line of credit fully comparable to that of our competitors, Australia and the United States. For other exports, the Export Development Corporation remained "off cover" or unavailable for credits for Iraq.

I recommended to Ottawa a more imaginative and flexible use of government financing for non-wheat exports, to stay abreast of our competitors, especially the U.S., Britain, France and Germany, all of which had renewed allocations of credit for a wide range of exports to Iraq. My plea for some loosening of EDC purse strings, at least for short-term credits, generated support in the Pearson building. EDC was sceptical and continued to regard Iraq as a bad risk. A lively in-house policy debate developed in Ottawa between the trade side of External Affairs and EDC, with the Baghdad Embassy putting its oar in when opportunities arose. I was authorized to inform the Iraqis, without commitment, that EDC credits were under review.

In the end, EDC caution, supported by Finance, prevailed. In retrospect, of course, this caution was amply justified. By the end of the war the Iraqis were increasingly defaulting on current commitments, even on confirmed letters of credit issued by the Iraqi central bank. They were squeezing their major creditors with demands for further rounds of credit, as the price for resumption of servicing of past debt. When the Iraqis invaded Kuwait two years later, suspending all debt repayment, the EDC was one of the few Western credit agencies not to be caught with its credits down. The Canadian Wheat Board still carries on its books a debt of $345 million owed by Iraq as of August 2, 1990.

For the United States, export credits were more than just an instrument of trade policy during this pre-Kuwait period. The Americans were careful to maintain formal neutrality as between Iraq and Iran. With deeper pockets and hopes of moderating Iraqi conduct the U.S. tilted in favour of Iraq in several ways, one of which was to increase allocations of credit. The White House intervened to override the misgivings of the export credit managers, even in the face of evidence that U.S. loans were being used by the Iraqis in ways and for purposes inconsistent with the applicable U.S. legislation. Recent evidence submitted in the Banca Nazionale del Lavoro (BNL) case suggests that U.S. loans may have contributed, inadvertently, to financing the Iraqi pre-Kuwait arms program. The U.S. persisted, however, in the hope that improved relations would encourage Iraq to take its place after the war as part of a new regional architecture of moderation and stability in the Middle East. Washington hoped to see emerge a pro-Western "three-pillar" alignment of Iraq, Saudi Arabia and Egypt for the '90s, to replace the failed "two-pillar" policy which had been built on Iran and Saudi Arabia in the '70s.

Canada, with more modest means and a more modest view of its role in the area, was constrained to maintain a stricter neutrality between the two combatants and to assess Iraq's creditworthiness on the basis of ability to repay. At the same time every effort was made to stress positive elements in the relationship, including our mutual desire to bring the war to an early end. Like the U.S., Canada hoped that growth and maturity in our bilateral relations with Iraq would contribute, in a wider strategic context, to the emergence of a more moderate Iraq in the postwar period.

Some commentators have since suggested that the U.S., by pursuing a policy of conciliation with Saddam Hussein through these years (some have drawn a parallel with appeasement of Hitler in the '30s), may have encouraged him to think that he could invade Kuwait with impunity. I do not share this view. A policy of conciliation—of trying to improve relations and to allay Saddam's mistrust of Western intentions—was, in my view, a worthwhile effort in the circumstances. It failed, but an attempt to confront or isolate Iraq would have had even less chance of success.

The invasion of Kuwait takes its place in Barbara Tuchman's catalogue of history's march of folly, an act contrary to the interests of Iraq, which should have been clearly recognized by Saddam as an act of folly. I know of no action or inaction on the part of the United States through the period leading up to August 2, 1990—including U.S. Ambassador April Glaspie's controversial meeting with Saddam Hussein eight days before the invasion—which could be construed by any reasonable person as condoning unprovoked aggression against a neighbouring state. The folly of Kuwait must be laid exclusively at the door of Saddam Hussein.

For Canada, Iraq's creditworthiness was not the only issue. Our trade-dominated relationship with Iraq gave rise to a number of sensitive policy issues for Canadian diplomacy, which we sought to track and shape, in Ottawa and in the Embassy in Baghdad. These concerns, relating to restrictions on arms exports, and respect for human rights and international law, represent major continuing themes in Canadian foreign policy. They were on the Canadian agenda but not on the Iraqi agenda, and our recurring efforts to raise them were sometimes liable to cut across our commercial interests. How were they brought to bear on Iraq during this 1986-88 period?

THE ARMS TRAFFIC

As the largest arms buyer in the world during this period, Iraq was the focus of avid attention from international arms salesmen from every corner of the world. The USSR and France were major, openly declared suppliers. Most Western governments, including Canada, prohibited arms sales to both belligerents. A major thrust of Iraqi procurement efforts was to circumvent such restrictions, chiefly through resort to intermediaries in third countries. Iraqi defence buyers, when allied with the ingenuity and resourcefulness of suppliers and intermediaries, formed a powerful coalition of forces challenging the integrity of even the most restrictive policies. In the aftermath of the second Gulf War, pointed questions have been raised—and in some cases formal judicial enquiries have been launched—about the conduct of arms salesmen who contributed to Iraq's war machine during and after the first Gulf War, in contravention of national policies and, in some cases, with active complicity of their governments. The BNL affair in the U.S. and Italy, and the Scott enquiry in the U.K., amongst others, have revealed how porous arms export barriers can be.

Iraq reacted angrily to the dramatic revelation in 1986 of secret U.S. weapons transfers to Iran. The "Irangate" arms-for-hostages episode rocked the Reagan administration. In Baghdad the U.S. ambassador struggled to contain the damage. He assured the Iraqis that these transfers were an aberration, did not reflect official U.S. government policy and, when brought to light, had been discontinued. With recurring outbursts of indignation and suspicion, levelled at "Western and imperialist circles," the Iraqis made it clear that they were unassuaged, and not without reason. Subsequent disclosures revealed that enterprising suppliers in Britain, France, West Germany, Italy, Belgium, Austria and Sweden, amongst others, had been involved in clandestine arms sales to one or often both belligerents, contrary to officially stated government policies.

Canada's policy on arms sales was clear, unambiguous and highly restrictive. Since the outbreak of the conflict in 1980 Canada had placed an embargo on exports of military equipment to both Iraq and Iran. The list of banned or restricted items was based on consultations within COCOM, the coordinating committee of like-minded countries, including Canada, which had been set up to curb arms exports to the Soviet Union. It was monitored and enforced by Ottawa under the Export and Import Permits Act. On the global scene, Canada was active at the UN in pressing for agreement on greater transparency and public disclosure of international arms sales and took a lead, unilaterally, in releasing annual reports on the nature, value and destination of Canadian arms exports.

The application of Canadian restrictions was, however, not entirely free from difficulty. I was called on the carpet several times by the Iraqis for perceived breaches of our policy, in favour of Iran. The Iraqi complaints invariably related to "dual use" items which were not on our prohibited list but which, according to the Iraqis, were being acquired by the Iranians from Canada and pressed into service in the war. Two examples may illustrate the issue. On one occasion I was called in by the senior official of the Foreign Ministry who laid before me photographs of some battered outboard motor boats. Scores of these small craft, he said, had been captured by Iraqi soldiers while repulsing a recent Iranian water-borne offensive through the southern marshes. A close-up of the manufacturer's label indicated the name of a well-known Canadian manufacturer of recreational water craft. Canada should take immediate action to halt any further shipments of this kind, which could only strengthen Iran's offensive military capability and prolong the war. I said I would convey this view to Ottawa but, since recreational water craft were not on the prohibited list under the Export and Import Permits Act, I doubted if the authorities in Ottawa were even aware of the shipments or had statutory powers to stop them. The Iraqi official said he hoped Ottawa was not being naive: in the context of the current Iranian offensives the Canadian authorities should be under no illusion that a shipment of recreational water craft to Iran was intended for recreational purposes.

After enquiries in Canada we learned that the manufacturer was as surprised as we were by this end-use of the boats, which had been ordered by a civilian agency of the Iranian government. Although this item was not on the Canadian export control list the company agreed voluntarily to decline any further orders from Iran.

A similar issue arose over a contract to supply Canadian-built replacement engines for Iranian helicopters. The Iraqis complained that this was inconsistent with Canadian arms export policy since helicopters could and, in the Iraqi view, undoubtedly would be used in military operations against Iraq. In this case we responded that the model of helicopter involved was classified as civilian, and the parts were accordingly not on the export control list. However, since we could not be confident that they were not being used for military operations, the Department consulted the engine manufacturer, who agreed voluntarily to halt further shipments.

These examples point up the difficulty of drawing distinctions between military and non-military equipment when an item might be "dual-use"—wholly harmless in its commonly accepted peacetime use, yet having a potential military use in another context. While condemning shipments of "dual-use" goods to Iran, the Iraqis were no less active in exploiting such ambiguities to procure equipment from Canada destined for their own military. A pickup truck is not normally considered military equipment, and it does not appear on the COCOM list of internationally restricted war material. But add camouflage, and a heavy machine gun on the back, and it may add significantly, under certain campaign circumstances, to the war-making capacity of a belligerent. An ambulance serves a clear humanitarian purpose. Can it be said to be objectionable when repainted dull khaki for service at the front, retrieving wounded soldiers so that they may live to fight again another day?

Doubts of this kind concerning the efficacy of an arms ban can be troubling, but I believe they should be placed in the perspective of the underlying purpose which the policy is intended to serve. In the Iran-Iraq context the important objective of Canada and other like-minded countries was not to impose a total embargo on all supplies (which could have crippled the economies of the two countries and inflicted additional hardships on civilian populations) but to maintain, to the greatest extent possible, international pressure on the belligerents to reduce the savagery and destructiveness of the hostilities, while at the same time encouraging them to move toward a peaceful resolution of the conflict. In this sense questions about dual-use relate to the margin rather than the substance of the policy, and to questions of practicality rather than morality.

I am not aware of any evidence of significant violations of Canada's export control laws or regulations in respect of Iraq or Iran. The only Canadian known to have been actively involved with the Iraqi military program was the ill-fated Gerald Bull, who operated from outside Canada, and whose "super gun" was assembled from a number of sources other than Canada. If indeed our record, unlike that of many other Western countries, is clean, I doubt that this can be attributed to greater vigilance of the Canadian authorities, or to a more timid or compliance-minded Canadian business community. A large proportion of Canada's defence production is closely integrated with that of the U.S. There are no Canadian export controls on military goods going to the U.S. for final use or for further manufacturing in that country. Canadian parts supplied to weapons systems of the U.S. could be re-exported. If so, they would be subject to *U.S.* export controls, and dependent on the rigour with which the U.S. monitored any subsequent transfers. Such parts would not necessarily be identified as Canadian in the end product.

Any arms ban will be vulnerable, at least at the margins, to deliberate and determined efforts to by-pass it by resort to international intermediaries. If the proverbial Man from Mars were informed of the total amount of war material imported during the eight years of the Iran-Iraq war by Jordan, Cyprus or Singapore (for example), ostensibly for their own end-use according to the shipping documents, he would have to conclude that each of these countries had been engaged in a most ferocious and protracted war with its neighbours. This flood of imports greatly exceeded the needs of their own modest defence forces, and many of these arms were obviously destined for transshipment to countries such as Iran and Iraq to which they could not be exported directly.

The Iran-Iraq war yielded, I think, three lessons in this regard. Efforts to curb the activities of intermediaries would be strengthened by greater transparency in the international arms trade. This would bring the cold light of international opprobrium to bear on those countries that engage in the trade, and those that, wittingly or unwittingly, allow themselves to be used for transshipment purposes. There will be strong resistance to this. However, the UN program to set up an effective register of international arms shipments is clearly worthy of the support of countries concerned about the integrity of their own military export controls.

Secondly, government efforts to monitor the destination of sensitive exports, and uncover falsified end-use declarations, may never be wholly effective. But a vigorous process of scrutiny, even if not always effective, will be beneficial in that it will slow down the flow and increase the cost of supplies to any illicit end-user. Each intermediary will exact his price and the more elaborate the subterfuge, the greater the exaction. The underlying purpose of the policy described above will be served.

Thirdly, Canada's regulatory powers based on the Act and COCOM listings need to be reviewed. Definitions of sensitive war material developed in a Cold War context may not be appropriate to a policy of export controls geared increasingly to trade with Third World countries. Distinctions between offensive and defensive or lethal and non-lethal military equipment are meaningless in the post-Cold War world, if indeed they ever had any relevance. At the same time one has to take into account important commercial interests in favour of maintaining Canada's competitive position, along with the associated jobs. Informed parliamentary debate of the whole issue of Canada's military export controls is clearly overdue if we are to avoid the contortions and duplicity that have infected this issue in other countries.

HUMAN RIGHTS AND THE LAWS OF WAR

"Your Excellency, I can assure you that the Iraqi military are under instructions to use no unnecessary brutality." I had queried a senior Iraqi official on the subject of a recent Red Cross report on ill-treatment of Iranian prisoners-of-war. With its implication that *some* brutality was the norm, this assurance was more revealing than he had intended. In fact brutalities were widespread on both sides in this war. Attacks on civilian targets were commonplace. Violations were so widespread and flagrant that they raised questions as to whether traditional rules of international law and civilized behaviour continued to have any restraining effect in this conflict. Was it not wholly futile and naive to keep reminding the belligerents of their obligations under the Geneva Conventions and other international accords?

The short answer is that, in the absence of persistent pressure from the international community, the abuses would undoubtedly have been much worse. This pressure was brought to bear in many ways, bilaterally and multilaterally. In the UN Security Council and General Assembly, and in other organs such as the Human Rights Commission, the Iraqi conduct of the war and the internal repression came under frequent scrutiny and condemnation. In Baghdad we sought useful opportunities to raise Canadian concerns with ministers and senior officials, usually on the basis of reports of specific violations issued by a variety of international watchdog organizations such as the International Committee of the Red Cross, whose representatives in Iraq (and Iran) were given selective access to POW camps and made dedicated efforts to improve conditions and bring to light abuses. Periodic reports on Iraq by Amnesty International also provided a useful platform from which to press concerns about Saddam's harsh repression of his own people.

The best line of approach, I found, in my efforts to develop substantive exchanges on these sensitive issues, was to appeal to Iraqi self-interest. It was all too easy to register a concern and elicit a perfunctory denial or rejection. If, however, I could place the concern in the context of, for example, the damaging effect which a specific report had on Canadian public and parliamentary opinion, thereby undermining our ability to support Iraq on some other issue of importance to it, I could sometimes strike a chord, or a nerve.

Iraq's use of chemical weapons, in violation of its own commitments as a signatory to the 1925 Geneva Protocol banning chemical weapons, was perhaps the most contentious item on our bilateral agenda. Here I could cite a special Canadian sensitivity. The standard Iraqi reply was a flat denial that any chemical weapons had been used. This began to wear thin after successive UN reports brought conclusive evidence of Iraqi use of nerve gas and a variant of mustard gas not unlike that inflicted on Canadian troops in the trenches of World War I. In private conversations with Iraqi officials a more sophisticated line began to emerge. Canadians should understand, said a close advisor to the President, that Iraq has used these weapons only as a last resort, in extremis, in defence of the homeland against imminent danger of Iranian offensives. "Let us have no hypocrisy here. Iraq particularly resents being lectured on this by the Americans, who saw fit to resort to weapons of mass destruction in 1945 against civilian populations far from their shores, against an enemy which no longer posed a serious military threat. We are fighting for our lives and for national survival."

My rejoinder was to question whether such a course was in Iraq's own interest, quite apart from the fundamental legal and moral objections. Resort to chemical weapons seemed to me, I said, to compound the mistake Iraq had made by invading Iran in 1980: in both cases the effect was to escalate a conflict which could have been contained at a lower level of intensity. I did not see how such escalation could be in the interests of the smaller party facing an enemy known to have the capability to retaliate at the same or higher levels of destructiveness.

Some would say that such protests about chemical weapons—the "poor man's bomb"—were bound to fall on deaf ears. Saddam's military commanders were no doubt reporting to him that these weapons were effective in halting human wave offensives. Saddam's diplomats in New York could report that efforts in the Security Council to have Iraq formally condemned for the use of these weapons were repeatedly deflected or muted, for one reason or another. Saddam continued to use chemical weapons selectively, even after the cease-fire of August 1988, against Kurdish insurgents who posed no serious threat to his security. In 1990, several months before the invasion of Kuwait, he threatened to use them against Israel, a gratuitous gesture which aroused anxieties and hostility throughout the world. Yet in the end I suspect that considerations of prudence, rather than legality or morality, persuaded him to refrain from unleashing these weapons of last resort in the final days of the Kuwait war.

To appeal to prudence and self-interest is not to dismiss the value or relevance of moral and legal principles. In this respect, perhaps, Saddam committed his greatest mistake. He failed to realize that by flouting these principles he incurred not merely opposition. He stirred deep currents of repugnance and outrage of the kind which swept the extraordinarily disparate coalition of countries that took the field against him over Kuwait.

The great tragedy of Saddam Hussein was that he allowed himself to indulge in misadventures beyond his borders. If he had concentrated on peaceful development at home he could have presided over a period of prosperity, based on oil wealth, which would have rivalled anything in the long and rich annals of Mesopotamian history. With prosperity, he could have lifted the heavy hand of internal repression. I doubt that he could ever have aspired to be a worthy successor to Hammurabi and Nebuchadnezzar, but the balance sheet could have been favourable. Instead he clings stubbornly to power in the wreckage of his country, with the bitter knowledge that his continued presence constitutes a major obstacle to recovery. He will face a severe judgement of history, as a tyrant who squandered his country's patrimony and brought nothing but grief to several generations of his people.

For Canada, a revived effort to reach out in friendship to the long suffering Iraqi people will have to await the departure of Saddam Hussein from the scene. A successor will face formidable challenges, from within and outside Iraq's borders. The Baath party has become an empty shell and will undoubtedly, like the Nazi party, collapse with its leader. This is a turbulent neighbourhood. With their resources, talents and ambitions the Iraqi people are bound to be a force for stability and prosperity in the region, or for unrest and conflict. Either way, it will be in the Canadian interest to persevere.

Erik B. Wang was born in Montreal in 1932. He joined External Affairs in 1958. He served abroad in Oslo, New Delhi and at the UN in New York. He was Canada's Ambassador to Denmark from 1983-86, and to Iraq from 1986-88. In Ottawa he was Director of the Legal Operations Division, Senior Negotiator for Maritime Affairs, Director General of the Middle East Bureau, and served twice as Inspector General of the Foreign Service. His publications include articles in *Behind the Headlines* and *Canadian Yearbook of International Law*.

INDEX

A

Abbotsford, B.C., 131
Accra, Ghana, 38
Aczd, Gyorgy, 15
Afghanistan, 12, 177-78, 189, 190-91, 209, 211
Africa, l'Afrique, ix-x *et sequi*
Ahsan, Vice-Admiral, 214, 224
Aitkin, Robert, 8
Alberta, 264
l'Allier, Jean-Paul, 92
Andreotti, Giulio, 89
Andropov, President Yuri, 191
Ankara, 59, 115
Anvers, 96
Arabie Saoudite, Saudi Arabia, 122, 123, 125-26, 130, 270, 276
Arbatov, Georgi, 194
Armstrong, Dorothy, 1-15
Arvida, 240
Asia, Asie, ix-x, 112, 147
Asgar Khan, 220
Aswan, 38
Athens, 59
Atwood, Margaret, 91
Australia, 4, 20, 42, 213, 218, 275
Autriche, Austria, 3, 121, 278
Ayub Khan, 209
Azerbaijan, 193

B

Baghdad, 120, 125, 130
Bangkok, 38
Bangladesh, 160, 209-37
Bantus, 72, 73
Baran, Emil, 227
Barbados, 203
Barisol, 224
Barton, William, 17-32
Bateman, Robert, 263

Baudoin, le Roi, 94, 96, 99
Bégin, Monique, 99
Beijing, 133, 136, 140, 235
Belgium, La Belgique, 92, 97, 98, 228, 278
Belize, 206
Berlin, 57
Berne, 52
Bethune, Norman, 133-34
Beyrouth, 115, 116, 119, 120, 123-32
Bhutto, Prime Minister Zulfikar Ali Bhutto, 209, 210, 222, 231-32
Biko, Steve, 23
Blanchette Arthur, 33-48
Bonn, 52, 174, 177
Bologne, 90
Botswana, 24, 71, 83
Bourassa, Premier Robert, 87
Brazil, 70, 249, 251
Brett, Bill, 229
Brezhnev, President Leonid, 190-91, 196
Britain, 213, 258, 265, 275
Brohi, A.K., 222
Brown, Gordon, 49-68
Brussels, Bruxelles, 92, 94-95, 98, 99, 106
Budapest, 2, 3, 12, 15
Bulgaria, 234
Burma, 161
Burnham, Prime Minister Forbes, 243, 245-51

C

Cadieux, Marcel, 64, 114, 248
Le Caire, Cairo, 37-38, 115
Caldwell, Ray, 65
California, 259
Cambodia, ix-x, 38-39, 42-43, 133
Campbell, J.G., 242, 250

INDEX

Canada, ix-x *et sequi*
Capetown, 69-70, 76-77, 80
Caribbean, 199-201, 203-04, 241
Carney, Pat, 142
Carrington, Lord, 186
Carter, Harry, 69-84
Carter, President James, 189-90
Central America, 191
Chaguarames, Trinidad and Tobago, 248
Chamberlain, Joseph, 72
Chan, Raymond, 139
Chiang Kai-shek, 134
Chili, 252
Chittagong, 223-24
Ciskei, 73
Chrétien, Prime Minister Jean, 101, 128, 129, 139, 155
China, Chine, 51, 103, 133-54, 168, 171, 232, 235
Chou-en-lai, 35
Chugoku, 266
Chumb, 228
Clark, Gen. Allen, 223
Clark, Gerald, 244
Clark, Joe, 154
Claude, Inis, 17
Congo, 103-05, 111
Cossiga, Francesco, 89
Coward, Noel, 139
Cyprus, 49-67

D

Dacca, 12, 13, 214, 218, 220, 227
Dale, Mac, 37
Davidson, Dr. George, 29
Davis, Premier William, 88
Davis, Nathaniel, 240, 250
Deng Xiao Ping, 136, 149, 151
Deslauriers, Omer, 92
Deutsch, John, 159
Dien-bien-phu, 34
Dimitrious, Nicos, 57, 60
Djeddah (Jiddah), 123, 126, 132
Doucet, André, 39
Durban, 81
Dunaujavos, 7

E

Eastern Cape, South Africa, 73
Eden, Anthony, 35
Egypt, 38, 270, 276
Elizabeth, H.M. Queen, 144
Ethiope, 114
Euphrates, 271
Europe, ix-x *et sequi*

F

Fao peninsula, 269
Faycal, le Roi, 123
Fenton, W.O., 39
Finland, 69
Flandre, 97
Ford, Robert, 186
Forrestal, Tom, 8
Fortier, D'Iberville, 85-114
Fox, Francis, 99
France, 19, 21, 23, 34, 92, 95, 104, 121, 153, 258, 265, 275, 278
Frangié, President Soeliman, 118-19
Fraser, Derek, 96
French-Beytagh, Archbishop Gonville, 82
Fukuoka, 255, 266
Fulford, Robert, 263

G

Gabcikovo, 14
Gaberone, 71
Gabon, 95
Gandhi, Prime Minister Indira, 169
Gardiner, James, 36
Gauvin, Michel, 103-14
Geneva, Genève, 107
Georgetown, Guyana, 243, 245-46, 250
George, James, 232, 235
Germany, 21, 228, 258
Ghana, 38, 107, 199
Ghotzbzadeh, Foreign Minister, 9
Gibson, Gibby, 227
Giglioli, Dr., 242
Gignac, Jacques, 115-32
Gill, Evan, 33, 38
Gillespie, Alastair, 124, 130

INDEX

Ginangzhous, 133
Girvan, Dr. Norman, 240
Gizenga, Ministre, 105
Glaspie, Ambassador April, 277
Glazebrook, George, 154
Goldberg, Justice, 249
Goodall, Joan, 15, 161
Gorbachev, Mikhail, 194, 197
Gorham, Richard, 133-54
Gotlieb, Under-Secretary Allan, 101
Goyer, Jean-Pierre, 51-52
Graham, William, 37
Greece, Grèce, 103
Greek Cypriots, 53, 65
Grenada, 200
Gretzky, Wayne, 193
Guyana, 239-53
Guyot, Daniel A., 266

H

Hadwen, J.G., 155-76
Hafiz Al-Assad, 117
Hague, The, 52
Hailé Sélassié, empereur, 107-10, 114
Halstead, John, 177-88
Hamid, Gen., 225
Hammarskjold, Dag, 104-05
Hammurabi, 272, 283
Hangzou, 133
Hanoi, 34, 45
Harare, 20
Hardenberg, Prince, 44-45
Helsinki, 12
Hiroshima, 255, 266
Hitler, Adolf, 276
Hoangzhous, 133
Ho Chi Minh, 34
Hokkaido, 266
Holmes, John, 35
Holy See, 59
Hong Kong, 136-37, 171-72
Howard, Leslie, 6
Howe, C.D., 36
Humboldt, Deputy Chancellor, 44-45
Hungary, 1-15, 83
Hussein, Roi de Jordanie, 130-32
Hu Yaobang, 151

I

India, 39, 44, 133, 151, 163-70, 205, 211, 228, 229, 230
Indochine, 34, 40, 171
Indonesia, 34
Iran, 4, 6, 120, 276
Iraq, 120, 269-84
Ireland, Republic of, 235
Isbister, C., 247
Islamabad, 151, 211, 216, 222, 230
Israel, 54
Ithaca, NY, 136
Italie, 88, 90, 121, 228, 258, 265, 278

J

Jack, Hubert, 244, 246
Jamaica, 199, 241
Jamieson, Donald, 24-25
Jancso, Miklos, 2
Japan, 133, 255-68
Jellenik, Donald, 142
Jerome, James, Speaker of the Commons, 91
Jessore, 224
Jinnah, Mohd. Ali, 222
Johannasburg, 82
Jordan, Eleanor, 136-37
Jordanie, Jordan, 115, 270
Jotti, Nilde, 90

K

Kadar, Janos, 1, 13-14
Kaifu, Prime Minister Toshiki, 262
Kampala, 111
Kansai, 265
Kaplan, Robert, 26
Karachi, 213, 216-17, 227, 229
Karbala, 272
Kasavubu, President, 104-05
Kashmir, 217, 228
Katanga, 104-05
Kaunda, President Kenneth, 66, 203
Keating, H.R.F., 171
Kelleher, 142
Kentridge, Mr., 82
Kenyatta, President, 108-10
Khaddam, Abdel, 114

287

INDEX

Khomeini, Ayatollah, 274
Khulne, 224
King, Martin Luther, 21
King, Ambassador S., 2, 245-46, 249, 250
Kirkwood, Kenneth, 159
Kitchener, Lord, 72
Kitimat, B.C., 240
Koki Tada, 266
Korea, 34, 155, 157, 171-74, 265
Kruger, Paul, 70
Krushchev, President Nikita, 148
Kuchuk, Fazil, 59
Kuwait, 270, 276, 283
Kuznetsov, Vice-President, 189
Kyprianous, Foreign Minister Spyros, 61, 64-65
Kyushu, 26

L

Lahore, 217
Landry, Bernard, 97
Lapointe, Paul, 24
Latin America, 147
Lee, Egmont, 91
Léger, Jean-Marc, 92, 95
Léger, Gouverneur General Jules, 100
Lenin, V.I., 149
Leopold, Roi, 105
Leopoldville, 105-07, 111, 112
Leslie, Brig.-Gen. E.M.D., 53, 56
Lesotho, 71, 73, 83
L'Espagne, 121
Lévesque, René, 87, 93, 95, 96, 97
Lévesque, Corinne, 96
le Liban, Lebanon, 115, 117, 118, 119, 120, 130
Liège, 96
Li Peng, Premier, 142
Lipkowski, Count Peter De, 62
Li Xiannien, President, 146
Lisbon, 52
London, 35, 52, 59, 174
Los Angeles, 265
Lumumba, Premier Ministre Patrice, 104-05
Luns, NATO Secretary General Joseph, 186

M

MacCallum, Elizabeth, 37
Macdonald, Donald, 130
MacGuigan, Mark, 13, 179, 183, 185, 192
Mackay, D.D., 240
Mackay, Dr. R.A., 37
Mackenzie, Guyana, 249
MacLennan, Hugh, 8
Macorquodale, Fraser, 244
Macquarrie, Heath, 247
Maine, 265
Makarios, President, 58-59, 62, 66
Malawi, 207
Malaysia, 156, 161, 265
Mao Zedong, 133, 135
Marler, Herbert, 256
Martens, Prime Minister Wilfred, 99
Martin, Paul (sr.), 36, 160, 161
Martola, Gen., 53
Maseru, 71
Masse, Marcel, 101
Massoud, Secrétaire General, 126
Marx, Karl, 149
Mbabane, 71
McCoy, Dr., 137
McCue, Doug, 229
McLuhan, Marshall, 91
Mekong River Basin, 42
Mendes-France, Premier Ministre Pierre, 34
Menelik, l'empereur, 114
Menzies, Arthur, 140
Mexico City, 33
Meyer, Assistant Secretary of State, 249
Milan, 89, 90
Mobutu, Gen., 105, 106, 111
Molotov, V.M., 35
Mongolia, 234
Monoghan, Tom, 159
Montevideo, 57
Moreau, Gertrude, 39
Moriyama, Raymond, 262, 264
Moro, Aldo, 87
Moscow, 1, 173, 177-78, 185-93
Moyent-Orient, 112, 115, 116, 117, 123, 129, 131-32

INDEX

Mozambique, 24, 207
Muller, Dr. Hilgaard, 83
Mulroney, Prime Minister Brian, 95, 97, 140, 142-43, 201, 262
Myanmar, Government of, 162

N

Nagoya, 266
Nagymaros, Hungary, 14
Nairobi, 108, 110, 111
Najaf, 272
Namibia, 21, 22, 24, 25
Namur, 96
Nanning, 45
Natal, 73
Nebuchadnezzar, 272, 283
Nehru, Prime Minister, 169
Nepal, 211, 234
Netherlands, 265
New Delhi, 34, 155, 163, 168, 225, 235
Newfoundland, 50
New York, 19, 26, 264
Nicol, Davidson, 18
Nicosia, 49-66
Norway, 160
Nothomb, Ferdinand, 94
Nujoma, Sam, 24, 26

O

Oglesby, Roy, 39
Osaka, 265-66
Ottawa, ix-x *et sequi*

P

Pakistan, West and/or East, 155-60, 162-76, 209-37
Pandelas, Helen, 66
Paris, 174
Parker, Jon Kimura, 263
Pascal, Blaise, 85
Pasco, Cerro de, 253
Pearson, Geoffrey, 189-97
Pearson, Prime Minister Lester B., 36, 104, 107, 109, 113, 160-61, 167
Peerzada, Lt. Gen., 225
Peleghias, George, 64

Pepin, Jean-Luc, 115, 247
Perez de Cuellar, 274
Persian Gulf, 177, 190
Peru, 253
Peterson, Premier David, 138
Pnom Penh, 38, 40, 42, 45
Poland, 178-84, 185-86, 187, 190, 234
Pope Jean-Paul I, 89
Pope Paul VI, 89
Polyani, John, 263
Port of Spain, 247
Pretoria, 69-70, 77, 81-83
Price, Prime Minister George, 206

Q

Quebec, 86, 90, 92
Quemoy and Matsu, 133
Quesnel, Joseph, 92
Quito, 57

R

Rahman, Mujibur, 209, 214-15, 218-20
Rajasthan, 228
Ramphal, Foreign Minister S., 243, 251
Rangoon, 161
Rankin, Bruce, 267
Rawalpindi, 217
Reagan, President Ronald, 189-92
Reece, David, ix-x, 85, 199-207
Reid, Gilbert, 91
Rhodes, Cecil, 72
Rhodesia, 21
Richler, Mordecai, 91
Riffou, Lt.-Col. Jean, 50
Ritchie, Ed, 160, 251
Riyad, 127
Roach, E. Hugh, 240
Robbins, Dr. John E., 59
Rome, 87, 90, 90, 174
Ronchey, Alberto, 88
Ronning, Chester, 33, 35
Rosanne, Robert E., 244
Rothschild, Brig. Bob, 37

S

Saddam Hussein, President, 269-73, 276, 277, 283-84

INDEX

Sakhalin Island, 191
Sami, Fuad, 64
Santo Domingo, 57
Sapporo, 255, 266
Sauvé, Jeanne, présidente de la Chambre des Communes, 90, 139, 194
Seaga, Prime Minister Edward, 199, 200
Seattle, 131
Sekou Touré, President, 108
Sendai, 255, 266
Shah of Iran, 63-64
Sharp, Mitchell, 51, 56-57, 60, 64, 124, 130, 132-33, 240
Shanghai, 133, 141, 153
Shatt-al-Arab, 269
Shearer, Prime Minister Hugh, 247
Shenstone, Michael, 125
Shenyang, 145
Shijizhuang, 133
Sialkot, 228
Sihanouk, Prince, 39-40, 42, 43-44
Sinclair, Mr. and Mrs. James, 159
Singapore, 38, 161
Slovakia, 15
Small, John, 209-37
Smith, Arnold, 234, 235
Somalia, 18
Sotho, 173
South Africa, 21-24, 38, 69-84, 86, 202
Soviet Union, 1, 3, 19, 51, 177, 179, 180-81, 182-83, 184-85, 189, 196-97, 232, 249, 277
Soweto, 74, 81
Stalin, Joseph, 148
Stanleyville, 103, 105-08, 110-12
Steers, Barry, 267
Stiles, John, 239-54
St. Laurent, Prime Minister Louis, 36
Sultan Khan, 226
Sultan, Mohd., 228
Sun Yat Sen, 144
Surinam, 241
Suzman, Helen, 81
Suzuki, David, 263

Swaziland, 71, 83
Sweden, 20, 228, 278
Syrie, Syria, 115, 117
Szabo, Istvan, 2

T

Taiwan, 9, 171, 265
Takamado, Prince and Princess, 262
Talleyrand, 44-45
Tamakawa, Toshio, 266
Tanzania, 24
Taylor, Archbishop Robert Selby, 78
Taylor, J.H., 255-68
Teheran, Tehran, 115, 230, 273
Tel Aviv, 63
Texas, 265
Thailand, 265
Thompson, Chief Justice Ogilvie, 82
Thompson, Robert, 107-10
Thordarson, Bruce, 51
Thorson, Inge, 20, 21
Tian An Men Square, 152
Tibet, 147
Tigris River, 271
Tindemans, Leo, 99
Tikka Khan, 219, 224
Tohoku, 266
Tokyo, 174, 255-67
Toronto, 136, 200, 241, 262-63
Transkei, 73
Tremblay, Michel, 92
Trinidad and Tobago, 199, 201, 203, 205, 241, 248
Trower, Col., 229
Trudeau, Prime Minister Pierre, 26, 50-52, 55, 58-59, 62, 87, 89, 97, 98, 131, 132, 150, 187, 192, 194, 226-27
Tschombe, 104, 106
Tunisia, 87
Turkey, 67

U

U.K., 19, 21, 23
Ulan Hu, Vice-President, 137
U.S.A., 4, 19, 21, 23, 109, 177, 183, 213, 235, 265, 275, 280
USSR, see *Soviet Union*

V

Vancouver, 203
Vatican, The, 58
Velasco, President, 253
Veniamin, Chris, 58, 64
Venice, 274
Vienna, ix-x, 18, 182, 204
Vientiane, 45, 57
Vietnam, 34, 36, 40
Vogel, directeur de l'Office Canadien du Blé, 124
Vorster, Prime Minister John, 83
Vreven, Freddy, 99

W

Waldheim, UN Secretary General Kurt, 27
Walvis Bay, 25
Wang, Erik, 269-84
Warsaw, 182
Washington, 59, 106, 174, 185, 190, 265, 276
Waterman Angie, 37
West Germany, 79, 278
Winnipeg, 122, 263
Wrong, Hume, 31

Y

Yahya Khan, 209-10, 215, 219, 222, 225-26, 228, 232
Yakovlev, Alexander, 192, 194
Yakub, Lt. Gen., 214, 219
Yangtze River, 141, 150
Yasu, Gen., 108
Yeltsin, Boris, 196
Yifru, Ketema, 108-10

Z

Zambia, 24, 199, 202, 203, 204, 206
Zhao Zi Yang, 144, 150
Zhou Enlai, Premier, 134
Zimbabwe, 204
Zulu areas, 73